Contemporary British Drama

Edinburgh Critical Guides to Literature
Series Editors: Martin Halliwell, University of Leicester and Andy
Mousley, De Montfort University

Contemporary British Drama

David Lane

Edinburgh University Press

© David Lane, 2010

Edinburgh University Press Ltd
22 George Square, Edinburgh

www.euppublishing.com

Typeset in 11.5/13 Monotype Ehrhardt
by Servis Filmsetting Ltd, Stockport, Cheshire, and
printed and bound in Great Britain by
CPI Antony Rowe, Chippenham and Eastbourne

A CIP record for this book is available from the British Library

ISBN 978 0 7486 3821 5 (hardback)
ISBN 978 0 7486 3822 2 (paperback)

The right of David Lane
to be identified as author of this work
has been asserted in accordance with
the Copyright, Designs and Patents Act 1988.

Contents

Series Preface

The study of English literature in the early twenty-first century is host to an exhilarating range of critical approaches, theories and historical perspectives. 'English' ranges from traditional modes of study such as Shakespeare and Romanticism to popular interest in national and area literatures such as the United States, Ireland and the Caribbean. The subject also spans a diverse array of genres from tragedy to cyberpunk, incorporates such hybrid fields of study as Asian American literature, Black British literature, creative writing and literary adaptations, and remains eclectic in its methodology.

Such diversity is cause for both celebration and consternation. English is varied enough to promise enrichment and enjoyment for all kinds of readers and to challenge preconceptions about what the study of literature might involve. But how are readers to navigate their way through such literary and cultural diversity? And how are students to make sense of the various literary categories and periodisations, such as modernism and the Renaissance, or the proliferating theories of literature, from feminism and marxism to queer theory and eco-criticism? The Edinburgh Critical Guides to Literature series reflects the challenges and pluralities of English today, but at the same time it offers readers clear and accessible routes through the texts, contexts, genres, historical periods and debates within the subject.

Martin Halliwell and Andy Mousley

Acknowledgements

Thanks to Andy Mousley, Martin Halliwell and the staff at Edinburgh University Press, to Graham Ley at Exeter University for his support and guidance on the book and for sending the opportunity in my direction, and to John Freeman, John Ginman and William Stanton for their continuing support and advice, and for the time spent teaching with each of them over the last 5 years. Thanks also to Barbara Norden and Chris Fallon at City University, and the Society of Authors for the Michael Meyer Award in support of this book being written.

Thanks to all those who took part in interviews or extended correspondence about their work: David Eldridge, Bryony Lavery, Anthony Neilson, Carl Grose, Alex Murdoch, Shiona Morton, Bill Wroath, Hugh Nankivell, Peter Oswald, Hugh Janes, Rachel Aspinwall, Ruth Mitchell, Sarah Dickenson, Tanika Gupta, Roy Williams, Kwame Kwei-Armah, Fin Kennedy, Chris Cooper, Suzy Graham Adriani, Dennis Kelly, Ben Power and Blake Morrison. Many thanks to all of the students who have pushed and challenged me with their searching questions in the various courses I have delivered, and thanks also to all the theatre professionals I have been lucky enough to work with and have advise me. Thanks to Margaret Bunce for providing the quiet space and time to construct the proposal, and of course to Lotte for her proof-reading, patience, love and endless support.

The biggest thanks go to Mum and Dad: thank you for the opportunities and for believing I could do it, and for everything really.

Chronology

Date	Contextual References	Theatre Events
January 1995		*Blasted* by Sarah Kane opens at Royal Court
July 1995	Serbian forces massacre nearly 10,000 people in Srebrenica, a designated UN safe area	
September 1995		*At The Inland Sea*, Edward Bond's first Theatre in Education play for Big Brum is produced
December 1995	Damien Hirst wins the Turner Prize with an exhibition titled *Some Went Mad, Some Ran Away*, including a cow and her calf in formaldehyde	

Date	Contextual References	Theatre Events
July 1996	Dolly the Sheep is the first animal to be cloned from an adult cell	
September 1996		*Shopping and Fucking* by Mark Ravenhill opens at Royal Court
May 1997	New Labour's Tony Blair voted in as Prime Minister	
June 1997		Shakespeare's Globe Theatre opens on the South Bank with *Henry V*
January 1998	Tony Blair announces the Saville Enquiry will revisit the events of Bloody Sunday	
July 1998		National Campaign for the Arts announces a cumulative loss of £12m in funding to producing theatres over a decade
January 1999		Tribunal play *The Colour of Justice* by Richard Norton-Taylor heralds a new interest in verbatim theatre
February 1999	The Macpherson Report on the case of Stephen Lawrence is released and finds the police institutionally racist	Writer Sarah Kane is found dead in London having committed suicide
May 1999	The new Welsh Assembly is officially opened	

Date	Contextual References	Theatre Events
July 1999	A new Scottish Parliament forms for the first time in nearly 300 years	
November 1999		Evening Standard Awards withhold the award for Best New Play
December 1999	British artist Tracey Emin's work *My Bed* – an unmade bed covered in detritus – is shortlisted for the Turner Prize	
May 2000		The Arts Council's Boyden Report recommends a £25m injection of funding for British theatre
July 2000	Channel 4 launches reality TV show *Big Brother*	
December 2000	George W. Bush is elected President of the United States of America	
January 2001	Online encyclopaedia Wikipedia is launched	Dominic Dromgoole's frank account of British playwrights, *The Full Room*, is published
March 2001		The seminal *In-Yer-Face Theatre: British Drama Today* by Aleks Sierz is published

Date	Contextual References	Theatre Events
June 2001		Eclipse conference held at Nottingham Playhouse to develop profile of national and regional Black theatre
September 2001	Terrorists fly two planes into the World Trade Center towers in New York	
October 2001		Artists Against The War is formed, led by Red Room Artistic Director Lisa Goldman, in response to the bombing campaign in Afghanistan
January 2002	The Euro is introduced as a new currency – Britain opts out	
August 2002	Ian Huntley is arrested for the murder of two schoolgirls in Soham, Cambridgeshire	
March 2002		The Dramaturgs' Network is created to help advocate and develop the role of British theatre
May 2002	A rail accident at Potters Bar kills seven people and becomes the fourth major accident on Britain's railways in 4 years	National Theatre creates the Loft to produce new small-scale work

Date	Contextual References	Theatre Events
September 2002		Creative Partnership programmes begin in schools, promoting arts across the country
November 2002		Soho Theatre splits the Verity Bargate Award three ways when none of the submissions provides a clear winner
February 2003	The largest peacetime anti-war demonstration in the UK takes place as millions march through London	The 'Monsterist' writers' manifesto on big plays for big spaces begins to spread; Hollywood actor Kevin Spacey is announced as the new Artistic Director of the Old Vic
March 2003	US–UK forces invade Iraq to end Saddam Hussein's reign	
April 2003		National Theatre begins a £10 ticket price scheme to encourage new audiences; it also hosts the transfer of *Jerry Springer The Opera*
May 2003	Two months after the invasion of Iraq, BBC correspondent Andrew Gillingham alleges the dossier on weapons of mass destruction to have been 'sexed up' by government officials	

Date	Contextual References	Theatre Events
June 2003	Liverpool is selected as the European Capital of Culture for 2008	
July 2003	Weapons expert Dr David Kelly commits suicide	
February 2004	Social networking site Facebook is launched from a dormitory room in Harvard	
April 2004	Reports arrive of torture and humiliation of Iraqi prisoners by US forces at Abu Ghraib	
September 2004		David Hare's new play *Stuff Happens* puts Blair, Bush, Rice and Powell on stage for scrutiny
November 2004	George Bush wins a second term as President	
December 2004	Troops from Scotland's Black Watch Regiment are sent to Fallujah	Sikh protestors smash the front of Birmingham Rep in response to *Behzti* by Gurpreet Bhatti which depicts a rape in a temple
April 2005		*Elmina's Kitchen* by Kwame Kwei-Armah, the first new play by a British-born Black writer in the West End
May 2005		*The Big Life* transfers from Stratford East to become the first Black British musical in the West End

Date	Contextual References	Theatre Events
July 2005	Terrorists explode four bombs on London's public transport network; London wins the bid to host the 2012 Olympics; Jean Charles de Menezes shot by police on underground network	Arts Council withdraws funding for a £9.5m home for Black theatre in Victoria, London
November 2005		Manchester Royal Exchange launches the nationwide Bruntwood Prize for new writing
February 2006		National Theatre of Scotland is launched
March 2006	Twitter is launched, providing a maximum of 140 characters for online updates and comment to those who join	
April 2006		The RSC opens a year-long season of Shakespeare's entire works, involving new versions and productions from international companies
June 2006		*On The Third Day* by Kate Betts premieres as the winner of Channel 4's 'The Play's The Thing', a reality TV search for a new West End drama

Date	Contextual References	Theatre Events
October 2006		Punchdrunk opens its immersive site-specific production of *Faust* in Wapping
December 2006	Saddam Hussein is executed	
March 2007		Katie Mitchell's radical multimedia revival of *Attempts on Her Life* by Martin Crimp opens at the National Theatre
May 2007	Three year-old Madeleine McCann is abducted from her parents' holiday apartment in the Algarve; the search goes global in a few weeks	
June 2007	Tony Blair resigns as Prime Minister; Britain begins to suffer the worst flooding since records began 200 years ago	
July 2007	Live Earth concerts take place worldwide	
December 2007		Arts Council announces severe cuts to some of Britain's most significant theatres
January 2008		Arts Council publishes the McMaster Report calling for a new focus on 'excellence' in art

Date	Contextual References	Theatre Events
February 2008	Northern Rock is nationalised at huge cost to the taxpayer	
April 2008	Austrian Josef Fritzl is arrested for keeping his daughter in a cellar for 24 years and fathering seven children by her	
May 2008		*That Face* by 21-year-old Polly Stenham transfers to West End, the youngest new writing debut since 1966
June 2008	Britain suffers a huge slump in the housing market as the country heads into recession	
July 2008		*Her Naked Skin* by Rebecca Lenkiewicz is the first new play by a living female writer on the Olivier stage
September 2008	The Large Hadron Collider is turned on by scientists searching for the Higgs boson particle	
November 2008	Barack Obama elected as the first African-American president of the United States of America	
December 2008	Statistics reveal 70 incidents of violent teenage deaths in the UK in 2008	Nobel prize-winning writer Harold Pinter dies aged 78

Date	Contextual References	Theatre Events
February 2009		*England People Very Nice* by Richard Bean attracts accusations of racism; *Seven Jewish Children* by Caryl Churchill is accused of anti–Semitism
April 2009	Protestors clash with riot police in the City of London during the G20 summit	
May 2009	The MP expenses scandal erupts with publication of former Conservative cabinet minister Douglas Hogg's claims for 'moat clearing' at his country estate	
June 2009	Global pop phenomenon Michael Jackson dies	The National Theatre trials NT Live, beaming Racine's *Phèdre* by satellite to independent cinemas
August 2009	Channel 4 plans to axe reality show *Big Brother* after 2010	
September 2009		Tricycle Theatre's 'Not Black and White' season of new plays by Black British writers
October 2009	Nick Griffin, leader of the British National Party, appears on BBC's *Question Time*	

Date	Contextual References	Theatre Events
November 2009		National Theatre of Wales is launched
December 2009	Copenhagen hosts a meeting of global politicians to discuss a deal on climate change; an appeal on Facebook prevents ITV's *The X Factor* from claiming a fifth successive Christmas number one single.	

Introduction

INTENTIONS AND CHAPTER OVERVIEW

This book presents a picture of contemporary British drama from the perspective of a dramaturg and playwright. It is not a comprehensive catalogue of theatrical activity and neither is it a book of theatre history. It takes as a guiding principle the exploration of the theatre writer's role and explores the practical and theoretical considerations they face when working in the contemporary theatre. Through offering a range of case studies and analyses across six different professional contexts, it is hoped that the reader will comprehend more fully the role of writing and the writer in contemporary drama.

The organisation of recognisable dramatic elements such as story, plot, character, location and theme in contemporary drama is no longer the writer's exclusive creative territory, and through an investigation of how and why the ground is shifting regarding our received notions of what writers (and performers, directors and dramaturgs) are actually doing when they create work, a picture emerges of writing for theatre as increasingly holistic and collaborative. Many writers are breaking through the staid and restrictive image of being simply autonomous providers of a list of lines, and moving closer towards what we might refer to as 'performance writing': a space where writers explore and develop their work in a direct and active relationship with other practitioners and spaces.[1]

This book is therefore an introduction to those unfamiliar with the breadth of theatrical forms, styles and creative processes involving writers since 1996. Its aim in part is to draw together what some may consider divergent forms of theatre such as devising, verbatim, theatre for young people and adaptation, by reassessing the figure of the writer as they navigate these different environments and studying the origin of what we may term 'authorial elements' in the work: the arrangement of plot, structure, character arcs and so forth.

For much of the past 15 years the figure of the writer has been a constant and visible fixture and a unique selling point of British theatre – perhaps even a marketable commodity – both on a domestic and international scale. By focusing almost exclusively on work that involves writers, I am also making a provocation: the contemporary theatre obviously need not begin and end with the writer, and there are always new forms emerging that eschew the figure of the writer altogether. The examples in Chapter 3 of Cartoon de Salvo's long-form improvisation show *Hard Hearted Hannah and Other Stories* (2008) or Punchdrunk Theatre's site-specific and immersive performance *Faust* (2006) are both a case in point. Their inclusion, and the inclusion of similar examples throughout this volume, is justified by their collective impact on our perspective of contemporary drama and the vocabulary we use for discussing it. Our assumptions regarding the use of common terminology are challenged when the practical activities of the 'writer' or the structural form of the 'drama' or 'play' go far beyond our habitual expectations of linear, realist depictions of life on stage, where 'the aesthetic gap between the world of the stage and the world of the audience [is] reduced to a minimum'.[2]

The main body of the book is arranged into six chapters, each exploring a particular professional context of writing for performance. Their order is deliberate, navigating the reader from the conventional demands of analysing 'New Writing' in context in Chapter 1 – plays performed largely in theatres and written by individual authors – to 'Adaptation and Transposition' in Chapter 6, where texts have been removed from their original context and reframed by theatre companies through dance, installation, mixed-media and site-specific performance. The interim chapters bridge this work through an exploration of verbatim theatre, writing and devising, Black and Asian theatre and theatre for young people.

Chapter 1 offers a comprehensive analysis of three major British writers whose bodies of work stretch across the book's timeframe: Simon Stephens, Gregory Burke and Caryl Churchill. The limited selection of writers is intentional, allowing more detailed script analyses that are not possible in other chapters due to the breadth of examples on offer. By focusing on shifts in the form and structure of their plays across 14 years and relating them to the context in which they were written, this first chapter provides an introduction to the mainstream of contemporary drama and an overarching perspective on the preoccupations of writers since 1996. The last 15 years have also seen the meteoric rise of verbatim theatre, where the writer is – or subsequently takes on the mantle of – journalist or editor, not of their own material but of words taken directly from written or spoken interviews, court hearings, newspapers and testimonials. Chapter 2 suggests reasons for the exponential growth of verbatim theatre and examines the writer's process of editing and selecting material. In contrast to Chapter 1 this section provides a bird's-eye view of the genre and resists a prolonged analysis of particular practitioners, including instead a range of work by David Hare, Robin Soans, Nicolas Kent and Richard Norton-Taylor at the Tricycle Theatre and Alecky Blythe's company Recorded Delivery, among others.

Chapter 3 combines the approaches of the first two chapters, offering an extended introduction to the key characteristics of writing and devising to place four longer case studies in context. Each case study contributes to a broader exploration of the different functions of writer, writing and text in the devising process, drawing on work by David Eldridge and Rufus Norris (*Market Boy* 2006); Frantic Assembly and Bryony Lavery (*Stockholm* 2007); three commissioned writers from Plymouth's 2008 site-specific and interdisciplinary festival 'Hidden City', created by Part Exchange, and the long-form improvisation show *Hard Hearted Hannah and Other Stories* (2008) by Cartoon de Salvo. The chapter also introduces the difficulty of imposing closed definitions on the different processes of making theatre; writing and devising stretch across many different disciplines and finding a categorical definition becomes less important than presenting the range of approaches in existence. This perspective is echoed by Chapter 4, taking as its starting point the author's potentially problematic decision to create a separate section exploring work by Black and Asian writers. It is a deliberate catalyst for teasing out the reasoning behind this choice, relating it to the history of British Black and Asian theatre before considering the tensions between representation, aesthetics and politics in work from the last three decades. Plays by debbie tucker green, Roy Williams, Kwame Kwei-Armah, Tanika Gupta and Gurpreet Kaur Bhatti provide a contemporary perspective on this historical issue, in particular the conflict between the writer's right to offend and the audience's right to offence in a multicultural world.

Chapter 5 continues the focus upon specific communities by considering the authors of plays written by, with and for young audiences and the different contexts in which they work. A brief history of theatre for young people reveals tensions between theatre as instrumentalism and theatre as art, encapsulated in various ways in the three subsequent case studies: Edward Bond's work for Birmingham's Theatre-in-Education company Big Brum; Fin Kennedy's collaborations with Mulberry School in Whitechapel, East London, and finally National Theatre Connections, which has commissioned up to ten new plays from professional writers every year for a decade, each specifically designed for productions by young people. The main body of the book concludes with Chapter 6, a substantial section on 'Adaptation and Transposition' that analyses the process of transposing texts from their original context to the contemporary theatre, looking at adapting companies with Filter Theatre's *Twelfth Night* (2006), Punchdrunk Theatre's *Faust* (2006) and Kneehigh Theatre's 2008 adaptation of *Brief Encounter*. This chapter also examines writers who have adapted work, such as Blake Morrison's *Lisa's Sex Strike* (a version of Aristophanes' *Lysistrata*) for West Yorkshire company Northern Broadsides in 2007, as well as writer-director adaptations such as Ben Power and Rupert Goold's radical 2008 reworking of Luigi Pirandello's *Six Characters in Search of an Author*. Each chapter finishes with a series of short paragraphs summarising the key points. Secondary reading (in addition to the texts referred to in the chapter end notes) is suggested in the Student Resources section along with online reference sites. On occasion, where references are from personal interview or correspondence with the author, or if it is useful to include some explanation on a particular point for the reader, this will appear in the chapter end notes.

It has become clear by investigating the breadth of the writer's role that the titles of 'playwright' and 'dramatist', taking their root from the words 'play' and 'drama', are not necessarily appropriate for work which no longer takes the form of what we may consider to be a drama, or even a play. We are often exploring work where elements commonly assumed to be derived from the writer's hand are present, but the writer is absent, or if not absent perhaps acting as a dramaturg, adapter, co-creator or director – sometimes performing more than one of these roles. The selection of the term 'writer' and its continued application through the rest of this book is conscious and deliberate; foregrounding our definitions of drama and theatre will be equally helpful in framing the chapters that follow.

WRITERS, THEATRE AND DRAMA

Theatre is derived from the Greek word *theatron* or 'place for viewing' and on the surface this root meaning does not appear to be problematic.[3] 'Theatre' is a clear adoption of the word by the English language: audiences view (or see) whilst performers perform, and this is true of many old and new forms of theatre. However, when a reader first approaches the analysis or interpretation of a play text, much of this activity is occupied not with seeing performances at all, but seeing words on a page. Reading, rather than seeing and experiencing a multidimensional form of communication, becomes the dominant mode of reception. At once this illustrates one of the central paradoxes of studying theatre in its written form, and one of its most exciting challenges: the play text exists in isolation from performance. The job of the director, dramaturg, performer and so on is to interpret it from a practical point of view, to creatively enquire how the play text will be realised on a multitude of practical levels.

Analysing a play text in isolation from performance has its

limitations, and to take a broad view of the task, 'one can argue that all dramatic works are, in some senses, open compositions'.[4] We cannot know for certain, 100 per cent, how the play will be received by an audience. This presents the reader with a problem, but not an insurmountable one. If a performance realises the text in three-dimensional form, including all the nuances of direction, acting and design that support the writing, the task of the reader must therefore be a search for 'performance potential'. This search relies on an understanding of theatre's immediacy as a performance language and its relationship to written text.

Playwright and academic Dan Rebellato further problematises this act of reading, stating that 'urging people to create sharp, vivid mental images of the plays is always to add information that is not contained in the play' – but the act of responding to a play text is a necessarily interpretative one, and the adding of information should not presuppose a move away from the intentions desired by the writer: in a perfect world, these additions only bring clarity and emphasis to what the text indicates.[5] Text is only the latent potential of performance bound to the page, but the more one becomes familiar with the translation of material from page to stage, the stronger our understanding and our instincts become. Reading and analysing text for performance is a creative process that can be honed and practised.

An element of theorising naturally accompanies this creative process of reading, and it is essential to recognise that in theatre, theory is tightly bound to practice. This is the basis of dramaturgy: the application of theory through practice, and the formulation of theory sprung from practical knowledge. Aristotle, as the first theatre theorist, could only have defined the mechanics of Greek tragedy in *Poetics* from studying the plays alongside the nature of the performances themselves. Theatre practice predates theatre theory, which is not to discredit theory but to recognise its symbiotic relationship with practice, and the usefulness of its application when faced with 'more than a hundred closely printed pieces of paper bound together in a cardboard sleeve'.[6] What is on the page is not yet the performance – it is only the beginning.

Exploring the origins of the word 'drama' we find movement through two historical definitions; the word stems initially from the

Greek verb *drãn* – to do – before shifting away from an active root meaning to be adopted by the language of Late Latin to mean 'a play': a much more fixed and rigid notion.[7] Whilst it is rare to hear somebody profess that they have written 'a drama' rather than 'a play', it is worth noting this tension between the fixed (the written word) and the ephemeral (the performance), which relates again to the reader's task. The phrase 'dramatic literature', commonly used to refer to play texts, only re-emphasises this unhelpful tension. Literature suggests the novel, the written form, the reader, an audience of one and the theatre of the mind; the dramatic suggests the immediate, the spoken, the experienced, and the communal theatre of human beings moving before us through space and time.

To conflate drama and literature carries not only challenges regarding definition, but it also challenges how we interpret the dramatic text. Once again, we must read it in a bid to discover its potential for transformation into live performance, not its qualities as literature to be read. Too often the study of play texts is carried out within the same realm as the study of a poem or book, for its literary qualities alone – particularly Shakespeare – as if the writer had never intended it to be performed. This approach indicates an ignorance of the theatrical form and of the process of creating theatre itself, which is necessarily collective, lived and shared, just as the performance will be.

Drama has long shared an association with the genres of naturalism and realism, and as such with the principles of those dramatic forms: linear narrative, action driven by causality, characters on clear journeys and a presentation of the physical world that closely matches reality. Drama, for want of a better description, has a strong association with accessible storytelling and naturalism remains, as writer Howard Barker rather cynically puts it, 'the official art of late democratic capitalism'.[8] But it is not only through naturalism and realism that the relationship between theatre and drama has solidified. Even across many diverse European forms of theatre, the use of paradigmatic dramatic features such as plot, imitative action, characters facing dilemmas and the resolution of conflicts to reach some sort of goal or super-objective has persisted. These elements remain present even in theatre that has moved increasingly away from a text-based culture; German academic

Hans-Thies Lehmann's influential study *Postdramatic Theatre* (2006, first English edition) finds evidence of theatre's literary legacy even through numerous 'new' forms of theatre which have rejected text as the dominant mode of discourse. The work may be 'post' drama as storytelling, but the repetition of dramatic characteristics only provides them with further cultural legitimacy, 'frequently still unquestioningly regarded as constitutive for "the" theatre' and resulting in theatre itself being commonly thought of as the '*theatre of dramas*'.[9]

In light of the thesis put forward by Lehmann, the avant-garde objectives in the first half of the twentieth century by art movements such as Dadaism and Surrealism – and more theatrically-inclined movements such as German Expressionism and Theatre of the Absurd – to unseat popular European theatre from the world of naturalism become nothing more than failed projects of the avant-garde, the terms 'drama' and 'theatre' maintaining a synonymous relationship despite their efforts. Unlike the more recent examples Lehmann explores – theatre-makers such as Robert Lepage or the Wooster Group, whose performances draw on languages beyond text – this failure is partly due to the dominance of the word. The assumed primacy of text above all other elements of the stage chained the avant-garde to theatre's literary pretensions. Even the radical theatrics of the inaugural Surrealist art movement's plays – Alfred Jarry's infamous *Ubu Roi* (1896) with its scatological opening torrent or Apollinaire's dreamscapes in *The Breasts of Tiresias* (1903) – were still dependent on action driven by character, communicated through text. The aim of the Surrealist movement to disrupt conventional forms of art, at least in its theatrical branch from Lehmann's perspective, was undone by an inescapable dramaturgical habit.

In fact, what these experiments did precipitate was something potentially far more important than an outright rejection of the dramatic theatre. Rather than destroying the form, the dramatic theatre was instead bestowed with new possibilities. It could begin to articulate something already tentatively explored by the Surrealists, and certainly by Dadaism: 'metaphysical anguish at the absurdity of the human condition'.[10] Rather than being totally eradicated, text-driven drama was given licence to go beyond the photographic representation of the real and instead embrace imaginative theatrical worlds, poetic language, symbolic and representative figures and darkly philosophical scenarios, embracing a true theatre of metaphor. These elements can be found throughout the body of work associated with the Theatre of the Absurd, plays by Genet, Ionesco and Beckett in particular: obvious precursors to the early work of British writers Harold Pinter and N. F. Simpson. In fact Peter Hall's English-language premiere of Beckett's *Waiting for Godot* in 1955 at the Arts Theatre in London pre-dated the first production of Harold Pinter's *The Birthday Party* (1958) by only a few years.

The incongruous interruption to this absurdist theatrical duo was John Osborne's infamous and fiercely realist kitchen-sink drama *Look Back in Anger* in 1956. Beckett's play was routinely subjected to walk-outs by the audience and Pinter's was described by the press as 'one of those plays in which an author wallows in symbols and revels in obscurity'.[11] The director of Osborne's play, Tony Richardson, described the reviews as 'almost universally disastrous'.[12] It was Osborne's legacy of social realism that ultimately fixed itself in the nation's consciousness, piercing a political artery that was waiting to burst: the genre of social(ist) realism was awakened. The characteristics of the dramatic theatre would continue to dominate the work of new theatre writers, from the living room of Osborne's incandescent Jimmy Porter straight through to the anonymously opulent hotel room of Sarah Kane's 1995 play *Blasted*.

British theatre may have maintained the binary of theatre and drama into the twenty-first century, but this maintenance does not represent a wholesale fidelity to the genres of realism and naturalism; the examples in the following chapters show this quite clearly. John Freeman writes that 'the grand narratives of mainstream dramatic invention are built on the classical modernist idea that there are certain truths that can unify humankind', and in doing so casts glances in the direction of Aristotle's unities of space and time found in *Poetics*, and the unities of space and time that form the backbone of realism and naturalism.[13] In 1979 the postmodern philosopher François Lyotard articulated in *The Postmodern Condition* the inadequacies of such grand narratives as religion, the

Enlightenment and a knowable history; Freeman argues that in a postmodern world, the result is the birth of a multiplicity of narratives. Our thirst for story is now quenched through the day-to-day narratisation of life through the media, television, film and a technological world that offers audiences the ability to narrate, engage and even live in their own virtual performances. Chapter 3 explores the impact of new media on writing and performance in more detail, but such arguments are usually followed closely by claims that the writers' theatre is somehow dead, despite the still-prolific output of new plays since the mid-nineties.[14]

The assumption is that to write for the theatre implies writing a story, ergo if the play as a form of theatre is dead or diminishing, then so too is the role of the writer. Whilst this is inaccurate scaremongering, it returns us conveniently to our original concern with the title of 'dramatist': it implies a writer of drama but not a writer practising the multitude of other forms of which the contemporary theatre is comprised, such as live art, installation art, theatre as event, autobiographical performance or site-specific promenades. Although 'drama' and 'theatre' have maintained a stable relationship for over a century, a study of contemporary British drama and our comprehension of the writer's role must be one that can relinquish 'story' from 'drama'.

One could argue that our desire for theatre is not a specific desire for plot-led narrative, but what this can engender in us as spectators: a feeling of recognition that what we are experiencing matters to us as human beings, and that a connection is formed between the performance and ourselves. Plot-led narrative is not the only route to achieving this. We must extend the remit of drama to work that not only echoes characteristics of the dramatic theatre – a basis in spoken text, action and human agency – but also shows innovation in form, performance environment, concept or audience-performer relationships. This means including work that is contemporary not only for its place in recent history, but because it displays originality of thought, vitality of imagination, or creates a challenge to our accepted ideas about what performance can encompass: 'creating unique forms of theatre that express what it is like to be alive today'.[15]

It is perhaps for this reason that Tim Etchells, Artistic Director of ensemble company Forced Entertainment and a leading force in contemporary performance – not playwriting – recently found himself rubbing shoulders with writers David Edgar, David Greig, Mark Ravenhill and Tanika Gupta in *At The Sharp End* (2007), a collected volume of interviews by Peter Billingham that examines the work of five 'leading dramatists'. This is a vital form of recognition, acknowledging not only Etchells' successful history as performer, writer and artistic entrepreneur, but also our need to adapt our terminology. We need to transform our long-held ideas about roles in the creative process and what they are, and to keep moving forward in a medium that is constantly evolving.

The selection of writers and work in this book reflects this perspective and attempts to look forward rather than create a static picture: definition is in truth a reductive and theoretical process, ever-limiting like the snake eating its tail. The third part of this Introduction attempts to explore what theatre theory is in relation to contemporary drama, and presents the role of the dramaturg: an increasingly visible role in British theatre and a potential bridge between theory and practice.

THEATRE AND THEORY

A common enquiry from students of theatre is to ask what and whom theatre theory is actually for. At times it can seem perverse to be studying what appears to be reflective, analytical, dry or even obvious theoretical material, when we desire to work in a medium that is so often spontaneous, unpredictable, exciting and eager to break established conventions. Theory in the classroom can seem so far divorced from practical activity that the connection is missed. As a general rule of thumb, a beneficial response has been drawing a comparison with the act of making theatre itself. The processes for doing so are multitudinous, but there is one fundamental dynamic that underpins the collaborative act of making theatre: conversation.

We are constantly communicating with one another. We are seeking communication with an audience. We are always in dialogue, even if it is with ourselves or our work. We make artistic decisions, argue over these choices and fight our case. Without a common terminology, shared vocabulary and ability to stretch our understanding across different forms of theatre we are less supple practitioners. It is true that we can learn to practice making theatre through just doing and seeing, but we can also learn to practice through re-doing, re-seeing and analysing – theorising – by asking the question 'why did they do it like that?' It is the same question we are constantly asking ourselves as practitioners, studying our theatrical choices: 'why are we doing it like this?'

Performance theory and performance studies has emerged in the last 20 years as a field arguably derived from theatre studies, somewhat dislodged from the practice of staging drama or theatre as we have defined it thus far. Through encompassing the hugely variable notions of what performance is – sport, ritual, play, psychotherapy, role-playing, teaching – the definition of performance can reach a point where it becomes completely divorced from the theatre space, demonstrating an absence of 'many or all of the signposts we associate with theatre production'.[16] Whilst we can probably speak of an audience existing for these types of 'performance' – a sports match or a teacher speaking to a class of students – those who comprise that audience are unlikely to perceive either event as 'performance'; their self-identity as an audience and the way they read the performance is therefore also disrupted. An audience of sports fans or students is not an audience watching theatre, and reactions in the theatre are always informed by the role an audience assumes or is instructed to assume by the work.

Considering the role of the audience is potentially useful, particularly with some of the work that follows that requires an audience to become actively engaged with the performance. This is true for the relatively static 'experiential' nature of in-yer-face theatre, the full-blown masked 'immersive' role required at the performances of Punchdrunk Theatre and the involvement of young people in the creation of plays they will later perform in, or see performed. The sprawling field of performance theory described above is still one that needs careful navigation; 'performance' in the context of this book is therefore assumed to refer to a theatre event consciously produced for a theatre audience. This may seem like a limiting definition considering the broad scope of performance theory, but it allows us to consider some of the progressive work falling under the category of contemporary drama, particularly that which is probing for greater flexibility in the role of the theatre audience

In terms of theatre theory, the twentieth century sees a gradual exchange of theories that were artistically introspective, exploring the rules of how to make theatre, for theories that linked together society and theatre in a bid to find a space where 'the stage and the society around it were perfectly united in form and content'.[17] By the end of the 1970s these theories (of Expressionism, epic theatre, Surrealism and so on, as mentioned above) had been repeatedly discarded and replaced, leaving what is referred to as 'a dimension mystically referred to as "beyond theatre"' and an invitation for a 'torrent of words': a cyclical but ultimately paralysing stasis of theoretical ideas that could lead to few practice-based outcomes.[18] This is the apparent black hole of theory and practice we inhabit in the early twenty-first century.

One of the possible reasons for theory's (or even theatre's) perceived obscurity, at least in the eyes of students pursuing a practice-based profession, may therefore be the shift away from theory created by those working in theatre (often collected in 'how to' manuals introducing the basics of writing, directing, acting and so on – theories *of* theatre) towards theory written by those not involved in it as professional practitioners. Their understanding is derived far less from practical experience in the field and instead taken largely (if not exclusively) from academic and pedagogic discourse focusing on niche areas – theories *about* theatre.[19] This tendency suggests a worrying drift of theatre theory away from the material theatre itself, or even of material theatre away from its own existence. Andy Field's *Guardian* Theatre blog of 23 January 2009, citing Forced Entertainment's *Nights in this City* as an unseen mental inspiration, quite sincerely floated the concept of 'a theatre of the mind' as a viable alternative to the real thing if playhouses and the Arts Council were to suddenly fold.

The separation of theatre practice and the academy is symptomatic of a broader suspicion of theory within professional British theatre and in turn towards the burgeoning profession of dramaturgy. The practice of dramaturgy has its origins in the work of playwright and theorist Gotthold Lessing in the mid-eighteenth century, as he attempted to employ a working model for a new German national theatre in Hamburg.[20] Among his responsibilities was the analysis of plays and productions at the theatre, and the task outline echoes the principles of the reader outlined above. Lessing was 'expected to assess a play from a literary viewpoint – providing background information on the plays themselves, the sources of plays and their structural and linguistic merits and demerits – and from the practical viewpoint of production'.[21] Lessing also recorded his findings in a journal of theatre criticism designed for both professional and public readership, the *Hamburgische Dramaturgie*; he was 'Germany's foremost man of letters, polemicist, and playwright'.[22] The continental perspective of the dramaturg is founded on an understanding of the role belonging to somebody who is academically and theoretically informed, but can bring that knowledge to bear on the practical decisions involved in creating work.

The role of the dramaturg in Britain is largely associated with the growing development culture for new plays and the processes of script-reading, workshops, one-to-one meetings with writers and rehearsed readings that often comprise a new script's journey to production, but they also work in devised theatre, revivals of classics, dance and site-specific theatre. Unfortunately their effective deployment in the field of both contemporary drama, offering opportunities for new writers to gain a greater understanding of the craft of writing for performance, and classical drama – the Royal Shakespeare Company has a dramaturg on its permanent staff – has not deterred critics from portraying them as 'unwelcome intruders into a domain not traditionally regarded as their territory in the UK'.[23] At worst they are perceived as 'meddlesome sounding creatures . . . highly paid, highly academic and notoriously highly strung'.[24] What these comments overlook is that Lessing's work, and the theories of the Epic theatre developed by the writer and dramaturg Bertolt Brecht 200 years later, were a development of theory for use through practical means. They both sought to employ a detailed and rigorous approach to actor training, writing, directing, design and production, and the education of audiences to not only create a more culturally and socially significant theatre, but also simply to craft a higher quality of work.

The potential advantage of the scholar–practitioner or the dramaturg above the academic theorist, therefore, is their ability to deploy theory through practice as a means to achieving clarity of expression in their own work or the work of their collaborators. Playwright and essayist George Hunka rather poetically likens those with these dual identities to 'moles underneath their aesthetic ground, examining the soil from which the art of drama springs'.[25] This metaphor again suggests a deep exploration of conditions informing the construction of dramatic art, but from a helpfully subjective perspective that allows research to directly inform practice and vice versa. The appearance of theory or theoretical principles in this book is therefore linked, where possible, to their further application in practice, or to illuminate processes that writers, companies and performances have followed which then lead to specific practical outcomes in the generation of work.

This book is not an instruction manual for theatre makers and is not a guide to theory or practice; it is designed to illustrate the varied influences that have shaped contemporary drama's creation and reception. They are influences we need to be aware of in both our analysis and composition of drama: the social and political contexts of the world we live in; the models of theatre history that frame our work and the vocabulary we use to both talk about practice and market or label the work. These aspects of theatre are in constant conversation and are explored in the final part of this Introduction, creating the beginning of the book's much longer dialogue between text and context.

CONTEMPORARY THEATRE IN CONTEXT – A BRIEF HISTORY

As forms of playwriting and writer-led performance evolve, the play text becomes an increasingly poor substitute for recording a performance. This has always been true of play texts, which as Rebellato noted rely on the imagination of the reader to fill in the gaps, but even more so in a theatre that has begun to merge physical performance, music, interactive film, site-specific environments and even acrobatics with scripted work.

The recent plays of Cornish-based ensemble company Kneehigh Theatre (*Don John*, 2009; *Brief Encounter*, 2008) or the collaboration between David Farr (Lyric Hammersmith's Artistic Director from 2006–2009), musician Nick Cave and the practitioners of Iceland's Vesturport company for *Metamorphosis* (2007) are, for example, rich with theatrical languages that go far beyond the limitations of the spoken word; yet the play texts are still available after the production. British practitioners have always existed in an author-centric theatre culture, and it is refreshing to see this position being called into question not only through the subordination of the text to an increasingly imaginative theatrical *langue*, but also the distinct mark of the auteur-director, perhaps best embodied by Katie Mitchell's radical staging of contemporary plays (*Attempts on Her Life*, 2007), classic literature (*The Waves*, after Virginia Woolf, 2005) and extant play texts (*Women of Troy*, 2007 and *The Seagull*, 2006).

Mitchell is still an anomaly, however, and critics and audiences are still coming to terms with her European-influenced style of directing and adventurous audio-visual theatrical experiments: following her production of Martin Crimp's new translation of *The Seagull* she received hate mail from spectators. Despite artistic entrepreneurs such as Mitchell, British theatre remains a place where the assumed mode of communication is that of realism, and where work that breaks these conventions is misinterpreted as an irritating interruption to a standardised form of dramatic theatre, compared to it in a reductive manner.

It is important to recognise that these changes to the status quo are not always welcomed and can have far-reaching consequences; for example, the arrival of contemporary British plays within other theatre cultures is not necessarily regarded as a positive influence. The interpretative challenges set by the work of some contemporary dramatists mean that the 'authorship' of the final production seems to lay in the hands of the directors rather than the writers, and occasionally to detrimental effect. For example, Croatian academic Sanja Nikcevic links the decline of the words 'play' and 'playwright' in continental Europe to the influx of contemporary

British dramatists in the European theatre (namely Sarah Kane, Mark Ravenhill and to a lesser extent Jez Butterworth) whose plays were simply seen as 'objects ready to be shaped into dramatic material'.[26] Illustrating the shift in vocabulary, she notes that 'the play became *pre-text*, *scenario* or *libretto*, *idea*, *words* – all these now appear on playbills all over Europe where once "play" was used'.[27] The plays' tendency to be open to interpretation, upon which these directors seized, is perceived by Nikcevic as an inability of the playwrights to communicate their vision coherently through a suitable theatrical language. Despite the claims that contemporary British drama from the late 1990s comprised an innovative new movement, she finds the plays 'lacked the usual criteria for this in not initiating new conventions of staging' and showed a habitual use of 'realistic and naturalistic procedures'.[28]

If this book is concerned with analysing drama, the implication above of 'usual criteria' – a norm or accepted convention against which new drama can be compared – is significant; in analysis it is a double bind that requires careful application. On the one hand it anchors us to the past, threatening a one-size-fits-all approach that, misused, becomes a barrier to the discovery of new theatrical forms: an attempt to 'dramaturgically "terraform"' the work without lending credence to the alternative rules the writer may be attempting to create.[29] On the other hand, we can use our existing knowledge of principles of drama even when they are deliberately absent in the play, applying them as a tool of translation, revealing the work rather than smothering its unique qualities. Elinor Fuchs, in a highly useful analysis of Samuel Beckett's absurdist classic *Waiting for Godot*, refers to this as a revealing of the play's 'super-text': discovering what is present through identifying what is absent.[30] The word 'revealing' suggests an important habit in the analysis of any play text of performance: focusing on what the writer is attempting to reveal to the reader or audience, and how effectively this is shown. A focus on the writer and new drama was a prominent feature of guides to British theatre occupying the years either side of the millennium, and this book is in part an attempt to roughly ring-fence the period. The most significant was Aleks Sierz's publication *In-Yer-Face Theatre: British Drama Today* in 2001, which offered a polemic commentary on writers whose plays were 'a theatre of sensation: it jolts both actors and spectators out of conventional responses, touching nerves and provoking alarm'.[31] Note here Sierz's precise use of the word sensation – implying a visceral, experiential environment for the audience – different from sensationalism, which implies an empty, shock-value tactic that is momentarily affecting, but lacks any dramatic rigour. It is true that these plays were often shocking in content for audiences, and Chapter 1 offers a more detailed perspective on this content; but it is important to mention at this early stage that the 'shock' of the content extended into unpalatable political opinions and surprising shifts in form, not just on-stage portrayals of violence.

Many of these plays clung on to the apron springs of linear, character-based dramatic conflict but there were distinct exceptions. The trajectory of the five plays of Sarah Kane, who committed suicide after suffering severe depression, show a progressive shift from character-based drama, through to plays awash with stunning theatrical imagery, and finishing with an open theatrical poem. Her writing was fiercely innovative, implementing forms and structures that expressed political and emotional states of mind.

Her first play *Blasted* (1995) is an appropriate example. In seeking to illustrate the moral degradation and fractured experience of civil war for both soldiers and civilians, the second half of her play is literally blown apart when a bomb rips through the naturalistic setting of 'a hotel room so expensive it could be anywhere in the world'.[32] The frame of the play is both physically and formally altered: the scenes become shorter and shattered, the experience for the audience disjointed and the timeframes concertinaed – the play's dramaturgy becomes a manifestation of the human experience it is depicting.

The plays referenced in Sierz's book came flowing from the pens of writers who spent their formative years under the shadow of a Conservative government. In response to a nation embracing the moral wasteland of a capitalist, free-market economy, and all at the expense of the socialist projects of the 1970s, their plays displayed a distinctly nihilistic attitude towards the world. The dynamics of Mark Ravenhill's *Shopping and Fucking* (1996), for example, are almost totally predicated on a basis of commercial transactions involving either sex or drugs, populated by characters lacking any sense of moral purpose. This was 'Cruel Britannia', not 'Cool Britannia'.[33]

Barely preceding Sierz's timely classification of the fresh young face of contemporary playwriting, Dominic Dromgoole offered a much more personal cataloguing of writers seen on British stages with *The Full Room* (2001), an unashamedly idiosyncratic offering that pulled no punches. David Hare is lampooned for waking up with a hard-on having dreamt of a knighthood, David Eldridge is described as 'the playwright as bloke' and Yasmina Reza, French writer of the Broadway and West End smash hit *Art* (1996) – a satirical comedy where a trio of friends have their relationship exposed when one of them pays thousands of pounds for a blank white canvas – has to make do with a single translated sentence for her entry, reading '*Yasmina Reza est très riche*' (Yasmina Reza is very rich).[34] The benefit of Dromgoole's encyclopaedia, however, is that he finds space for the stalwarts of British playwriting whom, in retrospect considering its now seminal status as a guidebook to late-1990s theatre, Sierz's volume disappointingly fails to acknowledge. Whilst Sierz never claims it is a comprehensive review of recent theatre history, the continuing presence of names such as Howard Barker, Steven Berkoff, David Hare, Howard Brenton, Caryl Churchill, Edward Bond and David Edgar in the 1990s and increasingly into the new millennium still helps to form a significant part of British drama's contemporary canon.

This more rounded approach is upheld by Edgar's own edited volume *State of Play* (1999), containing contributions from a wide range of theatre writers and directors and prefaced by a concise contextualising chapter, which offers a brief socio-political history from 1956 to the date of publication. It helps the reader to identify not only the isolated importance of the play text (or the performance, and its author) but also the conditions of its production and the forces that have formed waves of new writing through history, namely 'the aftermath of great national triumphs, at the point where the loss of the old calls into question the rise of the new'.[35] Used together, this formidable trio of authors – Sierz, Dromgoole and Edgar – can provide a particularly coherent picture of the conditions leading up to the theatre boom across the millennium, and at the centre of it all stand the plays and their writers.

The demerits of terms and labels should be viewed as part of the issue discussed above regarding vocabulary and terminology; Sierz's term 'theatre of sensation' has become a recognisable marker, and open to criticism as a misleading market-influenced phrase. He has since defended his choice on numerous occasions, at pains to point out that he merely chose a label from those already being circulated by the media and that this was inherently 'more democratic' than imposing one.[36] Others are more sceptical; in an interview with Mel Kenyon, the agent of In-Yer-Face writers Sarah Kane and Mark Ravenhill, she refers to the movement as 'a load of old shite. There's no movement. But there is a moment. There *was* a moment'.[37]

This sense of the momentary – of the moment passed, especially – is vital to our perception of theatre history and its relationship to theatre future. It is a shifting and sensitive medium, both informed and aggravated by its past, its development erratic rather than gradual. Edgar ascertains that whilst contemporary theatre culture clearly supports and reveres the work of writers, a review of 'the golden ages of creativity – Elizabethan and Jacobean, Restoration, Edwardian and postwar' suggests only 76 years from 350 as credible periods of new writing production: 1590–1620 (Shakespeare and his contemporaries), late 1670s–1707 (Restoration period) and 1890–1914 (Wilde, Granville-Barker, Pinero and Shaw).[38]

The purpose of revisiting, reassessing and taking stock of activities in the past as our knowledge in the present expands is not to nitpick at other's discoveries or claim the territory as our own. Theatre cannot evolve in a temporal vacuum; the act of labelling the past is a process whereby the messy and impulsive relationship between audiences, the work and the world may be better understood, and thus inform the work we make in the present. The day we stop and decide we know what we are doing once and for all is the day our work becomes most vulnerable. The first chapter of this book presents three writers who follow this principle closely, with bodies of work that are continually shifting in response to their environment, creating a fitting start to a broader consideration of contemporary British drama in context.

NOTES

1. Ric Allsopp, 'Performance Writing', *PAJ: A Journal of Performance and Art* 21:1, 1999, pp. 76–80 (76).
2. J. L. Styan, *Modern Drama in Theory and Practice Volume 1: Realism and Naturalism* (Cambridge: Cambridge University Press, 1981), pp. 162–3.
3. Definition taken from the *Collins English Dictionary: 21ˢᵗ Century Edition* (Glasgow: HarperCollins).
4. Cathy Turner and Synne K. Behrndt (eds), *Dramaturgy and Performance* (Basingstoke: Palgrave Macmillan, 2008), p. 35.
5. Dan Rebellato, 'When We Talk of Horses: Or, what do we see when we see a play?', *Performance Research* 14:1, 2009, pp. 17–28 (21).
6. Julian Meyrick, 'Cut and Paste: The Nature of Dramaturgical Development in the Theatre', *Theatre Research International* 31:1, 2006, pp. 270–82 (272).
7. Definition taken from the *Collins English Dictionary: 21st Century Edition* (Glasgow: HarperCollins).
8. Howard Barker, 'On Naturalism and its Pretensions', *Studies in Theatre and Performance* 27:3, 2007, pp. 289–93 (291).
9. Hans-Thies Lehmann, *Postdramatic Theatre* (Abingdon: Routledge, 2006), p. 21.
10. Martin Esslin, *The Theatre of the Absurd* (London: Pelican, 1968), p. 24.
11. Michael Anderson, *Anger and Detachment: A Study of Arden, Osborne and Pinter* (London: Pitman, 1976), p. 88.
12. Ruth Little and Emily McLaughlin, *The Royal Court Theatre: Inside Out* (London: Oberon, 2007), p. 25.
13. John Freeman, *New Performance / New Writing* (Basingstoke: Palgrave Macmillan, 2007), p. 20.
14. David Edgar, 'Theatre verite'. Paper presented for the At The Sharp End conference, 15 September 2007, University of Portsmouth, England. It is a threat commonly directed at writers in contemporary theatre, but rarely realised.
15. Theodore Shank, 'The Multiplicity of British Theatre', in Theodore Shank (ed.), *Contemporary British Theatre* (London: Macmillan Press, 1996), pp. 3–18 (p. 3).

16. Erin Striff, 'Introduction: Locating Performance Studies', in Erin Striff (ed.), *Performance Studies* (Basingstoke: Palgrave Macmillan, 2003), pp. 1–13 (p. 2).

17. Julian Meyrick, 'The Limits of Theory: Academic versus Professional Understanding of Theatre Problems', *New Theatre Quarterly* 19:3, 2003, pp. 230–42 (232).

18. Ibid., p. 232.

19. Ibid., p. 232.

20. Mary Luckhurst, *Dramaturgy: A Revolution in Theatre* (Cambridge: Cambridge University Press, 2006), p. 24.

21. Ibid., p. 28.

22. Ibid., p. 25.

23. Mary Luckhurst, "Gagging': Forum on Censorship', *Contemporary Theatre Review* 17:4, 2007, pp. 516–56 (550).

24. Lucy Powell, 'Whose Lines Are They Anyway?', *The Times*, 13 March 2006.

25. George Hunka, 'Playwrights Writing: Procedure and Polemic', *PAJ: A Journal of Performance and Art* 87, 2007, pp. 119–23 (119).

26. Sanja Nickevic, 'British Brutalism, the "New European Drama", and the Role of the Director', *New Theatre Quarterly* 21:3, pp. 255–72 (255).

27. Ibid., p. 255.

28. Ibid., p. 263.

29. Mark Bly, 'Pressing an Ear Against a Hive or New Play Explorations in the Twenty-First Century', *Theatre Topics* 13:1, 2003, pp. 19–22 (20).

30. Elinor Fuchs, 'Waiting for Recognition: An Aristotle for "Non-Aristotelian" Drama', *Modern Drama* 50:4, 2007, pp. 532–44 (540).

31. Aleks Sierz, *In-Yer-Face Theatre: British Drama Today* (London: Faber and Faber, 2001), p. 4.

32. Sarah Kane, *Complete Plays* (London: Methuen, 2001), p. 3.

33. Ken Urban, 'Towards a Theory of Cruel Britannia: Coolness, Cruelty, and the 'Nineties', *New Theatre Quarterly* 20:4, 2004, pp. 354–72 (354).

34. Dominic Dromgoole, *The Full Room: An A–Z of Contemporary Playwriting* (London: Methuen, 2001).

35. David Edgar, *State of Play: Playwrights on Playwriting* (London: Faber and Faber, 1999), p. 4.
36. Aleks Sierz, 'Still In-Yer-Face? Towards a Critique and a Summation', *New Theatre Quarterly* 18:1, 2002, pp. 17–24 (18).
37. Mel Kenyon quoted in Urban, 'Towards a Theory of Cruel Britannia: Coolness, Cruelty and the 'Nineties', p. 354.
38. Edgar, *State of Play*, p. 4.

CHAPTER I

In-Yer-Face Theatre and Legacies of the New Writing Boom

NEW WRITING, THEN AND NOW

It has been 15 years since 12 January 1995, when the Royal Court Theatre in London premiered a new play by an unknown 23-year-old writer called Sarah Kane. The play told the story of a troubled relationship between an abusive older male journalist, Ian, and a naïve young woman, Cate, sharing a hotel room in Leeds whilst the former collated a news story. He was racist, angry and sexually aggressive; she was outwardly timid but showed a willingness to give as good as she got. So far, so realism. At the end of the second scene a soldier burst in, demanded to see Ian's passport and claimed the town as occupied, shortly before a bomb ripped through the entire room and catapulted the play and its characters into an expressionistic depiction of the brutality of war and the worst excesses of human cruelty.

Blasted, with its now infamous scenes of cannibalism, rape and violence – moments embedded in the play's dramaturgy, but causing total outrage – heralded a period of new theatre writing with a distinct flavour. It would dominate contemporary British drama for the next 4 years. This was work by a new wave of angry young men and women lashing out against a world they saw as deeply flawed. They were highly critical of the most lamentable aspects of their generation: apathy, cynicism and commercialism, political violence at home and abroad, and the loss of any viable ideology other than nihilism and self-destruction to guide them out of it. This was a world increasingly secularised and divisive on a domestic scale, but unified through the operating tool of capitalism – commodification – on a global scale. The outlook seemed bleak and the plays were determined to reflect this.

Aggressive and eye-catching tactics were employed both within the work, as evidenced by Kane, and in how it was branded: titles such as *Shopping and Fucking* and *Some Explicit Polaroids* by Mark Ravenhill, *Penetrator* and *The Censor* by Anthony Neilson all helped to set the tone. The form of the work had its own characteristics too, offering a stylish and streetwise theatrical language that not only embraced the visceral and experiential nature of live theatre, but also echoed attitudes found in the more provocative cultural influences of the time. This was the era of the Brit Art pack including Damien Hirst and Tracey Emin, the Brit Pop battle between Oasis and Blur, the drug-and-club fuelled generation found in Irvine Welsh's *Trainspotting*, and from across the Atlantic, the films of Quentin Tarantino with their fast-talking gangster chic and slick narrative structures. Shortly after New Labour came to power in 1997, this new British theatre was amalgamated into the expanding 'Cool Britannia' image as the 'fifth leg' on the table of edgy and contemporary cultural offerings – or cultural products, to briefly adopt the rhetoric of New Labour.[1] By 2000, new writing in Britain was deemed 'more varied, more creative, and more optimistic than at any other time in the previous three decades'.[2]

'New writing', as it became branded within the industry, was fashionable, cutting-edge and embodied the spirit of the contemporary. Arts Council funding streams showed favour to programmes that could identify, develop and produce new writers and especially work by young writers. The Boyden Report in 2000, commissioned by the Arts Council, resulted in a huge increase in theatre investment promising a £25m injection. Regional festivals of new writing have since sprung up – Hotbed in Cambridge, High Tide in Suffolk, Momentum in the East Midlands – and regional development agencies such as New Writing South (South East), Theatre Writing Partnership (East Midlands), Script (West Midlands) and Yorkshire Playwrights (North West) strive to increase the support for their members, nurturing the writing of more and more new plays, establishing a rapidly increasing culture of workshops, development and opportunities for professional training.

In the same year of publication as Sierz's seminal book, the urgency for the 'new' was reflected in a nation facing an economic world growing faster and faster, beset with the immediacy of paranoia over the war on terror following 9/11, and experiencing civil disquiet as a renewed Anglo-American political relationship strengthened its fight against international terrorism, simultaneously placing the country in a more vulnerable position. Recognisable tenets of a materialist, capitalist culture imposed themselves on the theatre as searches continued for the new, the next best thing, the most fashionable product, the youngest writer and the freshest emerging talent. The dominance of new writing brought with it a reaffirmation of a characteristic British tendency: the author's seat placed firmly at the top of the creative hierarchy.

The 'moment' of In-Yer-Face theatre has been well documented (see Introduction), characterising a vibrant but short period of theatre history with energy and optimism. The years since 2000 have been accounted for disparately, and what does exist is much more critical of the state of new writing. As Sierz, Edgar, playwright David Eldridge and others began to record the general mood of the industry in the calm after the storm, a new picture emerged. It was increasingly critical of the In-Yer-Face grouping, and frequently bemoaned new writers' lack of imagination and their apparent banishment to black-box studios in front of coterie audiences. In 2002 Sierz was first to hold his In-Yer-Face categorisation to account, probing his conclusions from only the previous year by debating the quality, counter-productiveness, introspection and reactionary nature of the plays he had selected, and criticising the lack of new writing that would have the scope to fill any theatre seating more than a hundred people.[3] This was reflected in the emergence the same year of a self-styled group called the 'Monsterists', including influential writers such as Roy Williams, Ryan Craig, Richard Bean and David Eldridge, whose manifesto was 'a right to campaign for writers to create large-scale productions, with large casts, for large-scale spaces, to allow the elevation of new writers to main stages', including among their strategies a 'dead-writers' levy' for theatres reviving classic large-cast plays, that could create financial resources for the Monsterist cause.[4]

It was not only the physical size of plays or the imaginative scope of new writers that drew criticism, but the depth of their political commitment. Although writing in the early millennium was deemed 'more overtly political than ever' it was engaging with the death of political ideology and the corruption of public bodies and corporations.[5] A resistance to the value or possibility of actual political change, and even a resistance to 'the very sense that valuation is either desirable or possible' was reflected in plays that offered politics with a very small 'p', emphasised in 'the domestic and personal, on relationships, rather than "public" issues – or, when a play does explore public issues, they are not treated as *social* concerns'.[6] Plays were becoming gradually introspective, a pale imitation of the energy and exuberance of the 1990s that so excited critics, and now writers were playing safe by 'penning unprovocative plays that flatter their liberal-minded audiences in studio theatres'.[7]

Writer David Eldridge picked up the critical baton himself in 2003, suggesting that the In-Yer-Face period 'only really lasted from 1994 to 1997', ascribing the emergence of quieter, more lyrical work from writers such as Conor McPherson, David Greig and Peter Gill to a 'period from the mid-Nineties until 11 September 2001 as one of relative peace and stability in the West'.[8] Simon Stephens corroborates this perspective but continues with the critical political stance addressed above, connecting the shift in the energy and rhythm of new plays to the public's realisation that little seemed to have been achieved since New Labour's rise to power:

> There was a sense in 1996 that things needed urgently to be changed, and I think now, given the consequences of that change, the urgency seems slightly pointless . . . people just aren't bothered about how outlandish a play is anymore, because there's a greater sense now, I think, that change is kind of fundamentally redundant.[9]

The habits of new writing that seemed so radical at the end of the previous decade had not yet been replaced by something equally startling or fresh. No new wave or easily identifiable movement of writers had emerged, leaving an uneasy climate where by 2004 – thanks to a series of high-profile incidents regarding the 'quality' of new plays – the state of new writing was very publicly called into question. The Soho Theatre's biennial Verity Bargate Award for the best play by a new writer was not awarded in 2002 because 'none of the plays submitted was good enough to win' and Britain was suffering from new writing becoming synonymous with 'yoof' and 'the relentless search for novelty'.[10] In addition, the perceived crisis was not necessarily concerned with the writing's content, or even its political perspective, but with its form: the inability of contemporary plays to escape the clutches of social realism that had long defined British drama.

David Edgar's alternative reading of the years since 1997 offers a seed of hope. Like Eldridge he cites Conor McPherson's *The Weir* (1998) as a signpost towards a 'third way' of investigating the changes in new writing, positively asserting that 'the defining characteristic is not so much a particular style, nor a particular subject, but an attitude to form'.[11] His brief thesis goes on to explore plays such as Michael Frayn's *Copenhagen* (1998) which presents multiple possible scenarios of one short conversation between nuclear scientists during the war, his own play *Albert Speer* (2000) where a man reconstructing the events of his own life has them challenged by two other characters, and Caryl Churchill's *Far Away* in the same year, which is analysed in more detail later in this chapter. What unites them for Edgar is 'an oppositional response by theatre to the overwhelming dominance of narrative in popular drama': a desire for writers to problematise story, constructing plays that question their own narrative authenticity during the act of telling (Chapter 3 also explores this tendency in writing and devising).[12] Among the critical stances taken up against them, Ken Urban's re-reading of the In-Yer-Face plays also finds a countervailing positive perspective, questioning the usefulness of studying them from 'a strictly literary or textual perspective' when they clearly 'desire to give language a body, a shifting physical presence, real but changeable'.[13] Neither Edgar nor Urban's readings suggest drama in crisis: instead they indicate an adventurous and playful attitude towards form, structure and theatricality, heeding a call at the end of 2005 for 'the best antidote to timidity in British new writing . . . the irrepressible, untamed quality of the imagination'.[14]

Despite the identification of these optimistic signs, the critical gloom continued and in 2006, regardless of the exponential rise in new work, new opportunities for development, new bursaries and new writing festivals across the UK, there remained 'a real failure of theatrical imagination at the heart of the whole artistic endeavour . . . little sense of exploration, or experiment, or excitement . . . wherever the cutting edge is, it isn't with new writers'.[15] In England, perhaps this was the case: in Scotland the same year, the picture could not have been more different as the new National Theatre of Scotland (NTS) announced its first season by commissioning ten new pieces from Scottish practitioners to take place 'simultaneously in non-traditional venues throughout Scotland . . . to be devised and performed in collaboration with local companies, communities and artists', forming the backbone of their inaugural *Home* production.[16]

Whilst the commissions did not exclusively involve writers, the spirit of invention, imagination and ambition that was deemed lacking in new work was fervently challenged, including perform-ances that took place on boats (*Home Shetland*), a disued glass factory (*Home Caithness*), a tower-block in Glasgow's East End (*Home Glasgow*) and a converted museum and art gallery (*Home Dundee*). The benefits of being a nomadic company – the NTS is not a company with a permanent production site – were clearly illustrated by the breadth of work available, and sent out a clear message regarding the proposed direction of new Scottish theatre, offering 'a progressive, dynamic model of what a national theatre might be in the twenty-first century'.[17] Looking back in 2010, what is noticeable is that whilst many of the practitioners were not writers, they have since been involved with writers on productions of new plays, suggesting that the desire for a more imaginative or interdisciplinary approach to creating contemporary drama is being fulfilled. Playwright Anthony Neilson, composer Hugh Nankivell, director John Tiffany and choreographer Scott Graham, who worked respectively on projects in Edinburgh, Shetland, Glasgow and Inverness, all feature in the following chapters of this book.

As the decade approached its last couple of years, the 'crisis' of new writing was characterised as a 'slump'. Despondency set in as still, despite the inventiveness of small pockets of writers such as Dennis Kelly, debbie tucker green and Philip Ridley, they were 'too few to get excited about. Too few that you remember; too few that people get het up about'.[18] Whilst the complaint remained that new writing was still lacking in theatricality and imagination, 'grounded by the twin ballast of naturalism and social realism', the perspective was that no new movement seemed to have arrived that could shake up what had now become the old guard.[19] What this perspective achieves other than pure frustration is unclear. To bemoan the lack of a new singular force in contemporary drama is a form of misdirection, a diversion from the more useful conversation about how the landscape may have changed over the last decade.

As a result of the growing interest in new writing and the role of the writer in collaboration with other artists beyond the solo-authored play, the imaginations and skills of writers are being put to the test in new working environments. The processes of creating and producing theatre that involve the writer as a collaborating artist, or a structuring force behind a collage of raw material (among many other possible roles) are filtering into the mainstream, challenging our perception of drama simply being the realisation of a writer's singular vision. Individual writers have also taken on the mantle of being self-innovators. Mark Ravenhill, the celebrated writer of the In-Yer-Face era, has evolved his working process since *Shopping and Fucking* in 1996, writing two plays for teenagers, *Totally Over You* (2003) and *Citizenship* (2006); performing his own one-person satire on the Hollywood film industry and 9/11 in *Product* (2005); collaborating with dance-based company Frantic Assembly in 2006 on *Pool (No Water)*; composing an epic cycle of short plays *Shoot / Get Treasure / Repeat* (Edinburgh Festival 2007) about the effects of the Iraq war on personal and political life; and in March 2009 co-directing his most recent play *Over There* with the Royal Court's Ramin Gray.

The last play is a stark answer to Sierz's continued criticism of new writing lacking metaphor and theatricality. It depicts the political ramifications of West and East Germany's unification through the story of twin brothers, who live together after the fall of the Berlin Wall but become gradually estranged through the course of the narrative. Their deep-seated political differences become too much to bear and one, the figure of the capitalist West, is seen to literally consume the figure of the socialist East, by this point doused in an ugly mess of instant packaged food and sauces. This use of theatrical metaphor to illustrate a moment of political history does feel forced after an hour, but it is clear that the threatened collapse of capitalism in the present day is the writer's critical target, and we know that the West's cannibalistic victory is ultimately hollow, selfish and doomed to failure. A more politically relevant and theatrical play would be hard to find.

Chapters 3, 5 and 6 will investigate collaborative models in more detail, but has a similar change occurred in the solo-authored play? Have there been developments in the aesthetic, politics and voice of the writers who were newly identified (or simply present) during the 1990s boom and still produce new work today? And if so, what does this indicate to us about how contemporary British drama may have evolved over the last decade? In a volume on contemporary work it may seem reductive to focus on writers about whom much has been written, or who are no longer 'new' simply because they are established, but to avoid them would only continue a potential prejudice of the new writing culture: that new plays mean young and new writers, not work from recognised and established writers. Together, the following three individuals support the notion of an evolving writer – a writer who responds to the conditions of the political and theatrical world, develops their craft, reinvents their work and pushes stylistic boundaries.

SIMON STEPHENS, GREGORY BURKE AND CARYL CHURCHILL

Simon Stephens

Stephens' first play *Bluebird* was produced in 1998 and he has since averaged a professional production of a new play every year to date, the most recent being *Punk Rock* in 2009. He was identified via the Royal Court Young Writers' Festival at the age of twenty-seven and his first play *Bluebird* (1998) centred on taxi driver Jimmy, whose cab is populated by troubled characters from the metropolis, bringing with them stories of bereavement, depression, loneliness and desire for revenge. Their voices – a mixture of humour and blind determination – transcend the gritty world outside the cab window. Jimmy's very first 'fare', known only as the Guvnor, begins by cracking clichéd jokes but ends his drunken speech with a bewildered philosophical pondering, asking 'what does it all mean? Eh? Do you have any idea what it all means? At all?'[20] It is symptomatic of characters in many of Stephens' plays to be fascinated by discovering the world and always pushing at the limits of their experience.[21] Despite their unresolved problems and unanswerable questions, rather than inducing a down-at-heel atmosphere the desire for each character to keep struggling, to keep trying in the face of adversity endows the play with a poetic optimism. Taken together, Jimmy's 'fares' depict a pre-millennial metropolitan landscape, populated by individuals determined to live through broken and damaged lives with a mixture of humour, pathos and blind hope.

This is reflected in a prickly reunion between Jimmy and his ex-wife Claire where the biggest secrets of all emerge: he accidentally ran over their daughter 5 years previously, gave up his job as a novelist and has been living in the back of his cab for four and a half years. In retreating from the world and his job as a storyteller, he has now become a receptacle for the stories of thousands of lives, absorbing the vast and varied experiences of the metropolis yet rarely setting foot outside his Nissan 'Bluebird'. Jimmy's separation from the world is re-emphasised when he presents Claire with a gift: thousands of pounds of cash in a suitcase, earned from his work. Far from a bribe or an apology for the incident, Jimmy just states to Claire that 'I have no need for it. It is about as useful to me as a suitcase full of drawing pins. Or envelopes. Or shoelaces'.[22] There is a hopeful suggestion that they may meet again, as upon her request Jimmy gives Claire the number of the minicab firm he works for. It is tinged with sadness however: if she does choose to call, they won't even know his name, only his driver number. His gradual absorption into the organism of the city renders him without identity. She leaves him standing by the cab just before daybreak, the sounds of Otis Redding's 'My Girl' and taxi cab instructions merging together in the last gasps of the night. *Bluebird* introduces some dominant characteristics of Stephens' work that are present through all of his plays. He poeticises an otherwise naturalistic use of language, allowing his characters to speak with passion and verve. He has a belief in the kindness of the human spirit, and a political perspective expressed through the personal struggles of everyday people. Perhaps most consistently, he has a sense of the urban landscape as a force that shapes our lives for better or worse. Stephens' plays are often set either within or very near large British cities – Stockport, London, Manchester – and the characters that inhabit them have troubled relationships with their locations. His second play *Herons* (2001) is set around the locks of a canal in East London, where a young boy seeks refuge from the anarchic bullies that terrorise the school and the local neighbourhood; in his third and fourth plays *Port* (2002) and *Christmas* (2003), Stockport and inner-city London become constrictive environments threatening to choke the inhabitants' attempts to improve their lives. There is a palpable shift in two of his more recent full–length plays, *Motortown* (2006, Royal Court) and *Pornography* (UK 2008, Traverse Theatre) where the urban environment is a malevolent force provoking deeply unsettling reactions.

In *Motortown*, Danny, a young soldier recently returned from fighting in Basra, is disgusted by the state of the England he has risked his life to protect. Whilst he acts upon this by abducting, torturing and shooting a young girl called Jade, this air of disgust is articulated most vehemently by Paul, the man who converts a replica gun for Danny. An embittered but perceptive fix–it man, he appears for just one scene but has a lasting impact, frequently erupting into fatalistic speeches about the state of the nation, the world and the environment. Stephens puts an uncomfortable strain on the play's structure by using a character as little more than a soap–box, but the sheer force of Paul's argument somehow earns its right to a place in the drama:

You want to know the truth about the poor in this country? They're not cool. They're not soulful. They're not honest.

They're not the salt of the fucking earth. They're thick. They're myopic. They're violent . . . Every week entire towns are torn apart by the puking boozers and the French-cropped cunts of England. Whacked off their heads on customised national health prescription anti-depressants. And testosterone injections. And Turkey Twizzlers. They puke up in the lobbies of banks. They use bank cards to go and puke in a bit of peace and quiet. Leave it there. Welcome to Barclays![23]

Paul's invective is sharp, far right-wing and one-sided, but it is also an unsettlingly accurate picture of an urban Britain creeping towards the end of the decade, self-destructing with poor health, cheap alcohol prices and a desire for refuge that can only be sought in drunken obliteration and vomiting, perhaps ironically, in the seclusion of a multinational's foyer. Stephens revisits this cynicism of the city through the monologue of a suicide bomber in *Pornography*. Travelling to London King's Cross on 7 July 2005, armed with a rucksack carrying an explosive device, the nameless character shares his passing observations of the West's cultural decadence directly with the audience:

Disused Jet garage forecourts sit side by side with double driveways. Here there are food-makers and the food they make is chemical. It fattens the teenage and soaks up the pre-teen. Nine-year-old children all dazzled up in boob tubes and mini-skirts and spangly eyeliner as fat as little pigs stare out of the window of family estate cars. In the sunshine of mid-morning in the suburbs of the South Midlands heroin has never tasted so good. Internet sex contact pages have never seemed more alluring. Nine hundred television channels have never seemed more urgent. And everybody needs an iPod.[24]

The observations made have the same ring of underlying truth as Paul's in *Motortown*. Stephens' characters are strangely seductive in their ability to persuade the audience of their perspective. The examples above contextualise snapshots of Britain recognisable to the audience and reveal the rot beneath the surface image, as we find ourselves challenged to agree with the views of a nihilistic neo-fascist and a suicide bomber.

Although common thematic elements of Stephens' work are found in both *Bluebird* and *Pornography*, the decade separation between his first and ninth full-length plays is evident through broader shifts in their underlying dramaturgy. Whilst the first play is tightly bound by the structural conventions of naturalism (even televisual naturalism in its minicab setting), such as a linear narrative, largely naturalistic dialogue, realistic staging, titled characters and a central protagonist who binds together location, theme and action, *Pornography* consists of seven scenes that can be performed by any number of actors and in any order. There are no character names preceding monologue or dialogue. There are no stage directions other than silent 'images of hell' punctuating the different scenes. There is no specific physical setting, only a broadly temporal one: a week in London straddling the 2012 Olympics announcement, Live 8, G8 and the 7/7 bombings. There is no central protagonist except at a stretch, London itself. There are subtle clues in the writing that connect six of the seven scenes by plot as well as theme, but they are deliberately coincidental, a brushing together of stories in a disparate and disconnected city.

The characters we meet in *Bluebird* with their determined optimism are now replaced by those trapped in a world of hopelessness and moral transgression. A corporate businesswoman sells vital papers to her employer's rival; an incestuous affair destroys the relationship between a brother and sister; a lecturer struggles to find work and attempts to seduce a former student; a widow sits alone in her flat downloading pornography from the Internet and descending into alcoholism; and a schoolboy fantasises about attacking his teacher. A decade on, markers of security such as family, the economy, education and employment are crumbling, leaving despondency in their wake. A tiny moment of optimism does survive: upon smelling it wafting down her street, the widow requests food from a neighbour's barbecue. Despite being taken for a madwoman, she is rewarded with a piece of chicken. This simple act of kindness in the play, placed among a sea of destruction and terror, is suddenly amplified as a beacon of hope, a possibility that our capacity for acts of kindness can still exist in a world where the foundations are slipping away:

> I walk home. The chicken tastes good. I let myself in. I can't feel my feet any more. I can't understand why there are tears pouring down the sides of my face. This makes absolutely no sense to me at all.[25]

In the given order of the published script, this is the final moment we spend with an identifiable character before the last scene: a list describing the fifty-two victims of the 7/7 bombings with one or two sentences each. The widow's words arrive as a harrowing final suggestion that we have not only lost the capacity to understand other people, but we are also incapable of relating our experiences to our emotion. We are isolated even from ourselves.

Stephens' politics become more sharply defined from *Motortown* onwards, offering a deeper critical analysis. He moves from the optimism of the new millennium to the despair of a dark new age of terror and the putrefaction of moral values. Whilst these observations find a voice through Paul and the suicide bomber, respectively, they are also captured with an expressiveness of form. What *Bluebird* begins to articulate in the stories of the characters alone, *Pornography* captures in its very architecture. The openness of the text reflects the fractured and disintegrating urban landscape, populated with fluid identities and uncertain futures. In performance, the choice of order and of cast numbers is ours to make. We create our own structure from the raw material and are given free reign to create our very own narrative: a far cry from the relative limitations of structure and story in *Bluebird*. One could suggest Stephens is responsible for writing a quintessential twenty-first-century play in form, content and intention, indicating an exciting contemporary outlook for his future work.

Gregory Burke

When his first play *Gagarin Way* was produced in 2001 at the Edinburgh Festival, Burke occupied an unusual position. In a theatre culture rife with postgraduate writing courses, workshop and development opportunities and a growing industry of dramaturgy for new writers, all contributing to the professionalisation of the role and largely focused on London, Burke was an untrained, working-class Scottish playwright from Dunfermline. His talent for black comedy, combined with the politics of his self-educated working class characters presented a fierce and refreshing view of the world where the class divide was rupturing, and a capitalist fat-cat could be a Japanese CEO or a local Fife lad who grew up down the road.

In the same way that Mark Ravenhill in *Some Explicit Polaroids* (1999) had contrived to catapult a committed political activist with 15-year-old socialist values straight into a late-1990s world of dreary New Labour civic duties, Burke's protagonists Eddie and Gary find their political values unseated in *Gagarin Way*. Both are employees of a factory, one well-versed in political philosophy and determined to uphold the communist traditions of West Fife, in particular the 'Soviet Socialist Republic ay Lumphinnans', known in the inter-war years as one of the 'Little Moscows'.[26] They intend to make a stand against the march of globalisation by kidnapping one of the factory's top businessmen – a figure of the capitalist establishment – and murder him, reviving political violence. As Gary explains to security guard Tom:

> Gary   Intellectual propaganda means nothing. (*Beat.*) Nay cunt listens tay a fucking debate. (*Beat.*) This is the propaganda ay the deed. (*Beat. Indicates Frank.*) He's a message.
>
> Tom   A message?
>
> Gary   That we've had enough?
>
> Tom   Enough what?
>
> Gary   Enough ay fucking everything.[27]

Their hostage is not Japanese or even American but Frank, a consultant from Surrey who grew up in Fife and whose father was a miner. Burke's canny choice of characterisation reveals a globalised business world out of sync with the political expectations of the play's protagonists, creating a metaphor for globalisation's capacity to dismantle communities, disrupt political identities and seep quietly into the fabric of day-to-day life without us even noticing. Gary states that he can't be an anarchist because he quite enjoys a Big Mac, and whilst he despises labels, he can make an exception if they're on his clothes. One of Eddie's characteristically articulate explanations for this act of abduction and murder is that he's been 'outflanked by the fluid nature ay modern demographics' and whilst he suffers from a crisis in masculinity (one of Sierz's identified core themes from the In-Yer-Face cohort of playwrights) he 'might as well cause a bit of havoc while I adjust'.[28]

Fashion, mass-produced food and the use of management-speak have become part of the physical and verbal identities of two anti-capitalist supporters. At the other end of the scale, Frank sounds just as adrift in the corporate ocean. His speech about corporate exploitation is less an admission of guilt and more a depressing statement of blind facts: the view from the top is no better than the view from the bottom:

> Frank   If you want me to say I've exploited and robbed honest, working people? Caused my fair share of suffering? Destroyed the environment? Fine. I've done it. So has everybody else. You want arrogance? Greed? Stupidity? Look around. There's no need for defences when something's everywhere. (*Pause. To Gary.*) That's why you're beat. I dinnay hay to defend anything.[29]

Despite this admission, Eddie repeatedly stabs Frank. What remains when the dust settles is more arresting than a violent protestor with an assured political agenda: it is a violent protestor who knows he is beaten, and is therefore freed from any responsibility for his actions. This nihilistic attitude achieves little except a fleeting and indescribable feeling of anti–climax, a horrible echo of the dilemma of a never-satisfied consumer:

> Eddie   . . . Didnay feel very revolutionary. (*Beat.*) It felt like something . . . but I dinnay ken if it was revolution. (*Pause.*) Doesnay even feel real.
> *Pause.*

Gary   It doesnay mean anything.
Eddie   Aye well . . . I've done it.
Pause.
Gary   It's just murder.[30]

Both men are left disempowered, but it is only Gary who seems truly broken by the events of the play. Eddie's survival tactic is to simply forget about what's happened as 'It's your only chance'. It is a statement with two possible interpretations and neither realistically achievable: that survival is only a possibility if we act in a continual present of violent impulse with no consequence; or that we have to look beyond the present, in some way decoupling the weight of history from the future. Burke emphasises the helplessness of the workers' situation with a telling final line from Eddie that 'We better get a move on. We've got tay be back in here in two hours. We dinnay want tay be fucking late'.[31]

The play ably illustrates the complex relationship between self and political values in a globalised world: when faced with political disillusionment, our ideological positions dissolve and clear identities fade away. The sense of self is no longer secure, and the only option is to cut your losses, or join the capitalist party which treats the victors no better than the victims. In many ways Burke's early millennial vision is prophetic of the years that followed. As with Frank, capitalism punished its own during the economic collapse in late 2008 as bankers were fired from their jobs. A state of voter apathy was induced through distrust of politicians during the expenses scandal in summer 2009, and the fact that party boundaries between right and left were allegedly dissolving, creating a moderate middle ground that devalued the purpose of voting.

The compositional narrative of Burke's work across his first three plays shows some gradual changes, but in many ways prepares the ground for the biggest dramaturgical shift: the 'total-theatre' experience of the National Theatre of Scotland's *Black Watch* (2006). The structure of *Gagarin Way*, for example, presents a structural staple of psychological realism. There is a unity of space and action as we watch the hostage attempt unfold in real time in a single location: the storage facility of a factory in Fife. In *The Straits* (2003) the action is set in the military-dominated

British overseas territory of Gibraltar, to the backdrop of May 1982 and the Falklands conflict. The frame for the narrative is a coming-of-age story, as new boy Darren fights for status among his recently acquired friends Doink and Jock. The interplay of the boys and their surroundings become a microcosm of the bigger arguments about patriotism, belonging and pride being contested just off the coast of South America. For Gibraltar old-boy Doink, war is seen as a given for the English, and he echoes Eddie's sentiment for violence without clear motive, stating 'War's what we do innit. What we do best. Don't matter who we fight either. Spics or Germans or French or whatever. Reckon we'll always be at war with someone and we always win'.[32]

The action unfolds on a linear timeline in eight scenes over three weeks, with the mid-point offering a suitable dramatic climax – the sinking of the HMS Sheffield. In the first production this otherwise conventional shape was supplemented by choreographed movement sequences, bridging the scenes and introducing a dash of contemporary dance into an otherwise realist play. The production made use of a theatrical vocabulary to emphasise its scripted content, but was seen as a contrary aspect by many critics, who labelled them 'outbreaks of dreary physical theatre'.[33] The production had presented an unfamiliar partnership of styles, but was attempting to express the story to an audience through physical dynamics, rather than relying solely on the spoken word.

In comparison, *On Tour* (2005) reverted to more conventional, and perhaps for Burke now over-familiar choices. It is a two-act drama charting a three-way power play between working-class characters with a penchant for violence, acting variously as conmen, drug-dealers, counterfeiters and smugglers. Set in Scandinavia during an England football match, the first act takes place in a prison cell and the second in a hotel, as dodgy Mancunian 'H' lures Cockney Daz, an ex-marine, into a questionable business deal with Scouser Ray. It is Daz who turns the tables on both parties when he reveals he is the mystery figure Ray has travelled from England to see, and rather than playing an innocent bystander, he knows more about Ray and H's predicament than the two of them put together.

Unlike the characters in *Gagarin Way*, these figures are now exploiting the pervasive world of commerce for their own good, rather than attempting to fight it. Like Eddie, Daz is also willing to get ahead by eschewing moral dilemmas and forgetting everything: but he really means it. Daz has no factory job to worry about getting fired from at the end of the day, and even if he did it is unlikely he would care. With all three of his first plays, Burke's political ideas are presented through fictional personal stories. In contrast, *Black Watch* (2006) is a response to a real political story, precipitated by the global crisis of the war on terror and populated by characters representing those directly involved. It is also, to a certain extent, drama–documentary or 'faction' – fictional material based on (very recent) historical fact, gleaned from research and interviews. The raw material is transformed through a striking collage of text, song, dance, movement and video that led to it being hailed in its Edinburgh premiere as 'one of the clearest artistic statements yet on the futility of war' and 'a major tipping point for the potential of what theatre can be in this country'.[34]

Behind the rich theatrical language of *Black Watch* was a collaborative approach. It was a story generated through text from a writer, dance and movement by *The Straits* choreographer Steven Hoggett, music and song from a composer, sequences from film makers and direction by John Tiffany, who worked on Burke's first two plays. The cast did not even have a final script until the previews. The overarching story is the dissolving of the 300–year–old Highlands Black Watch regiment, and the death of three of their soldiers in a suicide car-bomb attack. Both events took place in 2004 during the regiment's replacement of 4,000 American marines with just 800 troops in an area of Iraq known as 'the triangle of death'.

The play moves between two locations and time frames. The first is a pub some time after these events, where an interview takes place between a writer (whom we imagine to be Burke) and a handful of soldiers who have since returned home. The second is the desert in Iraq in 2004, where the same soldiers' experiences leading up to the suicide bomb are played out. Essentially *Black Watch* is a storytelling of a storytelling of real events, creating an impressionistic layering of experiences. There are multiple narratives overlapping in the play: the writer has to win the trust of the soldiers; the soldiers have to revisit their memories of being in Iraq, which are also shown as action in real time, and the entire history of the regiment is depicted in the military drill-style transformation of a character wearing the uniforms of the last three centuries. If we are searching for common dramaturgical progressions, it echoes Simon Stephens' *Pornography* in a move away from the character-istics of psychological realism and towards an expressive structural form.

Burke's most recent play *Hoors* (2009) was a tale of four Scottish twenty-somethings gathering the night before the funeral of a mutual friend, one of the characters' fiancés. Burke wryly intro-duced himself on the first day of rehearsal for the play as 'the writer of the disappointing follow-up to Black Watch'.[35] This disclaimer fails to hide the play's weaknesses as a drama in its own right, regardless of any comparison to his previous work. Unfortunately the play's Ortonesque potential – the coffin is on stage throughout and the two male characters' desperation for sex is manipulated by two sisters – is not capitalised upon, and the play leaves the audience, as one critic put it, 'in dramatic limbo'.[36]

The style reverts to the straightforward realism of his earlier work, but the lack of momentum in the story is perhaps indica-tive of his intentions with the play: to depict a world in a reces-sion where the days of plenty are over, that money never made us happy anyway and the mood is one of doomed failure.[37] The plot's structure, moving through evening to morning but with the char-acters seemingly adrift and failing to achieve their goals, is perhaps another gesture towards an expressive dramaturgy; though in practice it is problematic, creating a play purporting to be a realist cause-and-effect drama, but seemingly without significant effects for its characters.

Burke's work illustrates his ability to commentate on problems of political importance by making compositional choices appropri-ate to his intention. From the edgy, clipped rhythms in the hostage drama *Gagarin Way* to the overlapping narrative structures of *Black Watch*, Burke is an adaptable writer exploring opportuni-ties to marry dramatic form with a changing theatrical landscape. Perhaps only one other writer takes this approach a step further, into the realms of the fantastical and absurd.

Caryl Churchill

Churchill has been one of Britain's most prominent theatre writers for almost 40 years. She is a hugely respected and influential writer, an incisive cultural commentator and a constant theatrical innovator. She has always been politically engaged, perhaps best known for her 1980s plays *Top Girls* (1982), which grappled with the problematic masculinisation of female identity during the Thatcher era, and her verse satire on the world of the stock market *Serious Money* (1987). Her desire to respond to current affairs is evident even in her first play for the stage *Owners* (1972) which responded to a property market boom and our ruthless desire to secure ownership of material wealth.

Since 1997 she has had seven new plays produced, exploring contemporary topics including the discovery of stem–cell research and the possibility of human cloning, the foreign policies and 'special relationship' of George Bush and Tony Blair, the rise of a secularised urban society disengaged from political realities, and Israel's ferocious attacks on Gaza at the end of 2008. Also among the work of the last 12 years is a double bill of short absurdist plays that pushes at the limits of language and theatrical logic, and the unsettling story of a total apocalypse as the whole world, including the weather, the animals and the grass, become engaged in conflict.

What characterises Churchill's writing over the last decade is a series of plays that are increasingly linguistically adventurous and structurally economical. These traits begin with half an hour of deliberately disjointed sketches in *This is a Chair* (1997), echoing the work of the surrealist painter Magritte, famous for titling pictures with names that bore no resemblance to the image. It displaced the action to a converted stage in the stalls, whilst the audience sat on the stage watching short scenes of urban mundanity that also bore no relation whatsoever to the projected titles that preceded them. The play's 'questioning of both theatrical and social reality' was given a more substantial treatment in the double–bill of short absurdist plays in the same year, *Blue Heart* (1997).[38]

Comprised of *Heart's Desire* and *Blue Kettle*, both plays present recognisable domestic scenarios: a daughter's homecoming and an adopted son in search of his real mother. Both are then gradually disrupted from within by absurd theatrical games, revealing uncomfortable truths and exposing the limitations of both language and objective reality. *Heart's Desire* presents the average scenario of a family awaiting the homecoming of their daughter from Australia. After the first two exchanges of dialogue the actors appear to falter in their lines. They disappear and then return to the stage to play the opening lines again, only the father is wearing a different item of clothing. The scene continues for a minute or so, and then 'resets' again, and again and again throughout the play, the structure of the scenario continually replayed, manipulated, distorted, sped up, constricted and invaded by crowds of children and at one point a ten foot tall bird.

Churchill creates an unsettling picture of slow domestic torture, but by withholding any explanation for the form of the play, asks an audience to engage imaginatively with the work. She offers an open text that replaces the security of dramatic constants such as linear time and cause-and-effect action with a dizzying multiplicity of perspectives. As a result she comes closer to representing the emotional truths of the scenario than a drama told from one subjective angle might be able.

Blue Kettle tells the story of Derek as he meets a number of different women who have given their sons up for adoption. He poses for each as their birth child, until he has a collection of five mothers and a con trick up his sleeve. At a dinner his girlfriend Enid tries to reveal his twisted plan to one of the mothers, but they refuse to listen. The truth eventually emerges in the penultimate scene as Derek's lie is unearthed when two of the women meet, and in the final scene Derek is made answerable for his actions by one of the women. Emerging along the way like a virus slowly taking hold, the surreal element of the play comes from the gradual replacement of words in the dialogue with the words 'blue' and 'kettle'. It creeps up unnoticed at first, perhaps a slip of the tongue, but by the end of the play comprehensible language has been decimated and Derek and the woman can only communicate in a mess of vowels and consonants taken from the two words. As the truth of his plans emerge, logical communication is challenged; just as Derek has 'replaced' each woman's son and drastically altered their perception of reality, Churchill ensures that her linguistic trick achieves the same effect for the audience and the characters.

Both plays are mindful of the fragility of language and the slipperiness of 'truth' on stage and in reality, but are also a portrayal of flawed characters, quickly but sympathetically drawn and with recognisable human desires: for recognition, for truth and for love. It is this ability to elicit an audience's compassion for her characters that prevents these plays from being just theatrical experiments, instead revealing 'something fascinating about the nature of language, identity and disintegrating family life'.[39]

Far Away (2000) moves from the domestic to the global, presenting a terrifying vision of the end of the world. Within a sleight and intentionally sparse dramatic structure, over three brief acts one can detect echoes of contemporary historical events. In the first act a young child, Joan, pieces together the clues of what she has seen and heard outside the bedroom window of her aunt Harper's farmhouse, whilst the aunt tries in vain to distract and deflect her discoveries:

JOAN	If it's a party, why was there so much blood?
HARPER	There isn't any blood.
JOAN	Yes.
HARPER	Where?
JOAN	On the ground.
HARPER	In the dark? How would you see that in the dark?
JOAN	I slipped in it.
	She holds up her bare foot.
	I mostly wiped it off.[40]

The sinister echoes with human trafficking, ethnic cleansing and genocide are clear, but what disturbs most of all is Harper's decision to embroil Joan in the brutal 'movement' she and her husband supports, rather than trying to protect her. 'You can be proud of that', she tells her, for being 'on the side of people who are putting things right'.[41] The second part, some years later, finds teenage Joan joined by Todd, working in a hat maker's to create outlandish and ridiculous creations. Across the six scenes of the second act we catch suggestions of an Orwellian political rule establishing itself.

Todd stays in to 'watch the trials'. Joan is attempting to get 'a room in a subway'. Conversations in the hat maker's are conducted with an air of trepidation and people are referred to with shadowy ambiguity, as Todd boasts of having influential contact with 'a certain person'. It is only in the last two scenes that the 'parades' for which the hats are prepared are explained – they are worn by a grotesque procession of 'ragged, beaten, chained prisoners' on their way to execution. The manner of death is unspecific, but when reflecting on her hat Joan plaintively states that 'it seems so sad to burn them with the bodies.' A brutal political regime has been established, but the characters turn a blind eye to the humanitarian injustices of the outside world. The resulting situation of this apathy, in the final act, is a world of total apocalypse where mallards commit rape on the side of the Koreans and the elephants, deer impale teenagers on the streets and the weather is on the side of the Japanese. Churchill sets ecological disaster and global war on a collision course, and their explosion creates a living nightmare.

Her portrait of a world crumbling inwards is painted with broad brushstrokes and, as a result, was found lacking in analytical depth by those who like their political theatre delivered with contextualising footnotes. Michael Billington accepted the play's portentousness as a credible prophecy, but 'would prefer the case to be argued'.[42] Rhoda Koenig in *The Independent* complained that the play failed to reconcile what is allegorical with what is fantasy, and demanded to know what the play was saying about totalitarianism and ecology.[43] Both arguments indicate an analysis that is at odds with the play's actual dramaturgy. They take a closed model of social-realist drama that requires reasons, solutions and answers, and try to apply it to a piece that is deliberately poetic, abstract and open. The form of Churchill's writing was more usefully characterised by Susannah Clapp in *The Observer*, who praised the Royal Court for pioneering a new genre of 'tableau theatre, in which installation art is given motion and voice'.[44] Whilst she also goes on to criticise the play for stating effects rather than analysing causes, her description acknowledges that the play's dramaturgy is predicated on a particular sort of trust: that the audience can search for cause and effect in a fragmented story world without having it spelled out for them. Churchill's story illuminates our capacity for cruelty and implicitly criticises our *laissez-faire* attitude to political events, escalating the ensuing violence to biblical proportions. The importance of the play as a humanitarian appeal rather than a political analysis, and an open theatrical artwork rather than a closed dramatic thesis, should not be overlooked.

A similar moral enquiry guides the action of *A Number* (2002). A father, Salter, comes face to face with the clones of his son, Bernard, who was sent into care as a young child after being neglected and abused by Salter. He has requested a single copy but 'a number' have been made, and the play charts the catastrophic results. Each of the 'sons' in the play are also performed by the same actor, a *coup de théâtre* that once again accentuates the issues the play investigates. Bernard finds out about the first clone, B2, with whom his father has established a relationship. He questions his father, then finds the clone and kills him before committing suicide. In the final scene another clone, now living by the name of Michael, goes to visit the broken Salter; through desperation for some sort of connection, he has asked to begin meeting all of the copies. His efforts are in vain as he searches for some clue from Michael, but slowly realises what he desires is something he cannot ever reclaim:

SALTER	I was somehow hoping
MICHAEL	yes
SALTER	further in
MICHAEL	yes
SALTER	just about yourself
MICHAEL	myself
SALTER	yes
MICHAEL	like maybe I'm lying in bed and it's not comfortable and then it gets slightly not so comfortable and I move my legs or even turn over and then it's
SALTER	no
MICHAEL	no
SALTER	no that's
MICHAEL	yes that's something everyone
SALTER	yes

> MICHAEL   well I don't know. I like blue socks. Banana ice
> cream. Does that help you?[45]

The possibility of cloning is a device for exposing our frailty as human beings: we only have one life and we cannot move time backwards. Salter's flawed choices in the past and present precipitate his downfall and the play becomes a drama about human responsibility. As with *Far Away*, Churchill is writing about the effect of her subject matter on human experience, which is what makes her such a successful dramatist. She considers a world of ever-expanding choices, 'where metaphysical speculation meets genetic possibilities, psychological puzzles and moral challenges'.[46]

The pared-back style of dialogue develops further still in *A Number*. At times punctuation makes itself scarce, appearing to offer little guidance for delivery. However, these sections of text tend to surface at times of high tension, indicating a loss of control in the speaker and creating a sense of emotional strain. Following a fight with Bernard in the second scene, Salter attempts to regroup but his language seems hampered by the situation:

> SALTER   Nobody regrets more than me the completely
> unforeseen unforeseeable which isn't my fault and
> does make it more upsetting but what I did did
> seem at the time the only and also it's a tribute, I
> could have had a different one, a new child alto-
> gether that's what most people but I wanted you
> again because I thought you were the best.[47]

The language she employs reflects the limitations mooted in *Blue Heart*, that words are merely signifiers and not objective truths. We have to make a choice about what they actually mean, and understand that language is only a system, and one that will falter under emotional pressure. Criticism of her last one–act play of the decade *Drunk Enough to Say I Love You?* (2006) was largely directed at this now fragmented sentence structure:

> SAM   sitting around
> JACK   not

SAM	so much to do because
JACK	thinking
SAM	no time for
JACK	all right I'm just
SAM	missing your
JACK	not at all
SAM	natural
JACK	get on with
SAM	because there's all these people we have to[48]

The tale of a gay romance between an American called Sam and a British man called Jack, with the latter giving up his family and then his principles to live and work with the former, was never going to be a subtle allegory for the Anglo–American political relationship that emerged shortly after 9/11. The style of language in this context creates various political statements: it's a private or 'special' form of communication, impenetrable to others; it's a lover's shorthand yet the subject matter is political atrocities; it's the now reductive nature of political speech set against the ruthlessness of taking political action. What it struggles to do is endear us to the characters, engage us with their plight or create a sense of momentum to the drama.

There were elements to the original stage design that accompanied the heightened language; throughout the play the two characters sat surrounded by darkness on a sofa that was lifted higher and higher into the air, as the couple drifted further from any grounded reality. At one point a lit cigarette was plucked from thin air. A teacup fell but made no sound. These characters are in a vacuum, a world of their own where they can plan and scheme to their hearts' content. The play occupies a strange middle ground, between the drama of *A Number* and the extended political metaphor of *Far Away*. It presents two–dimensional characters restricted by their allegorical nature, but in a political landscape that is palpably real and current. The previous two plays present human dilemmas in a striking and theatrical way; this play articulates a political problem with theatrical style, but without the heartbeat of human experience. It is a justifiable response to the unchecked rights of larger nations to bully smaller ones as they see fit, but its dramatic scope remains confined by the arch allegory.

Her final salvo of the decade was the provocatively one-sided ten-minute play *Seven Jewish Children: a play for Gaza* (2009), a response to Israel's retaliation against intensive bombing from the Islamist terror organisation Hamas after Christmas 2008. An unspecified number of Jewish adults (nine in the Royal Court production) gather in seven tightly written scenes to debate what they should tell a young girl about Israel's history. Each scene is located during a significant historical moment, stretching from pre-Holocaust Germany, through to the Six-Day War in 1967 and finally Gaza in 2009. Charting the rise of a nation from the persecuted to the aggressor, the dialogue is comprised as a list of statements rife with internal conflict over honesty versus the need to protect:

> Tell her it's a game
> Tell her it's serious
> But don't frighten her
> Don't tell her they'll kill her
> Tell her it's important to be quiet
> Tell her she'll have cake if she's good
> Tell her to curl up as if she's in bed
> But not to sing.[49]

Each section continues with the same pattern of conflict until the last, when there is a barrage of statements celebrating Israel's right to be among other things 'better haters' and 'chosen people', though still culminating with the contradictory line 'Don't tell her that.' The play uses a concise and intelligent structure to external-ise the troubled internal dialogue of a Jewish nation. It dramatises the awkward task of bequeathing a nation's history to its children, but reconciling it with a desire to protect them from lies and fear.

The play attracted accusations of anti-Semitism from the Jewish press, one national broadsheet and two evening tabloids for its 'ludicrous and utterly predictable lack of even-handedness'.[50] Churchill and director Dominic Cooke had written and directed a play 'critical of, and entirely populated by, characters from one community' and it was therefore indefensible regardless of its dramatic power, as neither of them were Jewish.[51] What this criticism overlooks is the play's core structural dynamic: indecision. If a nation's historical identity is constructed upon reportage of past events, the perspective from which they are reported is crucial. This is the struggle the characters face. They are simultaneously heroes and villains. Their pride is at stake but they are aware of their own fallibility and therefore show a confused humility, rather than Machiavellian cunning. They are struggling to create a fixed version of history when history is perpetually fluid, terminally insecure and one sided. Churchill's portrayal of the Jewish people may have been critical, but it therefore comes with an understanding that they are only exercising part of an eternal and global human conundrum: 'we're just like everybody else and we're nothing like anybody else'.[52] As a writer with an acute sense of what it means to suffer from the human condition, it is a fitting description for her most recent work.

NEW WRITING TOMORROW

The analyses of these selected writers suggest an emergent pattern in the composition of 'new writing' in contemporary drama: more fractured time frames, non-linear narratives, open performance text, politically committed work and expressive forms. Whilst it is undeniable that the emergence of these elements is a tendency that has emerged with more frequency since 1996, one must remember that the shape of contemporary drama is not fixed. Just as a story is amorphous and formless until the writer fixes it down and arranges the various components in some way, so theatre history is also formless until shaped and arranged by other forces. The forms available to writers with which they can craft their work only multiply, rather than replacing one another outright. Despite similarities between the plays explored above, psychological realism is not yet redundant, but it is part of a broadening pool of strategies for expressing story, and the most effective dramas are often the ones most adept at creating hybridised forms by bringing different styles together to create unexpected outcomes.

David Harrower's *Blackbird* (2005), for example, is a paradigmatic 'homecoming' tale of a fifty-something man confronted by his grown-up child lover – or possibly victim, but the distinction is deliberately ambiguous – and the action unwinds with a unity of space and time. The text, however, is written as free verse with little punctuation other than one sentence hovering in mid air and the next one beginning below. There is no punctuation to provide rhythm, because the text is notated on the page as rhythm itself, the rhythm of the character's thoughts and words as they appear to arrive fresh in the performer's mouths. It is realism, but with a poetic wash, and one that heightens the presence of conflict and tension by providing it with a distinct immediacy.

The theatricality or poetic sensibility of contemporary drama is not a new phenomenon. Shakespeare, for example, belonged to a school far from the conventions of realism. His body of work transcends literalism to occupy a wide metaphysical plane, full of poetry and fantasy, fairies and magic, witches and spirits, metaphor and imagination, often found colliding with sweeping historical and political dramas and majestic set-pieces such as battles and shipwrecks. The writers selected within this volume to comprise a picture of contemporary British drama are those whose work not only captures a mood or 'a moment', offering the audience a story that is critical of the culture from which it has sprung, but also embraces innovation, implementing forms and structures that progress our idea of what drama can be.

This exploratory approach is reflected in a commitment by theatres to challenge how audiences engage with drama, as well as a commitment to developing the craft of the writers themselves. In the last few years the Royal Court has staged two new plays by writer Mike Bartlett, *My Child* (2007) and *Contractions* (2008), and for the first it redesigned the theatre as a tube carriage, within which the performance was staged. For the second, only a limited number of tickets were available as audience members took their places around a conference table, embedded within the performance frame to watch a story unfold over a series of meetings between a manager and her beleaguered employee. In 2009 the Bush Theatre, National Theatre and High Tide produced Adam Brace's play *Stovepipe* which follows the stories of the soldiers and managers of a private military company, but was performed in a converted shopping centre in Shepherd's Bush. It is a promenade performance where spoken dialogue still has priority, but the audience experience remains that of implicitly-involved performers, as we are ushered into an arms fair as potential buyers, harassed by eager salespeople. It is drama, but the performance context feels contemporary, modern and challenging.

If there was a legacy from the new writing boom, it was the desire for innovation, a recognition that drama cannot stand still and that 'a fusion of text, dance and music was still one of the best ways of avoiding the banality of suffocating dramas set in sitting rooms dominated by center-stage sofas'.[53] From writers to audiences, the desire to challenge practice and the way in which stories are told is now being embraced fully, and the sheer range of approaches being explored in contemporary drama is the subject of the next five chapters.

CHAPTER SUMMARY

Following a surge of activity and interest in new writing at the end of the 1990s, imaginative scope, political commitment and theatricality were felt to be in decline. An identifiable schism between social realism and a more theatrical questioning of conventional storytelling began to emerge in the middle of the decade. The purpose and expression of dramatic narrative then began to diversify, and in 2006 the new National Theatre of Scotland helped to promote a model of working that was collaborative, site-specific and targeted at specific communities. Writers sought diversification in their work and broadened the scope of their role, although no new 'movement' emerged as it had during the previous decade.

Writers Simon Stephens, Gregory Burke and Caryl Churchill all offer bodies of work that show a transformation in form and content in direct relation to the social and political landscape of Britain. Their ideas are communicated through increasingly expressive styles of writing that move from social realism to a total theatre of dance, music and text (Burke), from linear television naturalism to open performance text (Stephens) and from absurdist sketches to fragmented, politicised linguistic games (Churchill).

The progress of drama is identifiable through innovation in production choices, as well as those made by the writer, as drama's frame moves from the theatre auditorium to the constructed or site-specific space. New patterns and tendencies may have emerged over the last decade but this suggests diversification, rather than a total relinquishing of more conventional forms of drama. Audiences are being challenged to read drama in new ways, immersed in performance physically and sensually.

NOTES

1. David Edgar, *State of Play: Playwrights on Playwriting* (London: Faber and Faber, 1999), p. 28.
2. Aleks Sierz, '"Art flourishes in times of struggle": Creativity, Funding and New Writing', *Contemporary Theatre Review* 13:1, 2003, pp. 33–45 (36).
3. Aleks Sierz, 'Still In-Yer-Face? Towards a Critique and a Summation', *New Theatre Quarterly* 18:1, 2002, pp. 17–24 (22–3).
4. Robert Johnson, "New Theatres – New Writing?" in NTQ 'Reports and Announcements', *New Theatre Quarterly* 19:3, 2003, pp. 286–90 (288).
5. Aleks Sierz, '"we all need stories": the politics of in-yer-face theatre' in Rebecca D'Monté and Graham Saunders (eds), *Cool Britannia? British Political Drama in the 1990s* (Basingstoke: Palgrave Macmillan, 2008), pp. 23–37 (p. 34).
6. Vera Gottlieb, 'Theatre Today – the "new realities"', *Contemporary Theatre Review* 13:2, 2003, pp. 5–14 (7–8).
7. Aleks Sierz, '"Big Ideas" for Big Stages, 2004' in NTQ Reports and Announcements, *New Theatre Quarterly* 21:1, 2004, pp. 96–98 (98).
8. David Eldridge, 'In-yer-face and after', *Studies in Theatre and Performance* 23:1, 2003, pp. 55–8 (55).

9. Simon Stephens, speaking at 'New Writing: The TheatreVoice Debate', 28 May, Theatre Museum, London: transcript from www.theatrevoice.com (accessed 25 September 2009).

10. Aleks Sierz, '"Me and My Mates": the State of English Playwriting, 2003', *New Theatre Quarterly* 20:1, 2004, pp. 79–83 (79).

11. David Edgar, 'Unsteady states: Theories of contemporary new writing', *Contemporary Theatre Review* 15:3, 2005, 297–308 (302).

12. Ibid., p. 306.

13. Ken Urban, 'Towards a Theory of Cruel Britannia: Coolness, Cruelty, and the 'Nineties', *New Theatre Quarterly* 20:4, 2004, pp. 354–72 (371).

14. Aleks Sierz, 'Beyond Timidity? The State of British New Writing', *PAJ: A Journal of Performance and Art* 81, 2005, pp. 55–61 (61).

15. Aleks Sierz, 'New Writing 2006' in Backpages, *Contemporary Theatre Review* 16:3, 2006, pp. 371–3 (371).

16. Trish Reid, '"From scenes like this old Scotia's grandeur springs": The New National Theatre of Scotland', *Contemporary Theatre Review* 17:2, 2007, pp. 192–201 (197).

17. Ibid., p. 194.

18. Aleks Sierz, 'Reality Sucks: The Slump in British New Writing', *PAJ: A Journal of Performance and Art* 89, 2008, pp. 102–7, (105).

19. Ibid, p. 104.

20. Simon Stephens, *Plays 1* (London: Methuen, 2005), p. 4.

21. Dan Rebellato, 'New Theatre Writing: Simon Stephens', *Contemporary Theatre Review* 15:1, 2005, pp. 174–7 (176).

22. Stephens, *Plays 1*, p. 70.

23. Simon Stephens, *Motortown* (London: Methuen, 2006), p. 36.

24. Simon Stephens, *Pornography* (London: Methuen, 2008), pp. 40–1.

25. Ibid., p. 63.

26. Gregory Burke, *Gagarin Way* (London: Faber and Faber, 2001), p. 68.

27. Ibid., p. 38.

28. Ibid., pp. 84–5.
29. Ibid., p. 86.
30. Ibid., p. 89.
31. Ibid., p. 39.
32. Gregory Burke, *The Straits* (London: Faber and Faber, 2003), p. 34.
33. Charles Spencer, Review of *The Straits* by Gregory Burke, *The Daily Telegraph*, 5 November 2003.
34. Neil Cooper, Review of *Black Watch* by Gregory Burke, *The Herald*, 7 August 2006.
35. Peter Ross, 'Gregory Burke interview: once more unto the breach', *Scotland on Sunday*, 19 April 2009.
36. Mark Fisher, Review of *Hoors* by Gregory Burke, *The Guardian*, 7 May 2009.
37. Mark Fisher, 'Gregory Burke on his Black Watch follow-up', *The Guardian*, 20 April 2009.
38. Michael Billington, Review of *This Is A Chair* by Caryl Churchill, *The Guardian*, 26 June 1997.
39. Michael Billington, Review of *Blue Heart* by Caryl Churchill, *The Guardian*, 25 September 1997.
40. Caryl Churchill, *Far Away* (London: Nick Hern Books, 2000), p. 10.
41. Ibid., p. 14.
42. Michael Billington, Review of *Far Away* by Caryl Churchill, *The Guardian*, 1 December 2000.
43. Rhoda Koenig, Review of *Far Away* by Caryl Churchill, *The Independent*, 2 December 2000.
44. Susannah Clapp, Review of *Far Away* by Caryl Churchill, *The Observer*, 3 December 2000.
45. Caryl Churchill, *A Number* (London: Nick Hern Books, 2002), p. 59.
46. John Peter, Review of *A Number* by Caryl Churchill, *The Sunday Times*, 6 October 2002.
47. Churchill, *A Number*, pp. 30–1.
48. Caryl Churchill, *Drunk Enough To Say I Love You?* (London: Nick Hern Books, 2006), p. 12.
49. Caryl Churchill, *Seven Jewish Children* (London: Nick Hern Books, 2009), p. 1.

50. Christopher Hart, Review of *Seven Jewish Children* by Caryl Churchill, *The Sunday Times*, 15 February 2009.
51. John Nathan, Review of *Seven Jewish Children* by Caryl Churchill, *Jewish Chronicle*, 12 February 2009.
52. Dominic Maxwell, Review of *Seven Jewish Children* by Caryl Churchill, *The Times*, 13 February 2009.
53. Sierz, 'Beyond Timidity?', p. 57.

CHAPTER 2

Verbatim Theatre – The Rise of a Political Voice

A CLIMATE FOR VERBATIM

In June 1994 the Tricycle Theatre in Kilburn, North London, produced a play constructed from nearly 400 hours of evidence given at the Scott Inquiry, the investigation concerning the sale of arms to Iraq under the Thatcher government. As well as condensing the material into two and a half hours of stage time, almost all of *Half The Picture: the Scott Arms to Iraq Inquiry*, edited by journalist Richard Norton-Taylor, was constructed from words spoken by the lawyers and by those who had given evidence. The play was presented as a reconstruction of the tribunal itself, bringing the courtroom centre stage complete with a dutiful stenographer who appeared to record every word spoken by the characters. Appearances followed from actors playing the then Prime Minister John Major, future Deputy Prime Minister Michael Heseltine, ex-Conservative MP Alan Clark and Lady Thatcher herself.

In taking these figures' words 'verbatim', embodying them through performance and leaving the audience to draw their own conclusions about the evidence presented, the play revealed a 'subtext of social and psychological gamesmanship' in the language of politics that would have been unachievable on the page.[1] It also put the audience in a position they would find increasingly familiar at the Tricycle over the next 16 years, bearing witness to cases exploring the institutionalised racism of the police force

(*The Colour of Justice*, 1999), the legality of the war in Iraq (*Called to Account*, 2007), the culpability of the British Army during the events of Bloody Sunday (*Bloody Sunday*, 2005) and the massacre of over 10,000 Bosnian Muslims in a UN-protected enclave in 1995 (*Srebrenica*, 1995). Implicitly cast as members of a watching jury, audiences could now become directly 'implicated in events' and, in principle, 'compelled to take a stand'.[2]

Whilst the rapid growth of verbatim theatre is a recent phenomenon in Britain, it is not the first time the form has appeared. In 1930s America the 'Living Newspaper' was a company sponsored by the government to produce theatre based on documentary evidence and respond to the social issues of the day.[3] Post war, director Peter Weiss was a key figure in the early 1960s 'Theatre of Fact' in Germany, when he used documentary evidence from the 1963 Frankfurt Auschwitz trials as performance text in the five-hour long *The Investigation* (1965). The play, which includes harrowing testimonies from witnesses of the concentration camps, was poignantly re-staged by Rwandan theatre company Urwintore at the Young Vic in 2007, in a new eighty-minute version by philosopher Jean Beaudrillard that created 'a chilling, contemporary resonance' despite its age.[4]

In 1987 Derek Paget coined the term in a paper for *New Theatre Quarterly* titled '"Verbatim Theatre": Oral History and Documentary Techniques', one of the first attempts to identify common methodologies in documentary theatre. Mary Luckhurst notes that the paper was framed in a political context by the journal editors, emphasising verbatim theatre's ability to probe into the darker recesses of the socio-political arena, 'projecting voices and opinions which otherwise go unheard'.[5] Paget focuses in particular on the Victoria Theatre in Stoke-on-Trent, led by director Peter Cheeseman, that produced a series of documentary plays based on primary sources. The third, which focused on the demise of the local railway company (*The Knotty*, 1966) made use of recorded voices for the first time, a technique which then dominated his documentary productions until 1993.[6]

The technique of interviewing to gain first-hand experience of subject matter was then widely employed in the 1970s by Joint Stock Theatre Company, formed by director Max Stafford-Clark and playwright David Hare, both of whom have featured prominently in recent verbatim history. *Yesterday's News* (1976) was the company's first piece to be based on interviews conducted by the actors, writer and director, a practice that only emerged from a creative stalemate during the development of a new play, but one that saved the production. As Stafford-Clark remarks, 'once we found the people the show began [to] pull together very quickly'.[7] Hare later wrote the verbatim play *The Permanent Way* (2004) based on hundreds of interviews with victims and rail executives following four major train accidents in Britain. He also appeared as himself – but representing thirty-three separate characters – in *Via Dolorosa* (1998), a one-man account of his journey through the territories of Israel and Palestine. Stafford-Clark's company Out of Joint produced *The Permanent Way* and was also responsible for Robin Soans' verbatim plays *A State Affair* (2001) and *Talking to Terrorists* (2005). Into the twenty-first century, 'theatregoers were screaming for plays with strong contemporary resonance and political relevance'.[8]

In contemplating the renewed interest in political theatre and the verbatim form in the past decade, David Edgar looks back at the Theatre of Fact and notes that unlike recent verbatim theatre – which perceives the form as a practical tool for getting to the truth of contemporary political injustices – the work of Peter Weiss and his contemporaries articulated an admission of theatre's inadequacy, suggesting 'playwrights were saying that, after the enormities of Auschwitz and Hiroshima, the old concepts of cause and effect no longer apply'.[9] The context of recent history demanded a response: theatre's was to remove the mediating hand of creativity and lay the facts bare. Quantifying widespread human atrocity was deemed beyond the capabilities of dramatic fiction. Similarly, Joint Stock's interviewing technique was only stumbled upon when the company's collective imagination could not generate suitable material for the story they wanted to tell, so real life stepped in to lead the way. Cheeseman's pursuit of documentary theatre with a local agenda at the Victoria Theatre was strategic, born of a desire to put roots down and 'explore a relationship with one coherent community', as well as preventing the company from losing money, support and energy if they had gone touring.[10] Economic, political and creative circumstances, from the local to the global: all influence the direction theatre may take next. In the late 1990s and early millennium, it was a fierce combination of the latter two that helped pave the way for verbatim theatre.

Despite the surge of new plays across the millennium it was deemed by many that there was a paucity of work that provided any serious political comment. Tracking the trends of modern playwriting and the tendency for new writers to ape successful models, Edgar wryly observed that whilst there were many new 'bratpack' style plays set in flats, 'the political radicalism and the breadth of vision of Kane and Ravenhill in particular – the politics of Kane and Ravenhill – has burnt off, like alcohol, and what has been left is the young people in flats'.[11] Some were drawing comparisons between the forms as early as 1996: John Peter's 20 October review in the *Sunday Times* of Nicolas Kent's *Srebrenica* felt that Mark Ravenhill's seminal 'Generation X' play *Shopping and Fucking* 'pales into insignificance beside this account of large-scale genocidal murder'. Fiction could not compete with reality.

David Hare saw another end-of-the-decade tribunal play, *The Colour of Justice*, as a critical moment. Edited by Norton-Taylor and based on the transcripts from the Stephen Lawrence Inquiry, launched to investigate the Metropolitan Police's inept handling of the racist murder of a black teenager in 1993, Hare saw the play as 'a rebuke to the British theatre for its drift towards less and less important subject matter'.[12] A few years later the mood had turned mildly offensive, with the verbatim work of Norton-Taylor praised as 'honourable exceptions to the rule of shallow titillation, rehash, social myopia and audience condescension' that passed for new British drama.[13]

It was not only the perceived failure of new British writers to engage with the political that made way for verbatim theatre. The failures of the media to faithfully report events without manipulating evidence, and the repeated failures of hallowed institutions – the police, the army and the government – to conduct themselves with integrity were a significant contributory factor. Whilst the events of 9/11 in isolation were responsible for creating a renewed climate of political interest, the reactions of those guiding us through the aftermath – Bush's administration, Blair's Labour government, the BBC, the Metropolitan Police Force – were the real target of criticism.

Britain joined the US in invading Iraq in 2003 on the basis that Saddam Hussein could launch weapons of mass destruction in forty-five minutes; the BBC alleged that the dossier containing these facts had been 'sexed-up' and that they had a witness to prove it. The witness himself, scientist Dr David Kelly, was then hounded by the press and the government who had employed him, choosing to commit suicide only weeks later. Several conflicting fictions seemed to have been created for the British public, and theatre held them up for questioning. As Carol Martin has suggested, this manipulation of material creates a particular version of social reality, echoing a distinctly post-structural approach:

> It is no accident that this kind of theatre has re-emerged during a period of international crises of war, religion, government, truth, and information. Governments "spin" the facts in order to tell stories. Theatre spins them right back to tell different stories. Poststructuralist thought has correctly insisted that social reality – including reporting on social reality – is constructed.[14]

Two years after the invasion of Iraq, London suffered a terrorist attack at the hands of the 7/7 bombers: barely two weeks later the police, who had already lost public confidence when judged institutionally racist by the Macpherson report into Stephen Lawrence's death, shot dead innocent Brazilian national Jean Charles de Menezes at Stockwell tube station. They were under the false impression that he was a suicide bomber. Supporting the assertion that theatre has become more politicised in the later half of the decade, three separate responses to this calamitous error by the Metropolitan Police were all staged in 2009, two of them from verbatim sources. At the Landor in Clapham appeared *Stockwell: The Inquest into the Death of Jean Charles de Menezes* by Kieron Barry, edited from court transcripts; Theatre 503 in Battersea produced *This Much is True* by Paul Unwin and Sarah Beck, drawn from personal testimonies of those involved with the case, and Upstart Theatre premiered *Oh Well Never Mind Bye* by Stephen Lally, set in the offices of a fictional newspaper before and after the shooting but based on research into the media's response at the time.

Conflict borne of events concerned with domestic rather than global politics did not escape theatrical attention either. The year before 7/7 saw David Hare's *The Permanent Way* arrive at the National Theatre, illustrating the devastating effects of British Rail's privatisation upon the safety of rail travel, and the insensitivity shown to victims of the crashes by rail executives. In 2005 Richard Norton-Taylor's tribunal play *Bloody Sunday* illustrated the resoluteness of the British army to protect itself from criticism by routinely evading clear answers to vital questions during the Saville Inquiry. At the Sheffield Crucible Studio the same year, Tanika Gupta's hybrid theatre documentary *Gladiator Games* (part verbatim, part dramatic reconstruction) reported the systemic failures of the prison system in allowing Zahid Mubarek, a young Asian man, to share a cell with a mentally ill and clearly racist young white offender. The night before he was due to leave Feltham Young Offenders' unit, Mubarek was bludgeoned to death with a table leg as he slept. The Public Inquiry into his death was only launched after extreme pressure from his family. Two years ago Philip Ralph's *Deep Cut* (2008) focused on one of four young British soldiers who each died from gunshot wounds at the Deepcut Barracks between 1995 and 2002, and the insistence of the army that the deaths were all suicides. Independent forensic evidence showed one soldier would have to own arms fourteen foot long to shoot himself, and another managed to shoot himself twice in the head despite it being impossible: 'We conducted tests which we videoed that prove it can't be done. We videoed everything. It can't be done'.[15] Verbatim has even stretched to encompass environmental tragedy. The experiences of families flooded out in the wettest summer in British history in 2007 were captured in Look Left Look Right's site-specific show *The Caravan* (2008), where eight audience members at a time were squeezed into the eponymous temporary accommodation for forty minutes, to listen to excerpts of interviews from flood victims played by an ensemble cast. Jonathan Holmes' promenade theatrical installation *Katrina* (2009) used interview text, music and film to document the experiences of the citizens of New Orleans, victims in 2005 of not only 140-mph Hurricane Katrina, but the hopelessly stalled rescue response that was decried as 'a total failure of disaster management' and a worse blight on Bush's record than the Iraq war.[16]

It was unsurprising in the midst of so many events to hear Kate Kellaway's call in her 29 August 2004 article 'Theatre of War' in *The Guardian* that 'people want from political theatre a clarity they are not getting from politicians'. It was in fact a need for clarity that extended beyond politicians to all those in charge of public institutions, as the public's faith in them began to wane. As Hare stated, 'very, very complicated things are happening that people struggle to understand, and journalism is failing us, because it's not adequately representing or interpreting these things . . . now the theatre rushes to fill that void because journalism isn't doing the job'.[17] As such, the opportunity to share a space with the perpetrators of these events present, albeit mediated through the artifice of performance, becomes increasingly attractive. Stephen Bottoms characterises this idea of 'presence' in three ways: first, it is specific to 'the mythology' of theatre itself as a communal event; second, it is often specific to verbatim, and he cites the staging and scripting of Robin Soans' *Talking to Terrorists* as an example; third, it is imitative of TV – Soans' play in particular is found guilty of being 'staged very much as if it wanted to be on television'.[18]

The analogy with television is understandable. The growth of instant celebrity culture since the arrival of TV reality shows *Big Brother* (2000) and *Pop Idol* (2001) has been exponential, now proliferating into numerous other formats including talent shows *The X Factor* and *Britain's Got Talent* and the vast selection of other 'reality' documentaries covering subjects such as the property market (*Property Snakes and Ladders*), domestic hygiene (*How Clean is Your House?*), fashion (*How To Look Good Naked*) and entrepreneurial business (*Dragons' Den* and *The Apprentice*). Our culture is saturated in serving our desire for the 'real' experience, reaffirming that conditions for verbatim theatre are perhaps better than ever.

RESEARCH, EDITING AND TRUTH

Verbatim theatre has been presented in a variety of forms, with the 'tribunal' structure – practiced first by the Tricycle and initiated by its artistic director Nicolas Kent – one of many examples contributing to its continued growth. Creating a clear and consistent definition of verbatim theatre, however, is problematic. Like many genres of drama, an umbrella term cannot do justice to the idiosyncrasies of the many plays held beneath it. Verbatim 'defies any straightforward categorisation' and it has been suggested that rather than a form of theatre, it is perhaps best considered as a process or 'a technique'.[19] In this case, what collectively defines verbatim theatre is something all of the plays have in common: the selection and arrangement of verbatim material.

The manner by which that material is gathered and how it is framed in performance is what varies. It may be garnered from face-to-face discussions with the writer or actor, written testimonies, transcriptions of court hearings and print journalism or recordings of interviews and news reports. It could then be structured as a tribunal reconstruction, a fluid collage of written and spoken statements and interviews, a combination of statements and fictional scenes based on evidence, or even a mixture of interpretative dance and text as with dance company DV8's *To Be Straight With You* (2008) which explored homophobia in a liberal, multicultural and multi-faith Britain. Writers may 'edit and juxtapose material in order to create debate and narrative' as Robin Soans often achieves with his plays.[20] They may follow the linear narrative of a tribunal, such as Norton-Taylor's Tricycle plays, which offers the dramaturgical convenience of 'an inbuilt conflict to the proceedings'.[21] They can even construct live re-enactments of situations by fitting actors with headphones, so they can repeat voices with utter fidelity and 'present what was recorded privately and in the intimacy of an interview to a whole audience'.[22] Sometimes the people upon whom the play is based perform the play themselves, as with Manchester-based Quarantine theatre's *White Trash* (2004), an exploration of the lives of young white working-class men. Audiences have also been plunged into a reconstruction site of the subject matter itself; Jonathan Holmes' *Fallujah: Eyewitness*

Testimony from Iraq's Besieged City (2007) was a promenade verbatim play that led its audience around the theatre space 'bombarding
them with blinking lights, piercing explosions and a warehouse
stocked full of anti-contamination suits'.[23] It is a varied catalogue,
but what matters is the unifying element of 'verbatim' sources:
these words have already been written or spoken by others.

A common element of verbatim theatre is the focus on minority
groups and their unheard stories, or upon information demanding
to be presented to a wider public. In 1998, upon seeing the thread-
bare audience for the International Criminal Tribunal investigating the massacre of Bosnian Muslims in the former Yugoslavia,
Nicolas Kent was so perturbed by the lack of media attention
that the act of re-staging it in *Srebrenica* for a wider audience
'became a necessity'.[24] One of the driving forces for Robin Soans'
A State Affair was a need to hear the stories of Britain's forgotten sink-estate underclass; Victoria Brittain and Gillian Slovo's
Guantanamo: 'Honour Bound to Defend Freedom' (2004) brought
us eyewitness accounts of detainees from the US naval base in
Guantanamo Bay. Verbatim performs a worldwide civic function
of sorts, creating a democratic theatre that can document all four
corners of the globe and give an opportunity for people to talk, and
be listened to.

It is important to distinguish the label of verbatim from 'documentary' theatre which, as Bottoms notes, implies the consultation
of documentary evidence but not, as verbatim does, 'the notion that
we are getting things "word for word", straight from the mouths
of those "involved"'.[25] Problematically, verbatim theatre often
carries a promise to present the unmediated truth, 'not merely *a*
version but *the* version of what occurred', a promise that it cannot
hope to achieve.[26] For 'living journalism' to succeed as theatre 'it
has to have the shape and rhythm of art', thus rendering any claims
to objective truth redundant.[27] The necessity of creating an effective dramatic journey for an audience means that the structural
choices made are at the service of the drama – the art – not a sense
of objective truth. Crafting a drama then necessarily brings with
it the political sensibilities of the writer, director and production,
presenting to an audience only another 'version' of the truth: the
one they want us to hear.

A selection process is occurring even before the complete range of material is retrieved, because the conditions of retrieval may also influence its content. In verbatim (rather than tribunal) plays, interviews are not objective. They present the truth as the interviewee perceives it and wants it to be heard. Interviews are also encounters with a question–answer structure: an agenda of discovery surrounding a chosen topic is set, casting the interviewee into a particular identity – figure of parliament or rail-crash victim or terrorist – and they select the content of their answer, rejecting or confirming that identity, whilst the interviewer responds in turn by selecting further questions to direct the interviewee.

In the case of Out of Joint, this entire process may then be mediated through the interviewer later on, once the interview has finished. Performer Bella Merlin participated in the Out of Joint research process for *The Permanent Way*, interviewing subjects and then reporting back to the company in the rehearsal room 'in character' as the interviewee. Merlin states that 'our imaginations as actor-researchers served as a creative filter for that which we deemed sufficiently theatrical or dramatically provocative to pass on to Hare as a writer'.[28] She also applied the rubric of crafting effective dramatic narrative by quickly assessing her interviewee's 'super-objective', citing Stanislavksian practice as a guide to the selection and presentation of material for the group.[29]

Writer and performer Alecky Blythe, who formed the company Recorded Delivery, conducts interviews herself but employs the more direct approach in performance of equipping the cast with headphones so they can repeat with every inflection the voice of the interviewee. However, for her play *The Girlfriend Experience*, which documents the lives of women working in a brothel, she arranged equipment with the consent of the staff and was absent for much of the recording. Interviewees were now simply subjects getting on with their day-to-day life, circumventing the structured question–answer reportage dynamic and 'creating a non–pressurised, non-interview environment'.[30] For Blythe it is also a way of escaping what she sees as the 'talking heads' syndrome of much verbatim theatre which relies on juxtaposed monologues, and incorporating present-tense cause-and-effect dramatic action into the play. The structure of the play is more similar to a fly-on-the-wall television documentary, offering a far less mediated and static performance text, replete with the idiosyncrasies of 'natural' speech:

GROPER. What do you uhm (*Beat.*) – what do you charge normally?

POPPY. Ahhh-mmmm (*Beat.*) – sixty for, half an hour. Again I don't have any extras. The only thing I do ext-[ra] – would charge extra for is anal. I don't know if you're (*Beat.*) into that? / (*She laughs.*)

GROPER. Mm-hmm. (*Beat.*) You are obviously.

POPPY. Yeah.[31]

The target here is verisimilitude – the delightful and sometimes shocking minutiae of human experience, supported by a willingness to show an audience the provenance of the raw material. *The Girlfriend Experience* declares its process from the beginning, hiding none of its technology from view (the technician is clearly visible on stage, as are the earphones and packs of the performers) and bookending the production with Blythe's voice explaining to the interviewees why she wants to create an account of their experiences in the brothel. Nonetheless, the material is still subject to Blythe's selection process and despite the televisual dynamic of the text, the advantage of editing audio material is that it is not bound to the limitations of location and time. Blythe acknowledges that this allows her to manipulate the material even further to create continuous narratives from fragments, and whilst being mindful of the authenticity of lived experience, she accepts the continual paradox of verbatim theatre from project to project, facing 'the same struggle between being faithful to the interview and creating a dramatic narrative'.[32]

Tribunal plays differ at source. They carry their own dynamic of conflict which does not require prior construction by writers splicing conversations together, or actors carrying out a research exercise imbued with objectives and goals. Where there is present-tense action, the drama is driven forward by the thrust and parry of prosecution meeting defence or inquiry confronting witness. The plays hold the language of officialdom up to scrutiny. In the face of pressure to admit culpability, dramatic tension is generated by the evasive tactics employed by witnesses, exposing the 'dissembling, buck-passing, hiding behind euphemisms, word play, facetious use of aphorisms and, above all, the cynicism and amorality of arrogant and unaccountable officials'.[33] It is the act of condensing material into a manageable dramatic timeframe that Norton-Taylor faces in editing the tribunal plays, a task immense in comparison to Blythe's, who can control from how much material she works. Luckhurst comments that the word 'editing' is an 'insufficient term' for the activities of Norton-Taylor, who has faced quantities of tribunal material including fifty million pages from the War Crimes Trials that eventually formed *Nuremberg*, and 2,500 witness statements of the Saville Inquiry that became *Bloody Sunday*.[34] What Norton-Taylor believes theatre can bring to the public in a way journalism avoids is the creation of an overall coherence to the tribunal in question:

> The craft, the instinct, of the daily newspaper or broadcast journalist is to seize on the most striking revelation . . . each day is different and not necessarily connected. The value of a play is that you can put together in a single piece of work what, on the face of it, might seem a simple enough disclosure-a-day saga, but which, in fact, is much more complicated.[35]

Selection is still dependent on dramatic effectiveness, however, and as a journalist of many years Norton-Taylor also responds to the emotional impact of the material in front of him. Referring to *Bloody Sunday* he mentions that the witness stands of 'some of the worst soldiers' – the most evasive and well-drilled by the British Army to withhold evidence through various means – were not difficult to choose but that Martin McGuinness, reputed leader of the Provisional IRA at the time, was omitted because he 'didn't read very well as drama'.[36] More notable is the rearrangement in chronology of the final two witnesses in *Justifying War*, where evidence from the widow of the besieged weapons expert David Kelly and Dr Brian Jones of the Scientific and Technical Directorate of the Defence Intelligence Analysis Staff is reversed, despite director Nicolas Kent's claim that 'whenever you do anything for dramatic effect [in verbatim theatre] it's wrong, you know it's wrong'.[37]

In the play, Mrs Kelly is the last to take the stand (via telephone link-up) for James Dingemans QC, despite Dr Jones preceding her in the original inquiry. Whilst the published text declares this, it is not made explicit in performance. Mrs Kelly's personal recollections of her husband's last days, which includes the revelation that his attempted overdose was conducted with her own arthritis medication, clearly emphasises the personal, human tragedy of the loss of David Kelly in a way that the preceding material, more concerned with the ramifications of government and media decision-making processes, does not. The play therefore concludes with a markedly different tone, indicating that 'the creation of a coherent dramatic shape outweighed the necessity of adhering to the order of the Inquiry'.[38]

Whilst the tribunal plays follow the chronology of the original event (with noted exceptions), for writers such as Soans, Hare and Blythe, who work from an amorphous mass of interviews or documents connected only by theme rather than the sequential narrative of a tribunal, after selection comes organisation: the arrangement of material, where the hand of the writer/editor exercises its control. The organising principle of drama – to make sense of events by structuring a coherent narrative – becomes a problem in verbatim theatre, which is more answerable to the criticism of manipulation or distortion of sources. There is a suggestion that verbatim theatre merely dulls reality by artfully ordering chaos and reassuring audiences that there is a traceable sense and logic to world events, giving primacy to 'a presentation of the world as ordered, liberal and reasonable over the chaos, incoherence and fantastic of war and terror'.[39] This sense of reassurance is also articulated as a charge of preaching to the converted, as theatre makers seek what David Mamet reportedly calls 'false drama, the drama that changes no one and nothing from the moment the first lines are spoken to the moment the audience leaves the theatre'.[40] It is not a view shared by Dominic Dromgoole who, tired of this continual accusation against the theatre, argues that we need preaching for 'affirmation and definition', and that whilst many public forums – not just theatres – spend their time conveying familiar messages to known audiences, it is still theatre that is more pro-active at questioning the culture we live in than other mediums.[41]

The act of taking a position or posing a central question is characteristic of both verbatim and non-verbatim plays. Reflecting on Theatre 503's process in developing *This Much Is True*, resident dramaturg Sarah Dickenson commented that specifying the question the play was asking became central to its development, and that these questions often reached beyond the factual specificity of the case, elevated on a much broader moral plane. Although verbatim theatre is often exploring real events via testimonies of real people, the arrangement and presentation of material can serve a metaphorical purpose that goes beyond factual reportage. The use of dramatic metaphor and its function as an organising principle in the work is 'a characteristic shared between dramatic fiction and a common area of dramaturgical inquiry with new writers'.[42] Hare suggests the central question in *The Permanent Way* is nothing to do with the management of railways, but in fact a much bigger human question of 'what do we need to suffer and what do we not?'.[43] Director Stafford-Clark's version is a little different: he suggests that the play's thesis is 'that privatisation has not been a good thing; and are these crashes, Southfield, Hatfield, Potter's Bar, Paddington, connected with privatisation in any way?' He also challenges the notion of a predetermined line of attack from the writer, stating that what is shown is only what is found, and that the play is approached without any particular agenda.[44]

Nevertheless these two areas – privatisation and what we need to suffer – are organising principles guiding the composition of the play, which juxtaposes the different experiences of the bereaved and survivors' groups. They encounter the insensitivities of rail company executives post-crash, and then one another as two subtly different ways of coping – remembering and forgetting – come into conflict. The play is also a lament for the loss of Victorian engineering values and the rise of the customer-oriented business school, becoming another metaphor for the state of the (consumer) nation riddled with the desire for profit over quality or, in this case, safety. Our engagement with the play, however, is with a drama of emotions – anger, regret, bitterness, frustration, sadness and loss – which is borne of a characterised documentation of selected facts. The emphasis on a particular set of protagonists becomes the locus of the story, and the narrative that emerges carries the point of view that expresses the writer's position. Kent suggests that the Tricycle tribunal plays lack both metaphor and longevity because they're a journalistic response to the moment, but despite his house rule of maintaining an even-handed display of statements, an attitude still emerges.[45] Co-opting Picasso's maxim, Hare describes *The Colour of Justice* as Norton-Taylor's attempt to paint 'the anger you feel when you look at a tribunal' rather than the tribunal itself.[46] The writer's attitude to the material is an important mediating force in the process of selection.

The evidence above suggests a similarity between the process of arranging verbatim material and the process of writing a fictional drama. Referencing his own verbatim work, Hare comments that 'in its writing, Via Dolorosa involved me in as much structural labour as any story with twenty-five actors and a dozen changing locations. It was a play like any other'.[47] Soans describes the categorisation of his work as verbatim 'irksome' and with a sweeping generalisation, conflates the free imagination of the playwright with the process of verbatim research, claiming that it doesn't make much difference to the play itself where material comes from.[48] This suggests a misunderstanding of the relationship between process, content and form; Soans is bound to the material he is given whereas writers of fictional drama can invent anything they wish. His bald statement only serves to support his desire for partisan authorship; the attitude to the material is the same a writer might have for their fictional imaginings. It is clear from the evidence above that whilst work rate, research, the writer's position and the search for narrative might be constant features across both fiction and verbatim, the creation of verbatim performance text is characterised consistently by two factors: the ethical responsibility of the playwright not to invent new material, and the requirement to construct coherent drama from what they see laid out in front of them.

PROBLEMS IN PERFORMANCE

The search for consistent methodologies and ethical guidelines across so many forms of verbatim theatre reveals a few common principles in theory, but in practice many plays have been open to criticisms of misrepresentation, generalisation, bias, embellishment of the facts and political protest. Verbatim theatre might generate these particular questions, but it should also be engaged with as theatrical performance, not performed journalism, and as such held up to dramaturgical scrutiny with similar rigour. Robin Soans' *Talking to Terrorists*, Victoria Brittain and Gillian Slovo's *Guantanamo* and Alan Rickman and Katharine Viner's *My Name is Rachel Corrie* (2005) have all been on the receiving end of comments regarding their ineffectiveness as political theatre, rather than their authenticity.

The text of *My Name is Rachel Corrie* is taken from the writings of a young American left-wing activist run over by a bulldozer whilst protecting a Palestinian house from demolition by the Israeli army. Directed by Alan Rickman, it was the recipient of the 2006 Whatsonstage Theatregoers' Choice Award for Best New Play and has since toured internationally, though not without incident. New York Theatre Workshop decided to postpone the production of the play a week before it opened without confirming any rescheduled date. In an article by Jesse McKinley in *The New York Times* on 28 February 2006, artistic director James C. Nicola reports the mounting pressure from local Jewish groups who were polled about the play by the venue itself, saying 'the uniform answer we got was that the fantasy that we could present the work of this writer simply as a work of art without appearing to take a position was just that, a fantasy'. The play is constructed from one woman's point of view, and as such carries pro-Palestinian weighting and, by association, anti-Israeli sentiment – the theatre hosting the production was by implication seen as party to the same bias.

The play is in many ways a memorial to Corrie's life and, as such, reviewers trod carefully with their criticisms, aware that they could be judging not only the play but also the actions that led to Corrie's death. The writing is incredibly personal, including emails home to her separated parents, diary wish-lists from her childhood, phone messages and notebook entries from her time away. Corrie is portrayed as a hopeful and spirited campaigner, but the way her idealism was choreographed in the production left some critics wondering if she had been done a disservice. In his 'Prompt Corner' section of Theatre Record, Ian Shuttleworth lauds the powerful and personal propaganda of the piece but finds Corrie implausible when framed as art, '*too* perfect a protagonist for a solo play'. The structural and theatrical devices at work are also listed as unhelpfully over-dramatising the content with a manipulative emotional wash:

> the e-mail in which Rachel considers her future, which you just *know*, even without the gradually tightening lighting effects, is going to be the last segment of the play; her final exit walking (literally) into the light, followed by an audio-taped extract of a colleague's account of her death, and topped off with a winsome video snippet of fifth-grade Rachel making a school speech about ending world hunger.[49]

Shuttleworth's analysis comes with an overtly cynical touch, but his concern that Corrie is simply absorbed into artifice as 'an amalgam of dramatic devices' is a legitimate criticism of the play's effectiveness as political theatre.[50] If the protagonist becomes cari-catured by the arrangement of the text and its production, then the overall effect is reductive as the politics – which are bound up with the character's actions – somehow appear less credible.

Rickman and Viner's text presents propaganda knitted together with a tightly woven personal narrative; its one-sidedness is an inescapable element of a drama constructed from largely autobio-graphical sources. The year before, *Guantanamo* had also propa-gandised the contravention of basic human rights in Guantanamo Bay, but was comprised of several different sources rather than a singular dominant personality, and met less sympathetically as a theatrical performance. The amalgamation of press statements from Defence Secretary Donald Rumsfeld, ex-detainees of the facility, their families and human rights lawyers drives home a fierce condemnation of the situation – but, it is suggested, achieves little else. Michael Coveney in his *Observer* article on 6 June 2004 'Why Guantanamo is a political play too far', felt that 'the human rights issue has superseded any sort of responsibility to the truth (or its perversions) and, more important, to the basic demands of theatrical dynamics'. Critics of verbatim cite the inventiveness of fictional political dramas by writers such as Sean O'Casey, Shakespeare, Brendan Behan and Michael Frayn, bemoaning verbatim's limited theatrical scope. Steve Waters elucidates:

> The events docu-theatre precludes from its truths are often the most significant: moments of private reflection, moments of immediate choice. Equally, verbatim theatre forgoes image and scene: its narratives unfold in indeterminate space and time, it chooses to tell rather than show. Dramatic fiction plays action against place, gesture against speech, it works in multiple dimensions; documentation is by its nature a strictly verbal affair.[51]

What verbatim can do is play verbal testimony against verbal testimony, juxtaposing opposing statements from different times and places in the same theatrical space, turning what Waters sees as a deficiency of the form into a positive attribute. It is a technique used in *Guantanamo*: Rumsfeld's watery defence of the camp in the face of press questioning is spliced with letters home from a detainee, indicating to the audience the gulf between lived experience and political rhetoric.[52] It is also a feature of Soans' *Talking to Terrorists*. The most effective example from the play, noticed by many critics, was the intersecting testimonies of the ex-IRA member responsible for the Brighton bombings of 12 October 1984 at the Tory party conference, and a Tory landowner who was sleeping a few metres from the explosion. Their remembrance of the events as they stand next to one another on stage articulated 'the divergence of outlook and attitude between bomber and victim in a way that is unique to theatre'.[53] The emotional impact of this moment in the production is palpable, but the play's political and dramaturgical credentials were less stable. Sierz's assessment was that by conflating separate conflicts and bringing together terrorists from wildly different cultures and political causes, the play might be 'humanistic' in its storytelling but can only come at a price as Soans 'throws politics out of the window'.[54] The quantity of testimony in *Talking to Terrorists* and the insistence of creating a global picture results in a paradoxical dramaturgy: the more it presents, the less specific it becomes, and the more obscured any narrative momentum.

The political agendas of these three plays do not necessarily translate into effective theatre, and in each case it is both the provenance of the source material and the particular structural characteristics it carries that create problems. Verbatim theatre finds itself continually treading a treacherous fault line between the natural limitations of the material as performance text, and the demand for an effective drama.

DEALING WITH LIMITATIONS

Theatre-makers have applied some inventive strategies to challenge both the structural patterns of verbatim theatre and satisfy the calls for greater transparency, with varying success. In performance, Blythe's Recorded Delivery technique captures the unadulterated dialogue of its subjects and brings action rather than testimony to the stage; Norton-Taylor and Kent mounted their own mock tribunal in *Called to Account*, scrutinising Tony Blair's decision to take Britain to war with Iraq by interviewing lawyers and potential witnesses; the site-specific and promenade work of Look Left Look Right (*The Caravan*) and Jonathan Holmes' projects (*Fallujah* and *Katrina*) take the audience on sensory journeys through a theatrical landscape, and DV8 and Quarantine have translated the verbatim spoken word into dance and physical movement.

In print, the published text of *Deep Cut* in 2008 was meticulous in referencing every single section of verbatim material to its original source, as did the text of Tanika Gupta's *Gladiator Games*; unfortunately this is not yet visible in performance. Gupta also includes reconstructions in her play – dramatised versions of the events to which the testimonies bear witness – but written from a point of view clearly sympathetic to the young victim Mubarek. Our judgement of the verbatim material is weighted by their inclusion, ensuring a response that sides clearly with that of the playwright. Public opinion on the form is also still far from unanimous. In her theatre blog for *The Guardian* (7 May 2007, 'Does verbatim theatre still talk the talk?'), Lyn Gardner considers Holmes' and Kent's experiments as 'unsatisfactory as theatre and ineffective as politics'. Elsewhere *Called to Account* is labelled as 'simply an obsessive attempt to change history'.[55]

However, verbatim theatre has survived and evolved as a form for over half a century and shows little sign of slowing down, with recent productions transferring to flagship venues and touring nationally in the last 2 years including *Deep Cut*, *The Caravan* and *Stockwell*. New verbatim plays continue to appear, even those that revisit topics or revive extant material already tackled by the form: Theatre 503's *This Much is True* and *The Investigation* by Urwintore and Jean Beaudrillard respectively. Their impact has even been felt beyond the auditorium, with the MET using *The Colour of Justice* as training material and, more anecdotally, the Hague contacting the Tricycle Theatre before the trial of Slobodan Milosevic to borrow the desks used in the production of *Srebrenica*.[56] Other playwrights have responded to the growth of verbatim plays by holding the medium up to the spotlight in their own work; Dennis Kelly's entirely fictional *Taking Care of Baby* (2007) presents itself as verbatim, but slowly deteriorates into a wry critique of the very processes other theatre-makers are exploiting.

The statement that 'theatre has no obligation to give a complete picture. Its only duty is to be honest' is a realistic one that honours political theatre's oppositional tradition, but also its integrity.[57] Verbatim theatre cannot present an objective truth or it would not succeed as art − and it must succeed as art to be effective as theatre. This is the tension at the heart of verbatim plays which so intrigues us as audience members; we want to know what happened but we want to be shown it in a theatrically engaging way. In this sense, verbatim theatre's unavoidable failure to create the objective 'real' has always been drama's gain, but it is a delicate conversation between two different responsibilities: respecting the source material and crafting a theatrical experience. It remains a tension and a limitation that demands new creative responses in the future.

CHAPTER SUMMARY

Verbatim theatre grew in popularity across the millennium thanks to the public's increasing distrust of politicians, journalism and respected organisations such as the BBC and the Metropolitan Police Force, and the rise of celebrity 'real-life' drama via reality TV programmes and talent competitions. Theatre's reputation as a politicised and critical medium for exposing the truth fed a public desire for the 'real' answers to political scandal, providing an alleged clarity that other mediums could not provide.

The composition of verbatim plays relies on a process of research, selection and editing, distorting truth claims through the partisan nature of the writers' choices. The form of the verbatim source (tribunals, interviews, print journalism, letters) helps to inform the shape of the drama, but does not necessitate utter fidelity from the writer, who is free to disrupt the original structure of the sources. Unlike writers of dramatic fiction, writers in verbatim theatre are limited to making creative choices within the boundaries of the material they have gathered, encouraging invention that may help shape the drama, but distances the material from its original source and context.

Verbatim theatre lacks the flexibility of fictional drama, often tied to the act of telling rather than showing. The volume and variety of source material that is included can also cloud the issue, leading to a generic analysis of problems rather than a specific focus on a particular event. Innovations in verbatim have included site-specific and immersive work, blending of source material and drama-documentary, and the use of dance to express textual sources, but in pursuing a more effective theatrical experience, the sources are increasingly 'authored' rather than objectively presented. The tension between creating successful drama and maintaining respect for the source material is a continuing problem for verbatim theatre.

NOTES

1. Paul Taylor, Review of *Half The Picture* by Richard Norton-Taylor and John McGrath, *The Independent*, 17 June 1994.
2. Kerrie Schaefer, 'The spectator as witness? *Binlids* as case study', *Studies in Theatre and Performance* 23:1, 2003, pp. 5–20 (6).

3. Phyllis Hartnoll and P. Found, *Oxford Concise Companion to the Theatre*, 2nd edn (Oxford: Oxford University Press, 1993), p. 127.

4. Nicholas De Jongh, Review of *The Investigation* by Peter Weiss and Jean Beaudrillard, *Evening Standard*, 2 November 2007.

5. Mary Luckhurst, 'Verbatim Theatre, Media Relations and Ethics', in Nadine Holdsworth and Mary Luckhurst (eds), *A Concise Companion to Contemporary British and Irish Drama* (Oxford: Blackwell Publishing, 2008), pp. 200–22 (p. 201).

6. Peter Cheeseman, 'Peter Cheeseman . . . on documentary theatre' in Robin Soans, *Talking to Terrorists* (London: Oberon, 2006), pp. 104–7 (pp. 106–7).

7. Max Stafford-Clark, Interview with David Benedict, 9 January 2004, transcript at www.theatrevoice.com/tran_script/detail/?roundUpID=26 (accessed 18 August 2009).

8. Richard Norton-Taylor, 'Courtroom Drama', *The Guardian*, 4 November 2003.

9. David Edgar, 'Doc and Dram', *The Guardian*, 27 September 2008.

10. Cheeseman, 'Peter Cheeseman . . . on documentary theatre', p. 104.

11. David Edgar in Janette Reinelt, '"Politics, Playwriting, Postmodernism": An Interview with David Edgar', *Contemporary Theatre Review* 14:4, 2004, pp. 42–53 (48).

12. David Hare, *Obedience, Struggle & Revolt* (London: Faber and Faber, 2005), p. 77.

13. Ian Flintoff, 'Bloody Poor Show', *New Statesman*, 21 June 2004.

14. Carol Martin, 'Bodies of Evidence', *The Drama Review* 50:3, 2006, pp. 8–15 (14).

15. Philip Ralph, *Deep Cut* (London: Oberon, 2008), p. 62.

16. Clive Crook, 'Bush has learnt to weather the storm', *Financial Times*, 1 September 2008.

17. David Hare, 'David Hare & Max Stafford-Clark' in Will Hammond and Dan Steward (eds), *Verbatim Verbatim: Contemporary Documentary Theatre* (London: Oberon, 2008), pp. 45–75 (62).

18. Stephen Bottoms, 'Putting the Document into Documentary: An Unwelcome Corrective?', *The Drama Review* 50:3, 2006, pp. 56–68 (59).

19. Will Hammond and Dan Steward (eds), *Verbatim Verbatim: Contemporary Documentary Theatre* (London: Oberon, 2008), pp. 9–12.
20. Robin Soans, 'Robin Soans' in Hammond and Steward, *Verbatim Verbatim*, pp. 15–44 (26).
21. Richard Norton-Taylor, 'Richard Norton-Taylor' in Hammond and Steward, *Verbatim Verbatim*, pp. 103–31 (122).
22. Alecky Blythe, 'Alecky Blythe' in Hammond and Steward, *Verbatim Verbatim*, pp. 77–102 (100).
23. Malcolm Rock, Review of *Fallujah* by Jonathan Holmes, What's On Stage, 4 May 2007.
24. Nicolas Kent, *Srebrenica* (London: Oberon, 2005), p. 5.
25. Bottoms, 'Putting the Document into Documentary: An Unwelcome Corrective?', p. 59.
26. Stuart Young, 'Playing with Documentary Theatre: *Aalst* and *Taking Care of Baby*', *New Theatre Quarterly* 25:1, 2009, pp. 72–87 (72).
27. Michael Billington, Review of *Talking To Terrorists* by Robin Soans, *The Guardian*, 28 April 2005.
28. Bella Merlin, '*The Permanent Way* and the Impermanent Muse', *Contemporary Theatre Review* 17:1, 2007, pp. 41–9 (41).
29. Ibid., p. 43.
30. Alecky Blythe, *The Girlfriend Experience* (London: Nick Hern Books, 2008), p. 93.
31. Ibid., p. 40.
32. Ibid., p. 94.
33. Norton-Taylor in Hammond and Steward, *Verbatim Verbatim*, p. 108.
34. Luckhurst, 'Verbatim Theatre, Media Relations and Ethics', p. 206.
35. Richard Norton-Taylor, 'Courtroom Drama', *The Guardian*, 4 November 2003.
36. Richard Norton-Taylor in P. Stack, 'Interview of the Month: Reliving the War in an Irish Town', *Socialist Review*, April 2005.
37. Nicolas Kent, 'Nicolas Kent' in Hammond and Steward, *Verbatim Verbatim*, pp. 133–68 (p. 155).
38. Rachel Clements, '"What I see has indeed existed:" Mis-iteration

and British verbatim theatre'. Paper presented at Performance Studies international conference 15, Zagreb, 24–28 June 2009.

39. Jenny Hughes, 'Theatre, performance and the "war on terror": Ethical and political questions arising from British theatrical response to war and terrorism', *Contemporary Theatre Review* 17:2, 2007, pp. 149–64 (153).

40. David Aaronovitch, 'Does Blair deserve to be in the dock?', *The Times*, 22 April 2007.

41. Dominic Dromgoole, 'Reality check', *The Guardian*, 23 Oct. 2004.

42. Sarah Dickenson, telephone interview with author, 22 August 2009.

43. Hare in Hammond and Steward, *Verbatim Verbatim*, p. 53.

44. Max Stafford-Clark, Interview with David Benedict.

45. Kent in Hammond and Steward, *Verbatim Verbatim*, p. 165.

46. Hare, *Obedience, Struggle & Revolt*, p. 77.

47. Ibid., p. 78.

48. Soans in Hammond and Steward, *Verbatim Verbatim*, pp. 18–19.

49. Ian Shuttleworth, *Theatre Record*, Issue 8, 2005.

50. Ibid.

51. Steve Waters, 'The truth behind the facts', *The Guardian*, 11 February 2004.

52. Victoria Brittain and Gillian Slovo, *Guantanamo: Honour Bound to Defend Freedom* (London: Oberon, 2004), pp. 29–32.

53. Michael Billington, Review of *Talking To Terrorists* by Robin Soans, *The Guardian*, 28 April 2005.

54. Aleks Sierz, Review of *Talking to Terrorists* by Robin Soans, *Tribune*, 15 July 2005.

55. Aaronovitch, *The Times*.

56. Nicholas Wroe, 'Courtroom Dramas', *The Guardian*, 24 July 2004.

57. Michael Billington, Review of *My Name is Rachel Corrie* by Alan Rickman and Catherine Vinar, *The Guardian*, 14 April 2005.

CHAPTER 3

Writing and Devising – The Call for Collaboration

DRAMA AND COLLABORATION

The staging of a play text is an inherently collaborative task drawing on the expertise of numerous individuals including set designers, lighting designers, sound designers, composers, costume designer, dramaturg and the many assistants who bring specific skills to each of these creative departments. There is no fixed rule regarding the arrangement of these individuals in the theatre-making process, but in the context of British drama, historically they have been at the service of a finished play text awaiting rehearsal and production. Even during the wave of contemporary drama at the end of the 1990s, the phrase 'new writing' still retained 'close associations with notions of the "straight" play, the "proper" play, the "real" play'.[1]

The relationship between literature and drama has already been explored (see Introduction) but its relationship with theatre as a whole fares little better when 'the historical models that address the relationship between literature and theatre, or the script and performance [still] give text the dominant position in this pairing'.[2] As recently identified by Jen Harvie, this historical tendency results in most narratives of recent theatre history portraying British theatre as defined by its literary heritage, perpetuating 'a vision of the British theatre industry as not only romantically naïve but also hierarchical and fundamentally resistant to practices of devising and /

or collaborating'.[3] Whilst Harvie seeks to challenge these dominant histories – tracing influences such as theatre impresario Peter Daubney who brought a huge diversity of international theatre to the British stage in the 1950s and 1960s – they are responses to a theatre culture that has been arranged predominantly around the production of play texts.

By the 1970s Britain had witnessed the emergence of a fringe theatre that offered alternative processes for creating work. Often inspired by common political interest, ensemble theatre companies with a firmly collaborative ethos began to form, intent on articulating experiences from the margins and doing so through performances that were made collectively, rather than led by an individual writer's vision. Red Ladder (1968) and 7:84 (1971) had a focus on popular theatre made for a working class audience, Women's Theatre Group (1973) still running today as Sphinx Theatre Company sought to challenge the male-dominated theatre culture, Gay Sweatshop (1975) was led by an interest in issues affecting the homosexual community, and Black Theatre Co-operative (1979), running now as Nitro, sought to articulate the experiences of the Black community through music and theatre. The politics of these companies were reflected not just in the content of their work, but in their attempts to create a non-hierarchical process driven by a collective. This was not always a clear-cut division in practice, particularly concerning the writing of a text. John McGrath, writer and director of 7:84, had a dominant position in the company and was considered its main writer – although he did maintain a principle of keeping the writing process open for discussion, encouraging a 'shared ownership over the play, even if the act of writing remained an individual task'.[4]

It is with this notion of a shared authorship or a play influenced by the contributions of an ensemble that our exploration of devised work and its place in an account of contemporary drama begins. The processes that many writers are engaging with in the development and production of their texts are ones more closely associated with devising; companies themselves 'see no contradiction between working on pre-existing scripts and devising work, and move seamlessly between the two'.[5] Physical theatre, improvisation, pop culture, street dance, video installation, fragmented narratives, found text, location and community history all feature as influences on the following examples of work. It is the presence of the writer and the continued employment of text within these devised, semi-devised or improvised scripts and performances that is the focus of the chapter.

The increased employment of theatrical languages that exist beyond the spoken word has in turn required performers to focus on the body as a diverse theatrical tool; not one that simply 'becomes' character in a Stanislavskian sense, but instead acts as a 'repository of narrative', moving seamlessly between character, actor, narrator, object, symbol or figure, creating momentum in performance not via a character arc or through-line but instead 'crystallising a distinct and disjunctive moment in time, and thus in the narrative'.[6] The physical presence of the performer can be utilised in any number of ways, creating limitless options for the writer that stretch far beyond scripting dialogue.

Although the last 20 years of British theatre has been accompanied by 'a steady proliferation of companies who describe what they do as physical theatre', devised work does not mean exclusively physical or dance-based theatre.[7] The use of this term as a catch-all phrase for describing anything that is non-realist theatre (or everything that is devised) can be unhelpful. Cartoon de Salvo, a company formed in 1997 by actors Brian Logan and Alex Murdoch in reaction to 'a theatre that is arguably too in thrall of its literary heritage' was cautious of carrying any 'theatrical baggage' whilst it created its performance style.[8] The founders sought to devise playful, theatrical storytelling that exploited the risks of live performance (considering the In-Yer-Face climate of the 1990s, rather wryly described as risks beyond 'swearing and taking your clothes off'), but were then frustrated by the placement of their work in the 'physical theatre' category: a label that brought with it 'a whole set of baggage'. It becomes a particularly limiting term in the twenty-first century, when companies are beginning to make use of new technologies in performance and increasingly create work that is site-specific. The theatrical languages employed in these performances go beyond the expressive body to encompass the communicative potential of spatial, visual and demographic factors – such as work made in a specific site for a specific community – and digital or recorded media.

The tendency to compartmentalise theatre into easily identifi-able genres misunderstands the frequency with which the varied languages of theatre-making overlap, particularly in collaboratively written or devised work when influences on the composition of the work are multiple. What emerges is an aesthetic reaching beyond the literal mimesis of realism, embracing a more expressive or lateral style of communication. Lyn Gardner notes that 'at best, collaborative writing provides a new model for playwrights which pushes the boundaries and allows everyone involved to not just produce their best work but which has a cumulative power greater than the individual parts', suggesting a move towards a total theatre that is *autered* rather than authored and expands the the-atrical horizons of the writer.[9] Ben Payne describes the increased prominence of dance and movement within text-based work as 'an antidote to the more stilted manifestations of an overtly 'British' theatre characterised by dead-from-the-neck-down actors', sug-gesting that the theatre as a whole may be yearning for a move towards a more multidisciplinary style of work, which celebrates theatricality rather than relying on a default setting of TV-inspired naturalism.[10] An atmosphere of progressiveness and fearlessness pervades this particular area, willing to ask questions not just of the outside world but of the very habits of theatre-making.

Questioning the validity of theatre as a tool for communicating any fixed meaning is considered the particular preoccupation of postmodernism, and seen by some as a cynical rejection of trust in narrative representation. When this questioning occurs through theatre itself, it creates a paradoxical situation, for 'by challeng-ing the processes of representation itself . . . it must carry out this project by means of representation'.[11] Theatre cannot escape its own artifice, but it can draw attention to it by revealing the mechanisms of its creation. Doubts concerning the reliability of narrative might be articulated through the play's themes and inter-ests. Plays about storytelling and its reliability, purpose or politi-cal influence such as Martin McDonagh's *The Pillowman* (2003) or Conor McPherson's *The Weir* (1997), for example, tell stories about stories. Alternatively, these doubts can be expressed through the form and structure of the work. In Martin Crimp's *The City* (2008), which charts the stuttering breakdown of a relationship between a writer-turned-translator, her redundant husband, their young child and a sinister neighbour, the existence of the characters' world threatens to fold in on itself. In the final scene it is suggested that they are all clumsily constructed fictions from the translator's diary entries, and not part of a tangible material world at all. In a play that flirts with ideas around the telling of tales, sharing of stories and reported acts of others, often with disturbing results, this final shift in the play's logic is an appropriate formal device that helps express the play's themes more clearly.

Writer-performer Tim Crouch pushes these tensions between the real and the fictional even further in his play *An Oak Tree* (2005), where a different performer is cast every night in the role of a 'Father', who is attending a hypnotist's show (the hypnotist played by Crouch) to try and recover from his daughter's death in a road accident. He also believes that his daughter is still alive but has taken on the properties of an oak tree, which he now visits regularly. The actor is fed lines on clipboards and through an earpiece throughout the play, creating a performance that is rehearsed and prepared (by Crouch) but simultaneously spontaneous and immediate (the performer's reactions to instruction). The two also play multiple roles through the piece: Crouch plays the Hypnotist and the Father's wife and the performer plays seven different contestants during the Hypnotist's faltering stage show, and over time the worlds of the real, the simulated and the hypnotic begin to bleed and blur into one another until it is almost impossible to decipher the divisions.

Postmodernism does not define a specific mode of practice or consistent methodology. Heddon and Milling suggest postmodernism is better understood in a devising context 'less as an aesthetic model than as a critical position'.[12] However, when the problematising of narrative is the focus of the work, a shift in its composition will often follow: form still seeks to express content. This notion of an 'expressive dramaturgy' has been touched upon in Chapter 1, where the form of the play is just as responsible for communicating the critical position of the content as the action, serving as a structural sub-text, but the focus on narrative as problem also leads us to work that challenges its own authenticity.

Dramaturgs Cathy Turner and Synne Behrndt have identified this tendency in contemporary playwriting as a 'dramaturgy of process': a form of theatrical composition that deliberately externalises the mechanisms of performance-making through an increasing concern with the 'live event' of narrative, leading to work that 'traverses what have too often seemed different "camps" within the UK theatre ("text-based" and "non-text-based", "traditional" and "new", "new writing" and "performance")'.[13] Crouch's work in particular creates numerous crossovers between these categories, both 'performance' and 'new writing' in its aesthetic but also 'traditional' and 'text-based' in its pursuit of a story structured around the resolution of a character's internal conflicts. The next section explores in more detail the process of writing and devising, and what is kept or rejected from more conventional models of practice.

WRITING AS DEVISING

The phrase 'writing for performance' is useful for unshackling writers from the historical or ideological assumptions that come with the label 'playwright', and suggests a helpful leaping-off point for writers entering a collaborative relationship for the first time.[14] Writer Shiona Morton, who collaborated with installation artist Bill Wroath as one of three pairings creating site-specific performances for Part Exchange's 'Hidden City' festival in Plymouth (September 2008), was advised by the dramaturg assisting on the project to 'stop thinking of myself as a playwright and much more like a provider of text, and the different ways that text can happen'.[15] For a writer this may involve an unfamiliar relinquishing of control and a willingness to watch text play an equal or even subordinate role in process and performance.

Tim Etchells, founder member of Sheffield-based company Forced Entertainment, known for their collaborative and provocative approach to performance, has over the last 20 years become the identified 'writer' in the company. His text is not written in isolation or provided to performers and a director with the expectation of a conventional rehearsal process to follow; it is tightly bound up with a two-stage process involving 'a research and development time, where ideas are very free, and a structuring time, where ideas, through improvisation, editing and discussion are subjected to a rigorous questioning' and material is continually recycled, redeveloped or rejected by the company:[16]

> We don't really know what we're trying to make and I'll pitch in some ideas, some text – it might be a paragraph, it might be a page – it might just be me running onto the stage and whispering into someone's ear 'Talk about blah – blah – blah – blah' and very often these days that's what it is . . . I try to write quite little in that sense and we work an awful lot with improvisation and a lot of it will involve me shouting 'Do this, say that' and we also work with a lot of transcripts and videotapes.[17]

This fluid 'suggesting' role is a looser form of authorial control than the writer who provides a fixed script, but it still requires the skill of selective organisation that a writer might bring to plotting their material: choosing what to suggest, when to suggest it and how it might develop the ideas further. It is writing 'standing-up' – an immediately collaborative exploration, externalising the same pattern of decisions and choices made by the writer who works alone. It also means the creative environment is porous, not closed. Freeman describes Forced Entertainment's process as allowing 'permeability of boundaries in concepts, beliefs, perceptions and hypotheses', which in turn challenges practitioners to question their habits, engaging with ideas and practices that lie outside their own experience and creating a work that has multiple readings, rather than a single, controlled perspective that comes from a dominant authorial voice.[18]

A direct relationship with performers is also employed by writer Anthony Neilson with the benefits echoing those suggested by Freeman above. Collaboration allows Neilson to 'think outside of my own parameters; not only unfamiliar speech patterns but different viewpoints, different relationships, the development of rapport which can then be integrated into the writing'.[19] The process is more strictly authored than the dynamics of the rehearsal room outlined by Naden and Etchells at Forced Entertainment.

Neilson's performers are collaborating to assist the writer's vision rather than acting as part of an existing long-term company. Scenes of dialogue provide written stimulus for the actors and improvisation is used very sparingly, perhaps to explore performance style rather than content:

> I have always kept a fairly tight authorial grip on work, as I don't believe playwriting is something you can do by committee . . . what I'm looking for are ideas, reactions, inspirations, challenges, personal insights, accidental moments. The actors have a huge impact on the work but it's mostly a conceptual influence.

Over the past decade Neilson has collaborated frequently with actors from scratch to write his plays, utilising a free theatrical imagination to create work that is highly expressive and playful but still tackles subjects of serious emotional and political depth; what he describes as 'my personal grail: a truly theatrical theatre, intellectually accessible and satisfying to all, utilising populist methods to address serious subjects'.[20] Neilson also directs his own work, and with *The Wonderful World of Dissocia* (2004) and *Realism* (2006) brought 'significant weight to elements of performance other than written text', moving a step closer towards the 'auteur' role described above, and expanding the role of writer away from just a provider of text and into that of a hands-on theatre-maker.[21]

The first act of *Dissocia* and the whole of *Realism* externalise the central character's mental landscape through a range of theatrical devices. Neilson finds a merging of creative disciplines occurring in the performers' work as well as his own, which in turn relates to the situations both plays are exploring and illustrates the connection between process and form:

> The supporting actors tend to be playing facets or imaginings of the main character which denies them the ability to really invest emotionally in the parts. They've had to be much more detached about the concept than they would normally be; as collaborators, to think more like writers or directors; as

actors to rely more on their performance skills than any more immersive practices.[22]

Neilson's most recent play *Relocated* (2008) continued his fascination with 'theatricalising states of mind' by exploring the inner landscape of a character plagued by (potentially misplaced) guilt in the moments before their death. Maxine Carr, who covered up the murders of schoolgirls Jessica Chapman and Holly Wells by her husband Ian Huntley in 2002, was his initial reference point. During the play's development in spring 2008, however, due to its prominence in the media the play also spilled into exploring the actions of Joseph Fritzl, the Austrian who kept his daughter in a dungeon for 24 years and fathered seven of her children through a series of sexual assaults. Neilson felt these images could 'feed into her [the protagonist's] dream-scapes' and together these reference points helped inform the creation of a disquieting piece of 'theatre horror'. In response to critics who found it an unsavoury juxtaposition of form and content, Neilson shrugs off the principle that writers should somehow provide answers for the actions of such people:

> Perhaps it is an intellectual crime – that there is a wish for someone (anyone) to make sense of such things; to somehow restore – or to suggest a way to restore – moral order. Art can do that, I suppose, but it's not something that particularly interests me.[23]

Neilson's play exploited a number of theatrical effects, particularly the disruption of lighting states and the use of haunting visual imagery, chiming with Freeman's view that 'the written word is no longer the default determinant in theatrical performance'.[24] The processes by which theatre is made are also informed by other determinants; the direction of the work is not dictated by a pre-ordained script, and influences are instead sought from multiple sources including found text, music videos and pop culture. This rush for varied stimuli echoes another postmodern paradox; in the act of rejecting narrative authority, narrative is instead found everywhere, creating 'a massive expansion in the narratological remit, in the scope of objects for narratological analysis'.[25] The potential for so many constructs within modern culture to provide narrative direction engenders theatre-making with an appealing 'smash-and-grab' energy, a chaotic whirl of possibilities.

Frantic Assembly captures this spirit of adventure in their signature style of work, fizzing with high-tempo choreography, contemporary dance music and detailed physical motifs interspersed with text-based sequences. Artistic Directors Scott Graham and Steven Hoggett have collaborated frequently with many well-known writers since 2000 including Abi Morgan, Isobel Wright, Mark Ravenhill and Bryony Lavery. Their work combines a fascination with popular culture – including advertising, films, music and music videos – with a detailed approach to analysing text 'exactly the same way a text-based company like Paines Plough would'. They also have a healthy innocence regarding the established rules of theatre-making. Graham states: 'I've never picked up a book or learned anything about theatre or sat in a lecture and been told about any of the rituals. So it's only ever meant anything to me in the moment.'[26]

This emphasis on the experiential is characteristic of many companies who work across performance disciplines, and echoes the 'dramaturgy of process' mentioned above, as performances assert their theatrical credentials and happily acknowledge the audience as a collaborator within the event. Indeed, the sense of theatre as a communal 'event' that declares a direct and open relationship with the audience, celebrating its performativity rather than hiding behind artifice, creates a style of writing that 'seeks to exploit theatre's liveness and its theatricality, as it eschews both naturalism's techniques of literal production, and the passive spectatorship naturalism is perceived to encourage'.[27] It also shares the risks of live performance, whether this is created through challenging an audience to form their own reading of the work from multiple possibilities, as in the work of Forced Entertainment, or through witnessing and sharing in the risk of long-form improvisation, as practiced by Cartoon de Salvo in its show *Hard Hearted Hannah and Other Stories* where performers improvise entirely new text each night from a story title suggested by the audience. The following case studies will consider in more detail the collaborative processes that particular writers have followed, creating work that rejects naturalism or welcomes the active spectator – and which also, on occasion, does both.

CASE STUDIES: DAVID ELDRIDGE, *MARKET BOY*; BRYONY LAVERY, *STOCKHOLM*; THE HIDDEN CITY FESTIVAL AND CARTOON DE SALVO

David Eldridge's play *Market Boy* was produced at the National Theatre in May 2006. Described by one reviewer as 'a modern *Bartholomew Fair*, an affectionate visitation of his own youth in Romford market during the 1980s, and a rites-of-passage parable of withdrawn new lad on the block Boy finding his voice and losing his cherry', it was a theatrical tour-de-force and a culmination of a 4-year process that began with ten actors, Eldridge and the director Rufus Norris in a room for a week at the National Theatre Studio in March 2002.[28] With choreography by Frantic Assembly and a large ensemble cast, the play embraced a total theatre approach that combined movement, music, text, multiple characters and an ever-changing set design manipulated by the performers to create a changing perspective on Romford Market, as seen through the eyes of 'Boy' on his journey to adulthood. The writer is named as Eldridge, but from the outset the processes that stimulated the writing of the script were undertaken collectively.

Beginning with 15,000 words of autobiographical material written by Eldridge, the first workshop week at the Studio consisted of reading through his recollections and asking questions. 'We did do improvisations about buying and selling' he recalls, 'but we didn't try and improvise anything from that material. There were some elements to do with growing up, losing your virginity, turning from a boy to a man, but that was it. We came back six months later for a two-week workshop, set up these market stalls in the Studio and tried to bring aspects of my experience to life – then we also just made stuff up'.[29] The first two workshops were not followed by any writing, but created characters, themes and ideas that related to the world of the market, some of which would appear in Eldridge's script. For example, the character of Steve the Nutter or Nut-Nut, who has a prominent role as a drugs pusher in the play, came from somebody one of the actors had known in the 1980s, a mad raver who the actor 'suddenly arrived with one day.'[30]

The third three-week workshop began to concretise ideas about the world of the play, and tackled the impractical nature of getting a market on stage in a realistic manner. Perspective emerged as a crucial factor: the image of a new world unfolding before the Boy's eyes escaped the need for the market to be a literal representation, and instead signified a gradually expanding landscape, its meaning in the story more important than its material appearance. Eldridge suggests: 'it's about expansions of knowledge and widening horizons, and theatrically, that was a really interesting idea, how you do point of view in a theatrical context'.[31] After the third workshop a script was written for the first time, but the rehearsal process that eventually followed, even after subsequent drafts, continued to reflect the imaginative freedom and immediacy of these initial explorations with Eldridge 'rewriting and creating more new material than I have ever done with any other play', working on scenes, printing them out and then being able to work on them immediately with the actors.[32]

Eldridge is keen to point out, however, that the function of the improvisations and the collaborative atmosphere created within the company, whilst influential in the energy and tone of the writing, was not designed to create text to be copied down verbatim: 'Really there were only two bits where I went away and wrote down stuff that people had improvised; otherwise there were bits where I saw the seed of something, and then made it my own.'[33] The impact of the devising process is, in this case, an aesthetic one: evident in the atmosphere and energy of the script but not a direct transcription of the actors' contributions. Eldridge does, however, identify the fluidity of the script as a major result of this collaborative work:

> We always wanted it to be experiential, so that the form of the play and the feel of the whole evening, not just in its content, conveyed a sense of that 1980s madness and chaos and

free-for-all, the can-do money grab and can-do aspiration, the very un-English lurch towards it at that time.[34]

Echoing the collaborative work of the ensemble companies which formed in the 1960s and 1970s to express unified political perspectives, from the beginning of the process there was also political intent informing the style of *Market Boy*:

> It felt ludicrous to do a big play that was from the point of view of the working classes, emancipated by the eighties, and also for a young writer that was one of Thatcher's children to take a received form as the way of doing it. It somehow had to be a form that wasn't establishment. So we sort of knew what we wanted it to be, but not actually what it was going to be, at that stage. It was a vague idea of an 'anti-National Theatre play'.[35]

The contribution of Frantic Assembly during rehearsals was to develop a physical language for the production, based on a series of gestures influenced by the play's world and themes and constructing the grammar for a 'choreographic language' that could run through the entire show and was learned by the entire cast. This search for a shared language is a common one in the work of Frantic Assembly, particularly when text and movement are jostling for equal status as the dominant mode for expressing story. As Bryony Lavery, the writer who collaborated with the company to write *Stockholm* (2007, Drum Theatre Plymouth) states, 'text and movement are both big show-offs and want to be centre stage . . . often my words would just be wanting to occupy the same territory'.[36]

The title of *Stockholm* refers to Stockholm Syndrome, a 'fascinating bond between perceived victim and aggressor' where the captor shows kindness to their victims, resulting in a complex relationship where the latter is prepared to defend the former's actions.[37] This dynamic is played out between the characters of Todd and Kali as they prepare for a holiday to Stockholm in the confines of their ultra-modern IKEA-inspired flat, but are terrorised by paranoia, violence, fear, lust and the figure of 'Us/

Them' – voiced by the same actors and, as Lavery puts it, 'the hostage-taker villain of the piece . . . the perfect us'. This collision of antagonistic relationships is visibly expressed in performance. Dance-based sequences are marked around a push–pull exchange of movements, the characters travelling from mutual co-operation in some activities:

> They unpack and sort the shopping brilliantly.
> They show us that they could unpack shopping for England.
> Olympic Standard Unpack Team.[38]

To warring factions in others:

> And now, a terrible beautiful fight.
> . . .
> She, trying for his absolute annihilation.
> He, trying to hold her, contain her until the fury passes.
> But, it's probably a beautiful wild dance . . .[39]

Even just the description of these movement sequences notated in the play text, with annihilation, beauty and fury locking horns, suggests the complicated and contradictory tensions within the relationship. However, rather than creating all the movement sequences in response to the writer's finished text, as was the case with *Market Boy*, much of the spoken text was a response to two weeks of 'movement and scenario sessions' led by Graham and Hoggett, which Lavery observed and discussed along with the actors, dancers and an assistant director, later responding with written text. The work progressed in stages, with actors making and practising moves in pairs, sharing them with others and building up 'what becomes a sort of step-by-step template of the piece'.[40] The exercises were methodical and detailed, experimenting with thematically relevant scenarios of love, loss and urgency, or physical contradictions that reflected the conflicts of the subject matter, with 'their top half bodies doing one thing, their lower half doing something else', gradually setting a pattern for the structure of the play through repeated improvisations. Graham notes that 'you can actually only find the freedom in improv if you set yourself some very strict parameters, otherwise you just spin off and you find you rely on what you know and that's not freedom, that's actually trapping yourself'.[41]

The earlier tensions Lavery described, between movement and text trying to take centre stage at the same time, were reconciled by a complementary approach that paralleled the push and pull rhythm of the physical routines, creating 'movement which is subtext when the text is dominant, or the "melody" line when the text is the subtext'.[42] Although the script cannot fully capture the detail of *Stockholm*'s physical sequences, it does indicate the transformations that can occur when a more visual language is at a writer's disposal. As Graham states, 'if a writer's trying to create a world on a page, they've got to realise that when it becomes physical and three-dimensional there are other ways and there are other possibilities and we give writers ways to embrace that'.[43]

The examples of work given thus far have been considered largely in terms of their freedom, possibilities, spontaneity and desire for theatricality, but the presence of guidelines or boundaries, as Graham evidences above, is also part of the devising process. The function of 'strategy' is revisited by various commentators, and suggests the requirement of a methodology that can release creativity, rather than restrict it. Heddon and Milling frame their critical history of devised performance with a definition of devising that emphasises 'a set of strategies . . . evolved in relation to specific and continually changing cultural contexts'.[44] Ben Payne also prefers 'artistic strategies' when referring to performance writing and live art hybrids, rather than 'forms', which suggests limiting traditions of form and style.[45] Turner and Behrndt, in considering the 'labyrinthine' number of devising models are keen to warn that 'this seemingly free and open-ended process might require an even stronger sense of structural organization and overview than a production of a conventional play would demand'.[46]

Part Exchange's co-founders Ruth Mitchell and Rachel Aspinwall, creators of the Hidden City Festival in Plymouth, took a similar view when setting up new artistic collaborations, firmly endorsing that 'strong guidelines give people the freedom to be freer'.[47] Three writers were separately paired with a composer, choreographer and installation artist to explore three different sites within the city, but Part Exchange constructed several stages to the process around which each of the partnerships could begin constructing their material. Mitchell and Aspinwall outline the approach as follows:

Aspinwall: We set up 'inspire days' for each of the sites, which brought together people who'd used the building: local historians, people who had memories of it, architects and planners. It was about sharing information and knowledge with the artists and creating material – unearthing material – that could then also be made into an exhibition and archive.

Mitchell: It was a very simple structure: the inspire day, then encouraging links to be made with individuals, and further meetings to explore stories and engage people in the work, rather than artists just dropping in to the spaces. The communities needed to link with the work . . . they could have ownership of it too.[48]

The work of each pairing was intermittently overseen by dramaturg Phil Smith who had extensive experience of making site-specific work, and was considered 'very collaborative . . . really helping with the overall shape and direction'. Aspinwall notes 'we were very conscious of allowing writers to work within a new collaboration . . . it was an exploration, an attempt to explore a new form, and we didn't really know what would come out of that'.[49]

Site-specific theatre has been increasingly visible in the twenty-first century, with a number of reasons being suggested for its popularity. The atmosphere of a site and the rules of the space from the audience's perspective help to inform not only the mood and atmosphere of the performance but its shape, leading in some cases to 'radical' popular theatre. Diane Paulus' example is that if a play is performed in a nightclub, there is the opportunity to feed off the danger, risk and unpredictability the audience associates with that space, so that 'the attributes inform decisions as basic as the form your theatrical event will take', thus drawing an audience into the world of performance as a community with a shared expectation.[50]

The term 'site-specific theatre' itself 'privileges place' and removes theatre from the ideology of the theatre building and the (negative) associations that accompany it. It places work in direction relationship with the space, 'responding to and interrogating a range of current spatial concerns . . . investigating the spatial dimension of contemporary identities'.[51] As we experience the world increasingly through a global and mediatised lens, the formation of our identity through a direct relationship with space and location is severely affected. Individuals are gradually removed from the live and communal arena which sits in a specific space and time, preferring the lure of an online community with a vast reach, but which sports no tangible physical or historical dimension. Site-specific theatre counters this by using location as 'a potent mnemonic trigger, helping to evoke specific past times related to the place and time of performance and facilitating a negotiation between the meanings of those times'.[52]

Shiona Morton and Bill Wroath's *Sea/Worthy*, a hybrid of promenade theatre and installation in the Barbican's Mayflower Sailing Club provides a useful example of the trigger Harvie describes. Historically a site of emigration, the audience both observed and participated in the rigorous routines to which emigrants were subjected; carrying cumbersome suitcases into the clubhouse following security checks, witnessing the scrubbing and scouring clean of other emigrants, listening to their stories which conflated several timeframes from across 100 years, before spilling out onto the jetty and sailing out to sea whilst projections of sea voyages flickered against the wall of the building.

The immersive promenade experience provided linearity – moving sequentially through a physical journey – but the scenes, images and objects encountered on that journey were often deliberately fragmented and open to interpretation. This structural collision parallels the tensions at work between the two practices of installation and drama: Wroath describes the first as conceptual, offering plural readings 'so people are free to make links and connections mentally, almost as if another piece happens between all those individual parts', whereas Morton wants 'to follow things through, take a through line for the story'.[53] The form of the final performance therefore expresses not just the imprints of historical journeys ghosting through the site, but the collaborative journey of the artists as well. Morton recalls 'masses of rewriting, to fragment it in a way, out of the natural storytelling that I was used to' but also honours the concept of 'discord' that the collaboration naturally created, with both artists reaffirming that 'collaboration doesn't mean it has to fit.'

The experience of writer Peter Oswald and composer Hugh Nankivell in Catherine Street, a road dominated by religious architecture that provided the site for *Catherine*, was the opposite: a mutual convergence of practice that echoed the rituals of faith, congregation and song that pre-existed in the site. Oswald suggests that 'out of the meeting of a dramatist and composer, inevitably comes some form of ritual . . . the thoughts about the music and the thoughts about the drama went along together very powerfully, right from the start'.[54] The performance focused on the unsteady foundations of faith and mythology. The audience was accompanied on a journey of reconstructing their understanding of two spaces; the material properties of the site, which were fixed, and the fluid and unreliable space of memory. Unlike *Sea/Worthy*, which was embedded in historical research, *Catherine* exploited the contemporary cultural concern of a loss of faith: a 'forgetting', which the characters were struggling to overcome.

The language of the piece took on liturgical resonances as a result: choral singing, verse chanting, sermonising and congregating were all strong elements of the scripted text. For Nankivell, the underlying structure was created by a new language of music and memory, which impacted directly on his compositions. Words were translated into melody by taking their individual letters and then matching them up to notes on a musical scale, until 'I'd mapped out the whole street with little melodies that we could have picked up if we'd wanted to'.[55]

The third collaboration, between writer Hugh Janes and choreographer Jules Laville on *The Last King of Devonport* had a much stronger link with the site's local community. The 1820s Guildhall in Devonport provided an opportunity for a story that could take the audience on 'a journey through the lives of our main characters, the history of the building and the stories and feelings of the main area and its people'.[56] Following a journey through the building, audiences watched boxer 'Rocky Devonport' – a metaphor for the town's independence – fight off numerous assailants, creating a structure for the beleaguered journey of the community. Originally an independent town, Devonport was amalgamated into Plymouth shortly before the war and then severely damaged by bombing; post war building projects created an architectural dissonance, with 1960s constructions nestling next to sites such as the Guildhall.

Aspinwall recalls the first night as 'a very cathartic piece for the local community' but acknowledges the risk that artists take in entering communities as outsiders. 'Retrospectively, I was scared, because it meant so much to them. If it hadn't managed that, we would have been another invader, another assailant to the area'. Initial material for *The Last King of Devonport* was garnered from a pub crawl through the town, talking with individuals who would later comprise the audience for the show. Authorship in this sense is shared with the community, and the investment in the work stronger as a result. The mention of catharsis also suggests an element of celebration, of the carnivalesque, as Devonport reclaimed its independence through a 'socially and politically generative activity', revealing the people's history of the space through dance, theatre and spectacle.[57]

The audience and the performers' shared authorship, strategies for constructing narrative storytelling and the risk of improvisation are all combined in Cartoon de Salvo's *Heard Hearted Hannah and Other Stories*, which is entirely improvised each night. The individual writer is absent, but the desire for authorship in us all is given free reign. Although there is no text to rehearse, artistic director Alex Murdoch outlines the preparation for this show as a culmination of training in long-form improvisation, and intensive work on narrative through 'simply coming up with endless story starts'. Whilst there are no formal narrative structures dictating each show's direction, there are simple guidelines in place to allow clarity and spontaneity to operate simultaneously:

There are a few rules about the first two scenes. There should be 'no new trouble' in the first two scenes; we want to get to know the characters in their world. We try to establish names, relationships and location and that's all. After that there's no structures or shapes that we work towards . . . the most important rule is to follow every 'offer' your friend makes on stage, say yes and build upon it.[58]

Murdoch places great trust in the audience's instincts as storytellers, and the developed sense we have as human beings for identifying the potential sequence of a story. This is something she feels an audience can share with the performers, necessarily drawing on collectively-shared myths, genres and reference points, up to the point where the audience will overtake the performers: 'we're writing, directing and acting at the same time so our minds are very busy; the audience often get to the resolution a few paces before us'. This suggests that the audience 'shares' the role of the writer in their imaginations, identifying patterns and shapes and anticipating likely outcomes that might emerge from developing narrative structures. The performers and the audience are both experiencing the risk of improvisation in a similar way; the writer is absent, but the act of writing achieves a silent presence. Whilst this form of work is not the only one practiced by Cartoon de Salvo – much of its work is devised and rehearsed – it is an exemplar of its desire to allow all the participants to be 'complicit in the development of ideas and the realisation of the production', echoing a common desire of all the collaborations described above and emerging as a key tenet of devising contemporary drama.[59]

FUTURE NARRATIVES

From the writer-centred *Market Boy* to the echo of the writer in *Heard Hearted Hannah and Other Stories*, process and performance context in writing-devising collaborations illustrate a direct influence on the form of the work. It is also suggested that it has a subsequent impact on the shape of other forms of contemporary drama, as the 'repetition of fragmented dramaturgy has undoubtedly

altered our comprehension of 'narrative', and of the possible shapes
or trajectories by which narratives can or should be represented'.[60]
As writers continue to collaborate and delve into new territories,
the tools of character, plot, language and story become malleable,
re-employed to serve an increasingly broad range of performance
contexts – a view shared by Anthony Neilson:

> It seems we are slowly stepping away from realism and offer-
> ing genuinely theatrical experiences that can't be had else-
> where. New methods of working are being slowly embraced
> and I think we're seeing a nice cross-fertilisation between
> what would once have been called experimental companies
> and the mainstream.[61]

The vocabulary for expressing writing for performance shifts
accordingly, and we should be prepared for the terminology we
use in play analysis and the writing process to necessarily invite
innovative responses from playwrights, and these in turn to
suggest innovative solutions and suggestions regarding form and
its purpose. If each element of playwriting is considered as a site
of exploration, rather than as a fixed entity with a fixed function,
the writers' options extend and new forms can be discovered.
Ruth Ben-Tovim suggests this is an essential area of exploration
intimately connected to the wider environment beyond theatre,
and that 'we need to ask questions about whether the conventional
perception of dramatic structure and form are singularly appropriate to how we live our lives today'.[62]

However, despite benefiting from such processes himself,
Eldridge warns against treating the collaborative approach as a
'panacea' for creating contemporary drama. Content and subject
matter should also lead decisions regarding how the work is made,
rather than process influencing the artistic choices:

> The way that you make your work has to come from the world
> of what you're doing and what you're trying to achieve in the
> end. There's not one theatrical lexicon that fits over here, and
> another one that fits over there. It's got to come out of the
> world you're writing.[63]

The diversity of approaches in contemporary drama is certainly part of its strength, but the collaborative nature of the work discussed above generates a very useful perspective for both the analysis and creation of new performance texts, highlighting 'the inadequacy of looking at the script as a discrete object, a closed system, without reference to the event of the performance'.[64] If theatre is only truly collaborative once it is seen by an audience, writers involved with devising, ensemble, site-specific or improvised work have the opportunity to bring a fresh perspective to their scripted work, celebrating the live event and further exploring this unique element of writing for theatre.

CHAPTER SUMMARY

Although often compartmentalised separately in academic study, writing and devising in contemporary drama overlap in both process and aesthetic, creating a shift in the terminology we use for analysing text and performance and a change in the traditional view of British drama as text led. In drama created through writing and devising, text can become an equal or subordinate element, as physical, spatial and musical languages also combine to express the work to an audience. A particular characteristic of this work is a postmodern fragmentation of single narratives into multiple narratives, distorting the frames of artifice and reality to question the reliability of theatre as a representational form.

Writers may collaborate with actors, dancers, directors or whole companies, but the leading force behind the work varies. Anthony Neilson leads the actors in the pursuit of an idea he will write as a highly theatrical story, whereas Tim Etchells works collaboratively with the company of Forced Entertainment to create a collage of moments, ideas and accidents. Text is not sacrosanct but treated as stimulus for work, malleable and disposable depending on its effectiveness in particular circumstances. Narratives extend beyond plot-driven stories into sequences of images or impressions, and multiple influences from popular culture (film, music, dance videos, digital media) can have a significant effect on the final shape of the work.

Writing and devising extends the writer's range of skills and theatrical languages and suggests that straight drama is no longer the most effective form for exploring the contemporary world. The influence of non-text-based sources or performance languages on the work does not devalue the use of text, but encourages it to be employed in more innovative ways: as projected text, as stimulus, as pre-recorded voiceover, as historical information, as a guide through a site. The language and history of the performance space can also inform structure and content, with interdisciplinary work encouraging inventive responses from practitioners of different backgrounds. Audience experience can be bound together with knowledge of a site, and process impacts directly on composition: subsequent analysis of text or performance must remain aware of this.

NOTES

1. Ben Payne, 'In the Beginning Was the Word' in John Deeney (ed.), *Writing Live: an investigation into the relationship between writing and live art* (London: New Playwrights Trust, 1998), pp. 9–50 (11).
2. Helen Freshwater, 'Physical Theatre: Complicite and the Question of Authority', in Nadine Holdsworth and Mary Luckhurst (eds), *A Concise Companion to Contemporary British and Irish Drama* (Oxford: Blackwell, 2008), pp. 171–99 (179).
3. Jen Harvie, *Staging the UK* (Manchester: Manchester University Press, 2005), p. 117.
4. Dee Heddon and Jane Milling, *Devising Performance: A Critical History* (Basingstoke: Palgrave Macmillan, 2006), p. 111.
5. Ibid., p. 6.
6. Ibid., p. 182.
7. Freshwater, 'Physical Theatre: Complicite and the Question of Authority', p. 175.
8. Alex Murdoch, Artistic Director, Cartoon de Salvo. All further quotations from Murdoch are from e-mail correspondence with author, 24 November 2009.
9. Lyn Gardner, 'Writing as collaboration – experiments in

form' in J. Sumsion (ed.), *The Skeleton Key* (Cheshire: Action Transport Theatre Company, 2007), pp. 9–11 (11).

10. Payne, 'In The Beginning Was The Word', p. 35.
11. Marvin Carlson, *Performance: A Critical Introduction* (London: Routledge, 1996), p. 142.
12. Heddon and Milling, *Devising Performance*, p. 191.
13. Cathy Turner, 'Getting the "Now" into the Written Text (and vice versa): Developing dramaturgies of process', *Performance Research* 14:1, 2009, pp. 106–14 (106).
14. Payne, 'In The Beginning Was The Word', p. 28.
15. Shiona Morton and Bill Wroath. All further quotations from Morton and Wroath are from an interview with the authors, Theatre Royal Plymouth, 17 September 2009.
16. Cathy Naden, 'Inside Forced Entertainment: the route to *The Travels*', *Studies in Theatre and Performance* 22:3, 2003, pp. 133–8 (134).
17. Tim Etchells in Peter Billingham, *At the Sharp End: Uncovering the Work of Five Contemporary Dramatists* (London: A&C Black, 2007), p. 165.
18. John Freeman, *New Performance / New Writing* (Basingstoke: Palgrave Macmillan, 2007), p. 133.
19. Anthony Neilson, from e-mail correspondence with author, 8 December 2009.
20. Anthony Neilson, Introduction, *The Wonderful World of Dissocia and Realism* (London: Methuen, 2007).
21. Trish Reid, '"Deformities of the Frame": The Theatre of Anthony Neilson', *Contemporary Theatre Review* 17:4, 2007, pp. 487–98 (489).
22. Neilson, e-mail correspondence.
23. Ibid.
24. Freeman, *New Performance / New Writing*, p. 56.
25. Mark Currie, *Postmodern Narrative Theory* (Basingstoke: Macmillan Press, 1998), p. 2.
26. Scott Graham in Nina Steiger, '"Absolute Immediacy": A Conversation with Scott Graham', *Contemporary Theatre Review* 16:3, 2006, pp. 312–17 (313–17).
27. Freshwater, 'Physical Theatre: Complicite and the Question of Authority', p. 172.

28. Michael Coveney, Review of *Market Boy* by David Eldridge, 7 June 2006, www.whatsonstage.com (accessed 15 November 2009).

29. David Eldridge, quotation from interview with the author, Royal Festival Hall, 6 October 2009.

30. Ibid.

31. Ibid.

32. Ibid.

33. Ibid.

34. Ibid.

35. Ibid.

36. Bryony Lavery, from e-mail correspondence with the author, 23 November 2009.

37. Artistic Directors' Notes in Bryony Lavery, *Stockholm* (London: Oberon, 2007).

38. Bryony Lavery, *Stockholm* (London: Oberon 2007), p. 35.

39. Ibid., pp. 65–6.

40. Lavery, e-mail correspondence.

41. Graham in Steiger, 'Absolute Immediacy', p. 313.

42. Ibid., p. 314.

43. Lavery, e-mail correspondence.

44. Heddon and Milling, *Devising Performance*, p. 2.

45. Payne in Deeney, *Writing Live*, p. 46.

46. Cathy Turner and Synne K. Behrndt, *Dramaturgy and Performance* (Basingstoke: Palgrave Macmillan, 2007), p. 171.

47. Rachel Aspinwall and Ruth Mitchell, Artistic Directors, Part Exchange. All further quotations are taken from an interview with the authors in Plymouth, 4 November 2009.

48. Ibid.

49. Ibid.

50. Diane Paulus, 'It's All About the Audience', *Contemporary Theatre Review* 16:3, 2006, pp. 334–47 (341).

51. Fiona Wilkie, 'The Production of 'Site': Site-Specific Theatre', in Nadine Holdsworth and Mary Luckhurst (eds), *A Concise Companion to Contemporary British and Irish Drama* (Oxford: Blackwell, 2008), pp. 87–106 (89).

52. Harvie, *Staging the UK*, p. 42.

53. Bill Wroath and Shiona Morton, from interview.

54. Peter Oswald and Hugh Nankivell, writer and composer on *Catherine*. All further quotations are taken from an interview with the authors, Theatre Royal Plymouth, 17 September 2009.
55. Ibid.
56. Hugh Janes, writer of *The Last King of Devonport*. E-mail correspondence with author, 23 November 2009.
57. Richard Schechner, 'The Street is the Stage' in Erin Striff (ed.), *Performance Studies* (Basingstoke: Palgrave Macmillan, 2003), pp. 110–23 (111).
58. Murdoch, e-mail correspondence.
59. Cartoon de Salvo Website, www.cartoondesalvo.com/about/read_more (accessed 5 December 2009).
60. Heddon and Milling, *Devising Performance*, p. 221.
61. Neilson, from interview.
62. Ruth Ben-Tovim, 'Writing for Performance: Three Contrasting Approaches' in Deeney, *Writing Live*, pp. 51–83 (83).
63. Eldridge, from interview.
64. Turner, 'Getting the 'Now' into the Written Text', p. 111.

CHAPTER 4

Black and Asian Writers – A Question of Representation

SEPARATION, DIFFERENCE AND TERMINOLOGY

The inclusion of a chapter exploring the work of British Black and Asian writers is an act of conscious separation, and one that offers problematic areas for discussion. Through the latter half of the twentieth century, plays by writers from minority communities consistently struggled to achieve recognition within the mainstreams of both professional theatre and academia. This canon of work has a relatively recent written history: there is little evidence of written or devised texts by Black practitioners in Britain before the twentieth century, and the first play produced in Britain by a Black writer was Trinidadian Errol John's *Moon on a Rainbow Shawl* at the Royal Court in 1956. It was only in the late 1960s that new plays by Black writers began to receive productions, and they in turn inspired the formation of many independent all-Black companies.[1] Since the 1970s work by minority communities has 'gradually gained access to the white-dominated means of representation' and contributed to the richness of British theatre, despite initially being seen as 'outside mainstream culture' by both the mainstream itself and the writers who were trying to raise the profile of their work.[2] It was only in 2005 that the first Black repertory company was performing in London, during the Tricycle's African American Season.

In the years directly preceding this season (2003–2004) eleven new Black plays were staged in established buildings including the National Theatre and the Royal Court, and by 2005 a new production company was 'forcing theatres to address black work in terms of programming, in terms of delivery and . . . the audiences that come through the door'.[3] Eclipse, based in the East Midlands, issued five new commissions from different writers each partnered with regional theatres. Writers such as Roy Williams, Kwame Kwei-Armah, debbie tucker green, Tanika Gupta, Gurpreet Kaur Bhatti and Ayub Khan-Din were also establishing themselves as prominent figures in both contemporary theatre and screenwriting (Williams, Kwei-Armah and Khan-Din have all had screen versions of their plays produced), and many first-time Black and Asian writers would soon follow in the second half of the decade, such as Michael Bhim, Oladipo Agboluaje, Alia Bano and Bola Agbaje.

The struggle for visibility is not a problem of the distant past. In 2000, following years of dwindling Arts Council funding for theatre, the number of revenue-funded Black and Asian theatres had dwindled from eighteen to two and of 2,009 staff employed in English theatre only 80 (4%) were African Caribbean and Asian and only one member of staff of African Caribbean, Asian or Chinese descent was employed at senior management level.[4] Even halfway through the last decade, despite the development of cross-cultural programming, white men continued to dominate the artistic administration of most British theatres and to direct the new plays of Black writers.[5]

Lack of visibility is not restricted to the number of productions achieved or the level of representation within staffing infrastructures; recent theatre histories have also been criticised for their lack of focus on Black and Asian work. Richard Eyre and Nicholas Wright's *Changing Stages* (2000), a review of British theatre through the entire twentieth century 'does not even pretend to include British black and Asian theatres'.[6] Sierz's *In-Yer-Face Theatre* fails to include any Black writers at all.[7] If the continued objective is to '*achieve presence*' as Jatinder Verma, Artistic Director of Tara Arts describes it, the arena of academia is as crucial as productions in bringing Black and Asian theatre into mainstream cultural channels.[8] Kwame Kwei-Armah, whose plays are peppered with references to forgotten histories and the effects of the past upon the present (*Fix Up*, 2004 and *Statement of Regret*, 2007), states in an interview that 'it is not until our work goes into the realms of academia and can be studied that it can last and have some kind of longevity'.[9] As such, the separation of the work in this volume can be interpreted as a means to visibly identify the work as part of a broader picture, just as verbatim theatre, work for young people and adaptation are all component parts of contemporary British drama.

Even when work is brought into focus by academia it is usually presented (as it is here) through the terminology of difference and separation. Referring to academia's 'secondary reception' of Asian-led theatre via the British Asian Theatre Project at Exeter University, Sarah Dadswell acknowledges the paradoxical position of 'selecting a history' that has yet to be investigated. An unseen history is made visible to others, but at the same time risks perpetuating its separation by 'leading our subject out of the mainstream and into an ethnically bound corner'.[10] As will be seen later in the chapter, difference – of content, aesthetic and artistic mission – has also been consistently employed by Black and Asian theatre companies and writers as a means of forming an identity, self-consciously creating work that brings different stories and artistic sensibilities to British theatre. In the spirit of diversity and enrichment, difference seen through this rather more optimistic lens can perhaps be celebrated rather than criticised.

The fact remains, however, that the worlds of both professional theatre and academia have been dominated by white males, and choices regarding production and academic study have often reflected this demographic. This form of exclusion, it has been suggested, is unconscious: a subliminal and culturally embedded habit symptomatic of 'the system and its institutions – its classic works and markers of its worth – [which] by their very nature exclude'. Separation exists in theatre as a result of a white-dominated canon of work that provides a colourless barometer of artistic quality. Institutional racism in British theatre could therefore be deemed to occur 'before any people become involved'.[11] The textual heritage of British drama – its stories and writers – is out of step with the realities of a multicultural society, contributing to a theatre which is still 'very white, very eurocentric and extremely male dominated'.[12]

This 'invisible' form of racism was the same mindset identified in the police force by the Macpherson Report (1999) following the troubled investigation into the murder of Black teenager Stephen Lawrence. The parallel between the theatre's and the police force's history was noted by Sergeant Robyn Williams, who oversaw the recommendations of the Lawrence Enquiry Report:

> They are both institutions that have hundreds of years of customs and traditions that are inherently and persistently exclusionary and problematic for the diverse communities in this country. They are both institutions dominated by white men and they are both institutions that have excluded women and Black people.[13]

The word 'institutions' suggests the producers, theatre programmers and funding bodies that fulfil the pragmatic task of helping work reach the stage. In 1999 Jatinder Verma pinpointed a more disturbing form of racism that ejects non-white communities not only from the day-to-day running of theatres, but from the world of the imagination. Although migrant populations have settled in Britain since after World War II, he notes, the plays by mainstream writers that include members of these communities on stage are barely visible:

> This suggests that the migrants who are now citizens of the country do not exist in the imaginations of our David Hares, Michael Frayns, Tom Stoppards and the rest of the theatre community. To not be part of the imaginative universe is, really, to not exist.[14]

Even when the imagination of the white writer 'rarely and intermittently' includes non-white characters on stage, Gabrielle Griffin suggests, 'they do so to expose the racialized conventions which govern social interactions between racialized groups' – their function within the drama and their identity is therefore seen only through the prism of race.[15] It is clear that inclusion on stage does not necessarily mean that subtle forms of racism, such as Western xenophobia towards the 'Other', cease to operate. If non-white characters are only represented through the 'race-as-problem' matrix, theatre continues to portray Black and Asian characters in relation to a white mainstream, rather than part of it. It is for this reason that Dimple Godiwala firmly asserts the need for a separate space for Black writing, arising from '*the neglect of black and Asian theatre and culture by white female and male playwrights alike*' – perhaps another reason to investigate it separately in the context of academic study.[16]

The use of the umbrella terms 'Black' and 'Asian' to discuss the creative activity of non-white artists in any context carries a risk of homogenisation, employing terminology that is guilty of 'obliterating significant differences among the various people commonly subsumed under those labels'.[17] Kwei-Armah describes the word 'black' with similar connotations, as a political construction 'deemed necessary to unite people of African descent across the diaspora' in the 1970s, but ultimately becoming obsolete in the face of intracultural differentiations from the 1980s onwards, when even Asians were puzzlingly subsumed under the 'black theatre' label.[18] Writer Winsome Pinnock is also careful to define 'black theatre' with an eye on its political history, as a form of theatre founded by Black migrants from former colonies 'in resistance to the racism they encountered from mainstream (i.e. white) theatrical institutions'. She also acknowledges her discomfort at the phrase now, but recognises that it still 'articulates the reality of a division' in British theatre.[19] She goes on, however, to identify features of early Black theatre that are still relevant a decade later, describing it as a form of performance 'that explored notions of race, identity and Englishness'.[20] Explorations of this nature continue to typify many of the most successful plays from Black and Asian writers over the last 10 years, but it is the treatment of these subjects as intracultural problems rather than intercultural that is the most significant shift. Griffin sees this contemporary work, firmly sited in the modern multicultural diaspora, as 'forcing us to attend to the here and now, making dissociation difficult'.[21] Kwei-Armah's interpretation of this tendency is more troubled; from his perspective theatre's response to the problems of multiculturalism 'has been to stage black plays that deal with its own destruction rather than theatre of ideas'.[22]

Indeed, the strongest responses to the work of writer Roy Williams are often a result of his disconcerting portrayals of Black, white and dual heritage working-class young people growing up in a fracturing Britain of gang warfare and low aspirations. These unavoidable contemporary concerns are dramatised in *Fallout* (2003), which revolves around the black-on-black murder of young African student Kwame on a London estate; *Little Sweet Thing* (2005) which charts the journey of Kev, a recently released young offender struggling to cope with the societal and cultural pressures of his streetwise mates; and *Days of Significance* (2007) which opens with a riotous booze-fuelled vision of middle England's Saturday night city centres.

Williams' work often places young people at its core, but as a conduit to expressing a story, rather than the starting point for the play. 'I find that generation interesting' he says, 'they've got a lot of potential and struggles too. My stories seem to come from them . . . the character choices are secondary really'.[23] It is also his response to a media-saturated portrayal of young Black people that labels the experience in terms of race, rather than recognising it as a wider problem affecting the nation's youngest generation. As he points out, 'this concerns everyone because these are British kids'.[24] He is also a vehement believer in theatre's right to explore even the most uncomfortable points of view, and allows his characters to illustrate the stark realities of a modern, urban multicultural Britain.

In *Clubland* (2001), which explores the ways white and Black men clumsily manoeuvre themselves through the uncertain world of race and sexual politics, he succeeds in 'putting explosive words into the mouths of his working-class characters that would bring down the wrath of the Council for Racial Equality if they were coined by Richard Littlejohn in *The Sun*'.[25] In *Sing Yer Heart Out For The Lads* (2002), a racist BNP supporter is given space to deliver in great detail his intellectually-informed lecture on white supremacy. Many of Williams' plays, however, are an exploration of national identity rather than Black identity, 'peeling away layers of intolerance, resentment and confusion in black and white characters, to arrive at the core question of what it means to be English'.[26]

Rather than dramatising relationships between first-generation migrants and a native community or between the second-generation and older relatives striving to maintain their cultural habits, contemporary writers are increasingly embedding their stories in third-generation experiences. They are populated by characters that are born to second-generation parents and stage the intractable world of multiculturalism with all its flaws. Contemporary writers are 'actively and powerfully addressing what it means to be a black Briton as opposed to what it means to be an immigrant'.[27] The most recent celebration of new work in 2009 by Black British writers at the Tricycle Theatre in London, featuring plays by Kwei-Armah, Williams and Bola Agbaje, was fittingly titled the 'Not Black and White' season. As Williams states, 'the plays we're writing about reflect London, or England as it is now, in a twenty-first century multicultural Britain, and in all of the three plays that's coming out in a sophisticated, detailed way'. The title of the season recognises the shift away from simplistic oppositional debates of race relations towards a more complex arena of debate: one that reflects Britain's relationship with multiculturalism, faith and the global community.

MULTICULTURALISM, GLOBALISATION AND CENSORSHIP

At the turn of the century eyes turned towards the new millennium and Tony Blair's relatively young administration. How would they proceed in turning around not only the damaging deficits left by the Conservative government's 'bums-on-seats' approach to the cultural economy, but also a theatre in which 'you could easily assume we were a racially monolithic society in which ethnic minorities lived largely separate lives'?[28] Theatre's mission in the new millennium, from the point of view of Black and Asian practitioners, was to transform the range of work available into a microcosm of the country's evident cultural diversity, seeking to 'embrace the Other: to learn how to become neighbours across divides of colour, language and sensibility'.[29] The Arts Council's published report from Nottingham Theatre's Eclipse conference in June 2001 (Developing Strategies to Combat Racism in Theatre) spoke of the need for theatres to 'address their lack of understanding' and ensure that culturally diverse work was 'fully integrated into all theatres' operations and programming and should not be seen as an add-on'.

New Labour approached the arts from a distinctly utilitarian point of view with a firm eye on the problems of modern Britain. The Conservative's focus on 'heritage' was quickly changed to a focus on 'culture' – a far less dusty and backward-looking term – and theatre was seen as a means to achieve social cohesion, mend social fractures and identify new forms of citizenship, a mission reflected in the Arts Council's key funding priorities in Grants for the Arts applications.[30] This emphasis on 'accessibility' and 'social inclusion' was deeply unpopular among practitioners, who rounded on the Arts Council for 'judging companies less by their artistic excellence than by their ability to tick politically correct boxes'.[31] In light of these opinions, recent developments by the Arts Council include the commissioning of the McMaster report to consider how 'public sector support for the arts can encourage excellence, risk-taking and innovation' and 'establish a light touch and non-bureaucratic method to judge the quality of the arts in the future'.[32] This movement away from a thinly-veiled attempt at utilising the arts for purposes of social engineering towards the prioritisation of the artists' pursuit of innovation and excellence suggests a level of cautiousness. It is perhaps an acknowledgement that although theatre has a role to play in encouraging social diversity and intercultural tolerance, its most important function is to ask difficult questions of an increasingly divided society, through the highest quality artistic work possible.

The terrorist attacks of 9/11, the 7/7 bombings, increasing paranoia regarding immigration laws, revised legislation related to the prohibition of incitement to religious and racial hatred, and the tension between promoting a liberal line in tolerance but maintaining freedom of speech have complicated the optimistic objectives of multiculturalism. 'Hitherto suppressed tensions within and between ethnic and faith communities and what critics perceive as their negative tendencies and attributes' have been brought into sharp relief.[33] On the one hand the theatre wants to celebrate giving a voice to everyone – on the other, it is struggling to reconcile its own values with the rights of other faiths to express or practise theirs. Peter Billingham offers a pertinent comment whilst framing the work of writer Tanika Gupta:

> The debate surrounding the nature of Islam and the confla- tion of fundamentalist terrorist ideology has created difficul- ties for those seeking a vocabulary through which to defend religious and cultural plurality whilst retaining a more critical questioning stance on matters such as forced marriages, the role of women and the tolerance of other sexualities.[34]

Instead of the multicultural ideal of harmonious integration, the efforts of different cultures to express their own values cause tension and segregation. Both parties maintain a right to live as they want and, crucially when discussing theatre, to defend their right to be offended. As a result, protecting the artist's freedom of expression to probe areas of tension and antagonism is no longer a straightforward matter. It sits uncomfortably between the rise of 'two mutually supporting phenomena . . . the commodification of art (which has tended to diminish the moral status of artists) and the rise of victim power in and beyond the criminal justice system'.[35]

In a global economy so rife with consumer lawsuits that one cannot purchase a cup of coffee without being warned that the contents 'may be hot', the free speech debate has been relocated with the consumer – or audience – now fighting for their right to be offended, rather than the artist fighting for their right to risk offence whilst using theatre to dramatise problematic issues. As Edgar is keen to point out, the theatre 'provides a site in which you can say things that are riskier and more extreme than the things you can say elsewhere, because what you say is not real but repre- sented'.[36] The development in victim power creates a dangerous existential shift in theatre whereupon suddenly, to represent is to actually be, and to simulate is to actually do: it is by this logic that Christian Voice decided to picket the *Jerry Springer: The Opera* tour 'on the grounds that a metaphorical dramatisation of a TV presenter's nightmare is a literal representation of Jesus Christ'.[37] Provocative comment and opinion are no longer protected by the artifice of representation.

The problem of representation and offence is further complicated when a play is portraying minority communities on significant stages for the first time. This was the case when Gurpreet Kaur Bhatti's play *Behzti (Dishonour)* was performed at the Birmingham Rep in 2004: the theatre had to close for health and safety reasons when Sikh protestors smashed the glass frontage of the theatre building. Bhatti wrote *Behzti* because she was determined to make a stand against hypocrisy and injustice, was eager to create a play that engendered discussion and debate, and did so by exploring the 'outward appearance, wealth and the quest for power' in the Sikh faith that she felt was clouding its principles of compassion and equality.[38] The play introduced these tensions through a number of different devices, including racism from an Asian family directed towards the African Caribbean boyfriend of one of the characters, but most notoriously through a history of sexual abuse practiced by community elder Mr Sandhu. This abuse escalates with the rape of the main character Min, a Sikh woman who is sent to see Mr Sandhu to discuss the possibility of an arranged marriage. The location of the rape – in the *gurdwara*, or temple – was the locus of discussion not only after the first performances were seen, but before the production even began.

Birmingham Rep decided to enter a consultation process with representatives of the local Asian community prior to the play's production, where a request was made to move the location of Mr Sandhu's act from the *gurdwara* to a community centre. It was refused by Bhatti and the theatre. As a result, both the protest that ensued at the theatre and the criticisms that followed were conducted by people who had only heard what happened (or was due to happen) in the play, rather than those who had attended a full performance. The process of community engagement initiated by the Rep – a venue that serves the hugely diverse community of Birmingham – had an unintentionally detrimental effect, as they were judged to be ignoring a clear request to respect the community's wishes.

The Rep's decision to consult was also carried out in a particular climate of funding for Asian companies and those who staged work that engaged with Asian audiences. Quality-control measures included a count of the number of Asians who attended the performances: a highly questionable policy that assesses performance quality not by artistic excellence, but by a measure of specific ethnic engagement. It has been suggested that such policies are not only detrimental but in the case of *Behzti* did more harm than good.[39] A nervous venue, in an attempt to reach out with sensitivity to a community rarely seen on stage, ended up facing a highly uncomfortable choice: censor the incisiveness of the playwright's message but satisfy the community spokespeople's interests, or damage the artistic integrity of the play but maintain civil relations with an under-represented section of the city's community.

David Edgar is mindful of the fact that 'the communities to which theatres should perhaps be sensitive are by no means monolithic', and that the play and the theatre were in fact being sensitive but only to an already 'dissident community'.[40] There has also been criticism levied at the play's dramaturgical choices. Brian Crow's analysis of the play concludes that Bhatti was 'arguably misguided in using the tragicomic and satirical dramatic form of *Behzti* if she was really serious about engaging in constructive "debate" with various opinion leaders and spokespersons for a wide cross-section of the Sikh community'.[41] The slightly speculative argument is that many of the audience were likely to be first-time theatre-goers and therefore unable to untangle the conventions of satire from what they would see as 'an all-out attack on British Sikh culture'.[42]

Whether this argument is secure or not, in terms of the relationship between cultural sensitivity and dramatic form, it is interesting to compare Bhatti's choices with those of Tanika Gupta in her play *The Waiting Room* (2000) at the National Theatre, where she depicts a Muslim man having a relationship with a Hindu woman as well as conducting an extra-marital affair: all highly taboo areas among two dominant faiths of the Asian community. The incident is part of the historical framework of the male character, but not the main focus of the play, which is more concerned with themes of death, grief, overcoming loss and confronting the results of missed opportunities. It is also set both in the front room of a deceased woman's house and the purgatory she occupies with the spiritual guide of her (subconscious) choice: Hindi film idol Dilip Kumar. The result is a play that swings between the naturalistic and the overtly theatrical with a tongue-in-cheek treatment of traditional Hindi funeral rituals. Regarding the revelation of the actual affair, Gupta recalls the Asian audience 'all shouted about it, commented about it. It wasn't that they were being negative, it was "Yes, we've not seen this on stage before," and that's why I wanted to keep it subtle; I didn't want to be heavy-handed with it'.[43] Despite having to go into hiding following the incidents in Birmingham, Bhatti will uphold the writer's right to reply with a new play *Behud (Beyond Belief)* in April 2010, which tells the story of a writer using her imagination to revisit her past. The play is set 'amidst the theatre establishment, politicians and protesters . . . a playful and provocative response to the events surrounding *Behzti*, and the story of an artist struggling to be heard'.[44]

The Waiting Room and *Behzti* addressed new audiences in flagship venues, made visible under-represented communities and tackled problematic issues within them, but through slightly different dramatic forms. This relationship between representation, dramatic form and identity – in particular aesthetic 'difference' as a means to self-identify – has played a crucial role in Black and Asian theatre since the 1960s and continues to do so in the present day.

IDENTITY, AESTHETICS AND LANGUAGE

In a brief retrospective of Black British work, Caryl Phillips describes theatre as 'the most important form of literary self-expression for the black community' since the 1950s, providing a public space for the articulation of first-generation immigrants' experiences of British life and establishing the possibility of non-white writers jostling for position within mainstream culture.[45] His emphasis is on the content of the work, rather than the form, but companies and writers were also launching an 'aesthetic challenge' to the largely realist habits of British theatre.[46]

One of the most distinct plays from any Black writer, pre-dating the dramatic poems of Sarah Kane or the verbal gymnastics of Caryl Churchill, was the work of African American poet and playwright Ntozake Shange, whose play *for colored girls who have considered suicide when the rainbow is enuf* (1975) was a theatrical tour-de-force, a fragmented dramatic 'choreopoem' where inter-actions and voices overlap and blur into one another, creating a unique voice for expressing the collective perspectives of Black women. Her legacy is upheld to some extent by the contemporary African American writer Suzan-Lori Parks, whose work exhibits a similar playfulness with language, and whose views about Black realist plays in the USA are unleashed with an appropriately poetic zeal:

A black play in the united states of America was ripped from the bosom of its motherland, caught by the man or sold down the river by its brothers, crossed the atlantic in chains, had its gods smashed to bits and pieces . . . had its language ripped out its mouth, its family torn asunder – all this and more and a black play is still expected to play by the rules, is still expected to be interested in what the other deems interesting and valid and valued.[47]

The sense of one form of cultural expression being bullied by another is implicit in her criticism, but mirroring the characteristics of the dominant theatre culture is actually lauded by Gabrielle Griffin in her analysis of plays by British Black and Asian women from the 1980s and 1990s. Recognising that their stories were usually placed within the frame of realism and the dramaturgical conventions of issue-based plays, she interprets this work as 'staking its claim for recognition within that convention rather than as part of the traditions of a (post)colonial other' and in doing so 'refuses the transformation of the issues Black and Asian women face in the UK into purely aesthetic projects'.[48] Their chosen form of expression – social realism – rooted their experiences in a recognisable material reality for the audience, recognising Black and Asian artists and communities as part of the theatrical and social world. They were demanding attention by speaking the recognisable language of the British theatre.

By way of comparison, Tara Arts began its work in search of

a hybridised dramaturgy that drew consciously on international influences from contemporary Europe's avant-garde (Brecht, Grotowski and Brook) as well as 'the ancient Indian treatise on performance aesthetics, the *Natya Shastra*', with the deliberate intention of pulling away from the realistic conventions of British theatre to create 'the aesthetic of the migrant / marginal / black':[49]

> This discourse with classical Indian dramaturgy contributed to Tara's rejection of the dominant convention of the modern English stage – the spoken word. Gesture became speech, as much as a phrase of music a sentence – or the passage of time.[50]

This approach was deliberately provocative, a counter-cultural gesture held within the performance's dramaturgy rather than just the subject matter of the work. It formed part of the company's mission to create a unique theatrical style that could extend across multiple cultural boundaries, 'destabilising' the British–Asian binary and opening up a shared creative space and language.[51] Tara Arts was in search of an expression of identity that was fluid, something that was still 'becoming' rather than something that was fixed and finished. This continues a characteristic identified in other chapters, of theatre's form articulating contradictions and conflict as well as the content.

One of the most prominent contemporary 'hybrid' Asian–British performances of the last decade was *Bombay Dreams* (2002), the result of collaboration between West End impresario Andrew Lloyd Webber and A. R. Rahman, a prominent composer of Indian film music. Compared to the politicised nature of Tara Arts' interdisciplinary work and its specific aim of moving away from the mainstream to create a unique cultural space, this glitzy musical instead sold a disappointingly saccharine picture of the capitalist dream via the slums of Mumbai. Parks' evocation above, of a dominant culture choking the unique characteristics of another, seems particularly apposite in this context, and extends further to an exploitation of the Bollywood form. Lloyd Webber and Rahman's musical 'assimilates any cultural difference into a hegemonic ideology of a globalized utopia, where economic success equates with heterosexual fulfilment'.[52] A young boy, Akash, finds love, prosperity and happiness through his career as a Bollywood actor, and whilst the musical illustrates 'Indian flavourings', the presentation of the slums from which he escapes is largely tokenistic and stereotypical, 'part of the kitsch aesthetic, subsumed to the colour and spectacle of the big dance numbers'.[53] This commodification of culture, however, is perhaps less surprising when one considers the commercial context of the production, and its role as part of Lloyd Webber's global empire of uniform theatrical exports.

It is largely in the subsidised sector that the most prominent contemporary Black and Asian writers now operate, and one can trace the imprint of these politicised dramaturgies – Shange's poetry, Tara Arts' hybridised forms, issue-based realism – in the plays of the past decade. Osborne identifies the work of tucker green and Kwei-Armah in particular as 'constructing a black aesthetic' through the particularities of their dialogue.[54] The world of tucker green's work certainly echoes the style of Shange's dramatic poetry, but has a much tighter grasp on narrative structure.

Her first play *Dirty Butterfly* (2003) concerns three neighbours, and focuses on the voyeuristic behaviour of Jason as he listens to – but never meets – the abused Jo in the flat next door, which in turn has a destructive effect on his relationship with the third character Amelia. At no point has either character sought to intervene with Jo's abuse, yet their lives revolve around the horror of her situation. In the main part of the play, all three characters occupy the same stage space, free to address one another as they describe and re-enact their experiences of listening, being listened to and being ignored, but never meet in reality. The form of the play expresses the disquieting nature of voyeurism, as characters connect through a common event, but never actually attempt to communicate. Their relationships are formed through what they imagine to be happening to one another, through non-communication and frustration, existing in an uncertain theatrical space that disrupts event, location and character. Whilst race is not a key concern of the play, it is significant that unlike many other plays by contemporary Black writers, the identity of the characters is not culturally or socially defined. What defines the characters is their private relationship to a common experience, which tucker green chooses to express through an exteriorisation of internal psychological thought. Whether they actually address one another directly on stage is left up to the director and performers.[55]

This combination of the said, the unsaid and the interiorised is revisited in *Stoning Mary* (2005) where the 'ego' of the character is given an external voice alongside that of the character. Where two performers occupy a scene, they perform four voices and swap roles as they go, depending on the sequence of lines. Character identity becomes fragmented and ownership of the lines blurred, creating a distancing effect that requires the audience to renegotiate their relationship with the action of the scene:

HUSBAND	'Stand still will yer.'
WIFE EGO	Got nuthin good I can be bothered to say.
HUSBAND	'And y'look fine'
HUSBAND EGO	liar
WIFE EGO	he says.
HUSBAND	'Y'look well.'
HUSBAND EGO	Liar.
WIFE EGO	Gives it that.[56]

Stoning Mary is more politically aligned to Osborne's suggested 'black aesthetic' than *Dirty Butterfly* in its placement of the story: a couple with AIDS fight over a single prescription for medication, a child soldier comes home to face his parents and a young woman is going to be stoned. All the stories are connected, but all the characters are white and the stage directions for the play indicate it is set 'in the country it is performed in'. It is a clear political gesture and a Brechtian appeal to an audience: we must consider our reactions to these overseas atrocities and to whom they occur by reading them through the context of our own environment.[57]

In her most recent play, *Random* (2008), a single Black actress plays five main characters, four of whom are from the same family, and all of whom are connected to the fatal stabbing of a teenage boy during an act of random violence. Whilst the play does not interrogate the reasons for such acts, the drama is created as much through the shattering of a normal day in one family's life as it is through the channelling of their individual reactions through a single point of performative focus. The entire world of the story is communicated through one performer via shifts in dialect, tone and rhythm, again choosing to portray character and situation not through realism, but the dexterity of language. tucker green's work exemplifies a unique approach in Black British drama, where audiences are required to construct their own version of events through the multiple perspectives offered by the writing, rather than reducing character and event to an analysis dictated by the presence of conflicting sociocultural forces.

Roy Williams' plays also make a distinct use of language as a marker of identity, as characters shift between roles and adopt cultural attitudes depending on their circumstance. In both *Lift Off* (1999) and *Clubland* the relationships between Black and white male characters are complicated by the habits of cultural imitation and the gender stereotyping that comes with it, often expressed through the language chosen to discuss women, sex and relationships. Williams' characters are continually hiding behind the facades they adopt to survive, and beneath are often insecure or scared, desperate to achieve status or material wealth as a shield. They lack guidance and instead rely on role models borrowed from 'a hybrid subculture influenced by gang and gun cultures of Jamaica and Afro-American urban societies portrayed by rap culture'.[58]

In *Little Sweet Thing* white teenager Zoë gradually adopts the street dialect of her antagonistic 'friend' Tash, unaware that all Tash wants to do is be more like Zoë and stop hiding behind the front of verbal aggression and attitude that she uses. Tash ends up in an accidental shooting in a nightclub, and Zoë ends up as a distorted version of herself, imitating the argot of gang violence and rejecting her love of boy band music for her own protection. In *Joe Guy* (2007) the character of Joe Boateng rises from waiter to Premier League footballer and Black urban icon, a transition motivated in part by being ridiculed for his African heritage and manner. Over the course of one remarkable monologue delivered to the audience, he wrenches himself from his strong Ghanaian speech patterns to adopt those of a British-Caribbean, transforming himself through language:

I'm running things now – you get fresh, you get cut. You come reach for me now, I go school you now, you pussy hole, rass clart, boomba hole, batty bwoi! Seen? Aiiiiieeee! You is the African one now. Don't step up unless you gonna jump! *(Pleased with himself.)* Yes, that's good.[59]

Kwei-Armah's work also engages with the tensions and overlaps between African, Caribbean and British identities, employing varied dialogue to illustrate the poly-vocal nature of contemporary Black language. In *Elmina's Kitchen* (2003), a fast-food joint on Hackney's murder mile where owner Deli struggles to keep his son Ashley away from the swaggering gang member and debt-collector Digger, the characters 'shift from RP to native Grenadian to hardcore Jamaican to black London'.[60] It articulates the seductive nature of language not just as a tool for self-identification, but also to gain the respect of others or to belittle them when required:

Deli *(kisses his teeth)* Digger, fuck off.

Digger   Oh, it's alright for you to use all manner of Viking exple, exples, swear word, but as soon as a moth-erfucker uses language of our heritage you start to cuss. Dat is what I am talking about when I cuss you British blacks.

Deli kisses his teeth and ignores Digger. Digger's phone rings. He takes out three. He finds the right one. He switches his accent to hardcore Jamaican.

Digger   Yeah yeah? Trick wha you say rude bwoy? . . . Seen. . .Seen. . .Na!!! Wha you ah say? . . .Alright. . .usual tings ah go run. . .seen. . .tie him up wait for me. . .[61]

Whilst Kwei-Armah's work is vociferously political, his plays have been criticised for their didacticism, and the tendency of the writing to force agendas centre stage rather than allowing them to emerge directly from the characters' journeys, resulting in '1970s debate-style drama' with a limited scope.[62] Rather than slavishly imitating a social-realist form however, he has attempted to intro-duce culturally-specific choices to his plays, commenting that 'to leave out the "African" would be to somehow submit to an exclusive European framework and thus attack the very premise of my work'.

The text of *Elmina's Kitchen* suggests a Prologue section where a costumed man plays a gurkel – a traditional African guitar – and in doing so invokes the spirit of Africa, which links to the death of Ashley at the end of the play and the voice of Africa suggesting 'you need to overcome the shackles that started here'.[63] The sequence was removed from the National Theatre production because it was felt that audiences, primarily the 'host population', would not understand the specific use of the spiritual alongside the traditional structure of a three-act play. For Kwei-Armah, the different reactions from Black and white audiences are a continuing challenge as he seeks the most appropriate form for his writing, and considers the areas he should go into that can 'guarantee host-majority interest'.[64]

LOOKING FORWARD

Despite the recent successes of Black and Asian work, the removal of the Prologue in *Elmina's Kitchen* brings an important tension back into focus: even though theatres are beginning to stage a greater number of new plays, British drama still appears to be dominated by the theatrical language of realism. In the case above it could even be accused of acting as a cultural censor, seeking to appease white audiences with what they know rather than challenging them to negotiate the unfamiliar. It assumes a one-way form of integration (Black and Asian integrating with white culture) that is a source of irritation for other writers. Alia Bano, writer of *Shades* (2009) – one of the first new plays in British theatre to feature the Muslim community outside the world of terrorism and religious fundamentalism – recalls being 'pissed off' with the Royal Court for the title of 'Unheard Voices', a project for young Muslim writers designed to integrate their work into the mainstream. Her response was that 'I felt like there was a whole part of Britain that hadn't integrated with *me*'.[65]

Writer Ashmeed Sohoye, speaking in the same context as Alia

Bano above, also voices his suspicions about courses for writers from minority backgrounds, describing them as 'a lie' because production of writers is what is required, not continual development, and they are still not part of the mainstream's infrastructure. It is a perspective echoed by Sol B. River, who appeals for 'a genuine structure . . . that works in terms of opportunity, production and longevity'.[66] It is a structure that needs to extend beyond opportunities for writers as well. Kwei-Armah bemoans the lack of older Black actors (only four were available in the whole country for the part of a 55-year-old Caribbean character in *Statement of Regret*) as 'whole generations of talent have disappeared'.[67] New audiences also need to be made welcome for all plays in the repertoire, not just targeted for new Black and Asian plays by theatre's marketing departments.

Putting the terminology to one side may be the biggest gesture theatre (and academia) can perform in the future, allowing writers to take centre stage as writers first and foremost, not representatives of anything other than their plays. 'Young black and Asian writers are offering us vital social evidence every bit as important – probably more so – than that provided by their white counterparts' and as such, the last word is probably best left to the writers:[68]

> The phrase 'black theatre' can only do so much. It's the work that these writers produce that will decide, years from now, whether we can bury that phrase forever. The only way it's going to happen is that we keep doing good work: brilliant work.[69]

CHAPTER SUMMARY

Plays by Black and Asian writers have struggled for prominence since the middle of the twentieth century but the last decade has seen their work become increasingly prominent, thanks to Arts Council-funded initiatives and the exposing of theatre as institutionally racist at the beginning of the millennium. The separation of Black and Asian drama in an individual chapter is problematic, threatening to continue its division from plays considered as the dominant or mainstream (plays by white European males) and also imposing an unhelpful umbrella term for what is a broad and diverse field of work. Its recent history, the need for further recognition and the identity of Black British experience and aesthetic as different from the mainstream, however, provide counter-arguments to these points.

Multicultural Britain, globalisation and terrorism have led to increased sensitivity and consumer power, fuelling a desire for audiences to voice their right to offence, and disempowering the right for drama to offend. The writer's responsibility to the audience and the theatre's responsibility to the writer have been questioned in the light of protests against contemporary drama that criticises minority communities or lampoons the beliefs of major faiths. Oversensitivity can curb artistic choice when there is a need for somebody to be answerable, introducing covert censorship that limits drama's freedom of expression.

Innovation in language and aesthetic is employed by some Black and Asian writers as a deliberate strategy for expressing difference, providing an identity for the work that is intentionally separate from the mainstream. The content of contemporary drama has also developed in the last decade, tackling issues relevant to not only third-generation Black and Asian communities but the whole country, suggesting their view of Britain is one of integration even when the theatre industry's is not. More Black actors and directors are needed to help maintain an infrastructure for the work, but artistic censorship is still a problem as programmers pander to the majority culture, developing Black and Asian writers but not producing plays as frequently and even editing scripts to serve a white audience.

NOTES

1. Deirdre Osborne includes these historical flashpoints within a much more detailed review of Black Theatre: see Osborne, note 5.
2. D. Keith Peacock, 'Black British Drama and the Politics of Identity' in Nadine Holdsworth and Mary Luckhurst (eds), *A*

Concise Companion to Contemporary British and Irish Theatre (Oxford: Blackwell, 2008), pp. 48–65 (48).

3. Steven Luckie, in conversation at the Theatre Museum during Black History Month, 4 Dec 2004, recording available on www.theatrevoice.com (accessed 24 October 2009).

4. Statistics from The Arts Council of England Annual Statistics 1999 / 2000.

5. Deirdre Osborne, 'Writing Black Back: An Overview of Black Theatre and Performance in Britain' in Dimple Godiwala (ed.), *Alternatives Within the Mainstream: British Black and Asian Theatres* (Newcastle: Cambridge Scholars Press, 2006), pp. 82–100 (83).

6. Dimple Godiwala in Godiwala, *Alternatives Within The Mainstream*, p. 5.

7. Deirdre Osborne, '"Know Whence You Came": Dramatic Art and Black British Identity', *New Theatre Quarterly* 23:3, 2007, pp. 253–63 (255).

8. Jatinder Verma, 'Cultural Transformations' in Theodore Shank (ed.), *Contemporary British Theatre* (Basingstoke: Macmillan Press, 1996), pp. 55–61 (55).

9. Kwei-Armah in Osborne, "Know Whence You Came", p. 262.

10. Sarah Dadswell, 'What is this Thing Called British Asian Theatre?', *Contemporary Theatre Review* 19:2, 2009, pp. 221–6 (226).

11. Tyrone Huggins, then Artistic Director of Theatre of Darkness, speaking at the 'Eclipse Report: Developing strategies to combat racism in theatre' conference, Nottingham Playhouse, 12–13 June 2001. Transcript published by Arts Council, 2002.

12. Tanika Gupta, quotation from e-mail correspondence with author, 18 November 2009.

13. Sergeant Robyn Williams, also speaking at the Nottingham Playhouse conference: see note 11.

14. Jatinder Verma, 'Sorry, No Saris!' in Vera Gottlieb and Colin Chambers (eds), *Theatre in a Cool Climate* (Oxford: Amber Lane Press, 1999), pp. 191–200 (200).

15. Gabrielle Griffin, 'theatres of difference: the politics of

'redistribution' and 'recognition' in the plays of contemporary Black and Asian women playwrights in Britain', *Feminist Review* 84, 2006, pp. 10–28 (21).

16. Dimple Godiwala, 'Editorial Introduction: Alternatives within the mainstream: British black and Asian theatre', *Studies in Theatre and Performance* 26:1, 2006, pp. 3–12 (8).

17. Gabrielle Griffin, 'Constitutive Subjectivities: Contemporary Black and Asian Women Playwrights in Britain', *European Journal of Women's Studies* 10:4, 2003, pp. 377–94 (382).

18. Kwame Kwei-Armah in 'Kwame Kwei-Armah: Why I'm willing to be unfashionable in the search for true definition', *The Telegraph*, 10 November 2007.

19. Winsome Pinnock, 'Breaking Down the Door' in Gottlieb and Chambers (eds), *Theatre in a Cool Climate*, pp. 27–38 (29).

20. Ibid., p. 35.

21. Griffin, 'Constitutive Subjectivities', p. 389.

22. Kwame Kwei-Armah, quotation from e-mail correspondence with author, 19 November 2009.

23. Roy Williams; all subsequent unmarked quotations from Williams are taken from interview with author, National Theatre, 6 October 2009.

24. Roy Williams, 'What Kind of England Do We Want?', *New Theatre Quarterly* 22:2, 2006, pp. 113–21 (119).

25. Neil Smith, Review of *Clubland* by Roy Williams, *What's On*, 27 June 2001.

26. Laura Hemming, Review of *Sing Yer Heart Out For The Lads* by Roy Williams, *Financial Times*, 4 May 2004.

27. Caryl Phillips, 'Lost Generation', *The Guardian*, 23 April 2005.

28. Michael Billington, *State of the Nation: British Theatre Since 1945* (London: Faber and Faber, 2007), p. 393.

29. Verma, 'Sorry, No Saris!', p. 191.

30. David Edgar, speaking on 'Access Schmaccess' panel, *All Together Now? British Theatre After Multiculturalism*, 13–14 June 2009, Warwick University. Audio excerpts available at www2.warwick.ac.uk/newsandevents/audio/more/atn/ (accessed 25 July 2009).

31. Billington, *State of the Nation*, p. 392.

32. Brian McMaster, *Supporting Excellence in the Arts: From Measurement to Judgement*, published by the Department for Culture, Media and Sport, 2008, p. 6.
33. Brian Crow, 'The *Behzti* affair revisited: British multiculturalism, audiences and strategy', *Studies in Theatre and Performance* 27:3, 2007, pp. 211–22 (212).
34. Peter Billingham, *At the Sharp End* (London: A&C Black, 2007), p. 226.
35. David Edgar, "Gagging': Forum on Censorship', *Contemporary Theatre Review* 17:4, 2007, pp. 516–56 (527).
36. Ibid., 532.
37. Ibid., 529.
38. Gurpreet Kaur Bhatti, *Behzti (Dishonour)* (London: Oberon, 2004), pp. 17–18.
39. Dadswell, 'What is this Thing Called British Asian Theatre?', p. 223.
40. Edgar, 'Gagging', p. 531.
41. Crow, 'The *Behzti* affair revisited', p. 218.
42. Ibid., p. 18.
43. Gupta in Billingham, *At The Sharp End*, p. 213.
44. Aleks Sierz, www.theatrevoice.com/news (accessed 16 December 2009).
45. Caryl Phillips, 'Lost Generation', *The Guardian*, 23 April 2005.
46. Verma, 'Cultural Transformations', p. 56.
47. Suzan-Lori Parks, 'New black math', *Theatre Journal* 57, 2005, pp. 576–83 (579).
48. Griffin, 'theatres of difference', p. 19.
49. Jatinder Verma, 'The shape of a heart', *Studies in Theatre and Performance* 26:1, 2006, pp. 91–7 (93).
50. Jatinder Verma, "Binglishing' the stage: a generation of Asian theatre in England' in R. Boon and J. Plastow (eds), *Theatre Matters* (Cambridge: Cambridge University Press, 1998), pp. 126–34 (129).
51. Dominic Hingorani, 'Binglishing Britain: Tara Arts: *Journey to the West Trilogy*', *Contemporary Theatre Review* 14:4, 2008, pp. 12–22 (17–18).
52. Jerri Daboo, 'One Under the Sun: Globalization, Culture and

Utopia in Bombay Dreams', *Contemporary Theatre Review* 15:3, 2006, pp. 330–7 (336).

53. Ibid., p. 333.

54. Deirdre Osborne, 'Writing black back: an overview of black theatre and performance in Britain', *Studies in Theatre and Performance* 26:1, 2006, pp. 13–31 (28).

55. debbie tucker green, *Dirty Butterfly* (London: Nick Hern Books, 2003), p. 2.

56. debbie tucker green, *Stoning Mary* (London: Nick Hern Books, 2005), p. 8.

57. Peacock, 'Black British Drama and the Politics of Identity', p. 60.

58. Ibid., p. 49.

59. Roy Williams, *Joe Guy* (London: Methuen, 2007), p. 33.

60. Ian Johns, Review of *Elmina's Kitchen* by Kwame Kwei-Armah, *The Times*, 31 May 2003.

61. Kwame Kwei-Armah, *Plays: 1* (London: Methuen, 2009), p. 10.

62. Paul Taylor, Review of *Statement of Regret* by Kwame Kwei-Armah, *The Independent*, 15 November 2007.

63. Kwei-Armah in Osborne, "Know Whence You Came", p. 257.

64. Ibid., p. 256.

65. Alia Bano, talking on the panel 'Mistaken Identity': see note 30.

66. Sol B. River, 'Serious business', *Studies in Theatre and Performance* 26:1, 2006, pp. 85–9 (87).

67. Kwame Kwei-Armah, 'Bringing it Home', *New Statesman*, 25 October 2007.

68. Billington, *State of the Nation*, p. 395.

69. Roy Williams, from interview.

CHAPTER 5

Theatre for Young People – Audiences of Today

A RECENT HISTORY

Theatre for young people in Britain has been shaped by the government's educational reforms and the changing conditions of arts funding. There is a direct link between British politics and the content, aesthetic and intentions driving work made for young audiences over the last 60 years. This chapter traces these conditions through to the present day and considers their wider impact, before offering three case studies as examples of this diverse field of work.

At the end of World War II, the government introduced the Education Reform Act, which raised the school leaving age to fifteen, setting in motion a two-tier education system that separated children into the grammar schools and what were perceived to be the less effective secondary modern schools.[1] Drama was being developed as a holistic method of education (rather than a subject topic) that could promote the development of a child's creativity and social confidence. The drama in education work of Peter Slade, Brian Way and Dorothy Heathcote from the late 1930s to the mid-1960s had an enormous effect not only on education but also on the principles of Theatre in Education (TIE).[2] One of Heathcote's primary aims was participants developing a 'self-spectator' by initiating 'a re-examination and/or development by the students of fundamentally held values by which they lived'.[3] TIE was created to be a social and participatory form of theatre, that took place in a school environment and encouraged young people to examine their place in the world in a way that neither the curriculum nor the mainstream theatre could offer.

The first TIE company began in 1967 at the Belgrade Theatre in Coventry, and was soon followed by many others including the Bolton Octagon, Leeds Playhouse, Nottingham Roundabout and Greenwich Theatre. The rising profile of theatre for young people also took place outside the TIE movement: Caryl Jenner and Brian Way founded the Unicorn Theatre and Theatre Centre respectively, both developing companies that prioritised work for young audiences produced to a high artistic standard, the former in a building-based theatre from the 1970s and the latter through touring to schools.

TIE companies relied on subsidy to create affordable programmes, but in 1988 the introduction of the National Curriculum devolved financial responsibility from Local Educational Authorities to individual schools.[4] Financial and educational freedoms were immediately curtailed and, as a result, the artistic freedom of TIE companies constrained by the market. Schools now sought plays that complemented the curriculum rather than opposed or challenged it. At the same time the Standing Conference of Young People's Theatre (SCYPT) was taking an increasingly oppositional stance to the government as resources were reduced further and further, a position that proved 'unpopular and embarrassing' for both local and national funding bodies.[5] Work was refused by schools for fear of its inappropriate political content and TIE companies became answerable to the needs of the curriculum, not their own needs as artists.

As a matter of survival, TIE companies such as Tiebreak in Hampshire and Half Moon in London adapted their working practice towards 'Young People's Theatre' – touring professional productions into museums, arts centres and schools – a diversification in the sector that led to 'a pluralism of educational theatre which embraced Young People's Theatre, TIE, children's theatre, education theatre, theatre in schools, theatre for schools, and theatre workshops'.[6] However, despite the slow withdrawal of full-time TIE companies from the British theatre – in 2003 Theatre Powys in Wales was the only remaining TIE company to offer full-day programmes for children – theatre for young people has continued to grow, either in partnerships with educational institutions or as strictly artistically-led ventures.[7]

The pattern in the last 10 years has been one of gradual progression. Following the Arts Council's Boyden Report that injected a further £25m into British theatre, a 15% increase in funding for youth theatre was introduced in 2001. A year later, 'Citizenship' was introduced as a compulsory subject for 11–16-year-olds in England, offering some relief to the TIE companies. According to the 2007 curriculum the subject 'encourages [students] to take an interest in topical and controversial issues and to engage in discussion and debate. Pupils learn about their rights, responsibilities, duties and freedoms and about laws, justice and democracy'.[8] Citizenship chimed with TIE's general aims of 'developing a personal as well as group awareness through active audience involvement' and meant schools were more open to the challenging political agendas TIE companies might offer.[9]

At the beginning of the decade, the Arts Council introduced the Artsmark award to 'encourage schools to increase the range, quantity and type of arts that are provided to children [and] raise the profile of arts education'. In 2002 the Department for Culture, Media and Sport also set up 'Creative Partnerships', a scheme designed to introduce arts provision to some of the most disadvantaged young people in the country by initiating projects between artists, arts businesses and schools.[10] New theatre buildings specifically designed for young people also began to open, among them The Egg at Theatre Royal Bath and the new building for the Unicorn in Southwark in 2005. The following year, for the first time in its 10-year history, the National Theatre's Connections programme brought three of their ten specially-commissioned plays – originally written for teenagers to perform in school and youth theatre settings – to the Cottesloe: Mark Ravenhill's *Citizenship*, Deborah Gearing's *Burn* and Enda Walsh's *Chatroom* were performed in rep for a general audience. Significant new companies were also forming; John Retallack's Company of Angels was set up in 2001 to pursue new and experimental theatre with a European influence for young audiences, and is now a partner of

Theatre Café, the annual international symposium on children's theatre. En Masse Theatre in Lancashire, only formed in 2003, has toured its collaboratively-made work for children internationally, including visits to Poland and Malaysia, presenting a form of theatre that consistently challenges its own conventions and the imaginations of the audience.[11] At the present time, the sector appears to be one of positivity, ambition and increasing diversity. A brief consideration of some shared elements across the field will introduce the three case studies, and emphasise some of the challenges that are specific to this area of theatre writing.

COMMONALITIES AND CHALLENGES IN THEATRE FOR YOUNG PEOPLE

> I believe that children are born with an innate sense of justice. This has nothing to do with morality, or knowing the difference between right and wrong. It is to do with fairness . . . The vast majority of children instinctively want justice to prevail.[12]

The ability of drama to expose injustice and present not the problems of society, but the challenges human beings face in making choices within that society is seen as its greatest asset by many practitioners. Anthony Clark, formerly the Artistic Director of Hampstead Theatre, sees theatre as the perfect forum for an exploration of justice, allowing young people a chance to 'rehearse life experience in a safe environment, and as such [it] fulfils a vital function in every child's (and all our) development'.[13] On the subject of justice, Edward Bond is probably the most vocal practitioner in children's theatre. He has written seven of Big Brum TIE company's plays since 1995, and offers the following assessment of the relationship between drama, the pursuit of justice and the preoccupations of the child:

> As [the child] begins to move into the world, the need to feel at home becomes the need for justice . . . Once you have the concept of justice you have something absolutely unique and something that's human, and it is the sole subject of drama

and it is the sole interest of the child . . . the child gives us our humanness: what we tend to do, as a society, is give it its inhumanness'.[14]

As Wood points out above, the dramatisation of the problem of justice is not the same as educating audiences in right and wrong. For example, a demonstrator smashes a bank's window during the recession. What is just from the criminal's point of view is unjust for the victim, but both are now seeking vengeance: one against capitalism, and one against an anti-capitalist. The law may decide who is right, but that does nothing to answer who has acted most justly. The problem of justice should therefore be dramatised through a problem that the audience confronts, where their own choices when put in the character's position – unable to reach for ready-made solutions – are put to the test. As David Allen states, referencing the work of Bond, 'an author should not provide answers; rather, the audience must find its own answers to the problems of "humanness"'.[15] Faced by the immensity of the world and their place within it, children are grappling with the biggest questions of all, and need a space to explore them at an adult level without being patronised.

The provision of such a space is connected to a question of visibility: bringing the untold stories and situations of young people to the stage and sharing them within and beyond those communities. One of the key principles of the National Theatre's Connections programme is the provision of new plays for young actors to perform beyond the confines of their peer groups, avoiding the ghettoising of 'youth theatre'. This is exemplified by the National's decision to once again select three of the plays for the theatre's main programme in 2008: *Baby Girl* by Roy Williams, *DNA* by Dennis Kelly and *The Miracle* by Lin Coghlan. Paul Miller, director of all three plays, singles out the audience dynamic as one of the most significant outcomes of the programme, recalling how 'you could see older middle-class theatregoers, and not only were they seeing dramatic accounts of people's lives, but they were part of an audience of young people that were also being dramatised, which makes for a very vivid experience: these people that are on stage are also all around me'.[16]

Lack of visibility is symptomatic of a long-standing division within the field of theatre for young people: art for education, and art for art's sake. Historically, it is not a simple separation. Theatre has always been educational in the sense that it has frequently stimulated debate.[17] Bond suggests contentiously, 'up until a few hundred years ago, drama was the foundation of all education, and indeed of all culture, either in the form of stories, plays or religion, which is a form of drama'.[18] The persistent employment of theatre as a tool to serve educational targets has widened a perceived gap between the aesthetic quality of theatre for young people, and the level of professionalism associated with mainstream theatre for adults. The creation of this division was on the one hand systemic – the culture of survival created by educational policies in the 1980s and 1990s demanded target-led outcomes – and on the other hand dramaturgical, as the participatory nature of theatre in educational contexts can be thought to disqualify any claims for it being proper 'art'.

Anthony Jackson defines this latter issue as a problem of 'aesthetic distance': the belief held by some that a clear separation between stage world and audience world must be maintained. The risk in practice, he suggests, is that 'a theatrical device intended to reduce the distance and engage the audience more strongly can have the reverse effect', and that incorporating audience participation may mean aesthetic choices are also sacrificed for pedagogic aims.[19] The problem of aesthetic distance begins to dissolve, however, when participation becomes part of the aesthetic itself, and is central to defining the poetics of the form.

The techniques of South American practitioner Augusto Boal's 'Forum Theatre' invite the spectator to step into the action as 'spect-actor' and 'restore him to his capacity of action in all its fullness'.[20] They echo Heathcote's principles of human beings growing and becoming themselves, a highly regarded aim of TIE. Practitioners working within schools found Boal's participatory techniques beneficial in demonstrating how political values can be transformed into action.[21] In the same vein, TIE programmes offer a whole experience that combines the play and workshop participation; the ultimate aim is that of an 'integrated aesthetic totality' where the audience and performers are contained in a complete environment, so any 'aesthetic distance' disappears as a result.[22]

These aims of empowerment, growth, personal development, social and political awareness and self-identity do not necessarily require direct participation during the performance to be achieved. Each of these aims suggests a simple commitment to audience awareness, which may also include consultation at the development stage, where particular choices in the themes, characters and language of the play are designed to speak directly to a particular community. Fin Kennedy's urban hip-hop play *Locked In* (2006) for Half Moon Young People's Theatre is about a 16-year-old Bengali DJ and Black British MC who broadcast their own show on a pirate radio station. It was developed over 2 years in direct contact with a mixture of Half Moon's youth theatre group and students from local schools, many of whom gave advice and guidance about the script's political content during its first drafts, especially when one of the characters begins to flirt with radical Islam. Kennedy's choice was to site this transition in the mosque, but he was quickly informed the mosque was more a place of peace for young Muslims than a site of radicalisation. This action now takes place off-stage and as Kennedy notes, 'those kids can have a meaningful say – and veto – over what you write'.[23]

The possibility of veto by young people is an active part of Kennedy's collaborative writing process. Covert censorship, however, is often a problem when plays are being produced in schools and subject matter conflicts with prevailing ideologies over what should and should not be discussed. If writers are working with extreme situations and language, or politics sensitive with particular communities, the handling of relationships is crucial. With all three case studies that follow, these are problematic issues that are met with different strategies. The first – extremity and ideology – is intrinsically bound up with the work of Edward Bond and Big Brum.

CASE STUDIES: EDWARD BOND AND BIG BRUM, FIN KENNEDY AND MULBERRY SCHOOL, NATIONAL THEATRE CONNECTIONS

Bond's collaboration with Big Brum in 1995 saved the company from an uncertain future; they were struggling to find funding but determined not to bow to the market demands of schools. As a prominent supporter of SCYPT, which grew out of the TIE movement, Bond had written letters and poetry to help focus debate and highlight the importance of their work, but Big Brum was the first to approach him to request a play which, as Cooper states, 'played a significant role in keeping the company alive.'[24]

Bond's plays for young people are constructed around what he calls 'Theatre Events' (TEs). These are the extreme moments (not necessarily violent) where the audience 'is helped to analyse not just the mechanics and significance of the moment, but also the causes and implications of the short-term "event" on the drama as a whole'.[25] It is often achieved with the significant use of an object, which diverts the audience from either an emotional engagement with or alienation from a character (avoiding both Stanislavski and Brecht in one move). This is why it is called an 'event' – it is live for the audience because they are given no answers: instead they have to commit their imaginations to create the reason behind the dramatic action. 'Reason' is used here in a philosophical sense; it is what we must seek to make sense of the world. However, it must be autonomously created: it cannot be taught. One of Bond's maxims is that 'drama teaches nothing' because true reason can only come from the individual's imagination. Reason 'taught' by the dramatist is only true to him / her so cannot also be the 'reason' of the audience. The reason behind action for Stanislavksi was based in character emotion; for Brecht, it was socially constructed. Both sorts of reason were made explicit to the audience. TEs therefore, for Bond, carry the possibility of a truly just society: the audience creates their own reasons, and are therefore released from any taught ideology.

During the TE, the audience are returned to the point of 'radical innocence': the perspective of the child who has yet to be taught what society expects of it. It is at this moment that our 'humanness' is reassessed (or developed) because the only rules left for making a choice are those we create for ourselves in that moment, and we recreate the 'radically innocent' child in ourselves because we desire those rules and that choice to be just. The way Bond confronts audiences with the uncomfortable problems of an unjust society is a direct appeal; we must try to separate the 'false learning' of education from the truth of the human situation.[26]

Cooper recognises that as a company performing consistently in a school environment, it is often not the content of the stories in the Big Brum plays, but the manner in which Bond prises apart these two truths and lays them bare that can create strong emotional reactions from teachers:

> People object to Bond's plays, because they want to be told what's right and wrong, but the kids don't need to be told that it's wrong to kill people because they already know that. They need to know why, and what does it mean, to commit that act? It's a complex problem in our culture but that makes adults very, very angry . . . a lot of these plays are too challenging for some adults, because they're trying to identify a given answer, whereas kids experience it, and it's a very open and powerful tool, for the kids to fill it with meaning.

Bond's principles for drama challenge not only the prevailing ideologies of educational institutions (the pursuit of answers through provision of reason, not the discovery of reason through use of the imagination) but also the ideology of dramatic realism itself. The 'gap' which is opened by Bond is the one contemporary drama has filled with the knowable subtext, thus preventing the audience from stepping into the action imaginatively as participant. It only permits them to judge as an outsider, gratified in the identification of a 'correct' answer. TIE is an interventionist theatre practice in a changing society, which necessarily requires 'the need to constantly test, question and develop our practice, and where necessary to reconceptualise it'.[27] This is what Bond seeks from his audiences – reconceptualisation of that society. By making choices that avoid the ideological trappings of other contemporary work for the stage, Bond is shaping a unique dramaturgy for his plays, and one which has been developed and refined through the collaboration with Big Brum.

His first TIE play, *At The Inland Sea* (1995), was about the power of the imagination, the death camps at Auschwitz and the impact of history's sufferings upon the present. Reduced to a synopsis, the play is 'deceptively simple'.[28] A young boy is in his bedroom, studying for his exams, whilst his fussing mother intermittently arrives and talks at him; then a woman from Auschwitz appears before the boy. She wants him to save her and her baby from the gas chamber by telling them a story. Although he cannot save her, both he and his mother are irrevocably changed by his experiences. The appeal to the imagination is immediate and inherently theatrical: the power of the language and the boy's direct experience creates the gas chamber in the audience's minds, though the material objects of the stage are only those of the boy's bedroom:

> Woman   What's that? – the terrible squeaking? The dead are crying? No – the hinges! They're opening the doors. (*To baby*.) Wait, wait – it takes ten minutes – twenty! All that time! Something will save you! – The people are getting to their feet. Stumbling. The doors are open. The great wet mouth. Water dripping from the top like saliva. (*An old woman wailing*.) An old woman beating her neighbours. Beating. Kicking. The soldiers are beating – dragging! The soldiers are screaming as if *they're* going to die![29]

The power of the imagination is crucial to Bond's philosophies about drama, and helps to explain his opposition to what he calls the 'lie-truth': ideologies that are passed down to our children (through various systems) but only force the individual to conform, teaching them how to be moral human beings in a given system, not a system of their own choosing. Bond believes a human being's ability to project itself into the lives of others is where a concept of morality is grown; this concept can only be truthful if it is autonomous, not taught to us by others. His intention to confront audiences with the TE has 'nothing to do with the control of our behaviour . . . but everything to do with the free activity of uncorrupted imagination'.[30]

The use of the object at the centre of the TE is perhaps best exemplified in *The Under Room* (2005), where a dummy has represented a character for the play's duration. All of his words in the play are spoken by an actor, stood to one side of the stage. The play is set in 2077 and follows the story of Joan, who agrees to protect an immigrant who has broken into her house, when she realises he will be hunted down and killed by soldiers. After discovering his traumatic history from his war-torn home country, she becomes involved with a human trafficker, Jack, who agrees to move the immigrant to a new location and provide him with a new life. She is lied to by the immigrant and ends up owing the ruthless Jack money: a situation which completely destroys her life. In the penultimate scene of the play, this polite, well-spoken middle-class woman attacks the immigrant she has been housing. The immigrant is played by a dummy for the entire play:

> Confess! Confess! (*She stabs the Dummy. Stamps on it. Rips. Slashes. Tears.*) Wake up! Slice the sleep off your face! Cut it out of your eyes! Shred your tongue! Cut the vrgs kvrichs blotch blotch off it! (*The Dummy is destroyed. The stuffing explodes and spills out. Long strips of yellow plastic rubber two or three inches wide scatter and litter the floor.*) Get up! (*She pulls off her headscarf. Rips it. Slashes it.*) . . . Get rid of the evil! Where is it? (*She searches the strips and rags.*) Evil! Wickedness? Where?[31]

The object of a featureless human effigy, until this point cared for and humanised by Joan, is invested with value throughout the play and then annihilated by her. If it were a real actor, the scene would be literal, bloody and horrific for its gore and shock value. Our reaction may be sympathy for the immigrant, empathy for Joan or alienation through the graphic visual spectacle. Through the use of an object, however, our perspective as an audience is not interrupted by spectacle or effect: Joan's emotions are very specific, and our imaginations can search for reason in her actions rather than reject the moment. We ask why Joan does this before we ask anything else. Creating this response in an audience is the cornerstone of his work and, for Cooper, it is what makes Bond's work for children so unique and why their collaboration will continue for years to come:

His whole theory about the gap, nothingness, is actually all about making the audience the site of imagination, so even if you're sat in a chair watching, you're projecting yourself into the action, and he thinks he does that in a way that nobody does – nobody has ever done.

The audience as a site of imagination is utilised very differently for Fin Kennedy's work as Mulberry's artist-in-residence. His first audience is simultaneously the performers of the work, co-collaborators, subject of the drama and members of a specific community: the students of Mulberry school. Their imaginations are crucial to the development of Kennedy's scripts:

The playwright in residence is required to step out of her own subjective sphere and use her craft as a storyteller to draw out and express the lived experiences of the host community through the facilitation of collective story-making . . . the playwright is not a *member* of the community but rather a *visitor*, a conjuror who is invited to play a temporary shamanistic role in order to transform the community's lived experience into a story that is meaningful and owned by those who create it.[32]

Kennedy began as Mulberry's artist-in-residence in 2007. Fisher's description of the community storyteller is a close fit in defining Kennedy's experiences, but she delineates the role further, into three potential interactions for the writer in residence: the facilitator, who assists the community in writing their own play in their own words; the interpreter, who takes the stories of the community and then writes a play themselves; or the mediator, who shapes verbatim dialogue or written contributions into a coherent whole.[33] She does acknowledge that there is a slippage between these working definitions in practice, and there are certainly elements of all three roles present in Kennedy's work.

Kennedy did have previous contact with the school as a writer, following short-term projects coordinated by Half Moon Young People's Theatre, but the artist-in-residence post had been newly created by the school itself. For the last 3 years the residency has embedded him in the school between January and August, when the collaboratively-created work, shaped and scripted by Kennedy, is then performed at the Edinburgh Festival. His blog records the students' collective ownership of the work as palpable; upon being asked by a journalist who wrote the first play *Mehndi Night* (2007), they turned around in unison to declare 'we did'.[34]

This statement is testament to Kennedy's ability to work across all three of Fisher's suggested roles for the playwright-in-residence, but still allow the play to belong to the community. In the early stages of developing *Mehndi Night*, the students had been given improvisation exercises through which they created characters and situations taken from family experience (facilitator); Kennedy had then shaped these into a dramatic narrative that used these stories (interpreter); then lines of dialogue found their way into the play through further improvisation with the cast and discussion with former students (mediator) who worked as a focus group to provide what he calls 'a Bengali critique' of the work, in an effort 'to give it a sounding at every stage so it's convincing and watertight.' In the play, an estranged daughter returns to her family during the Mehndi celebration of her sister's forthcoming marriage (a female-only ritual). This event and location were only identified after several attempts by Kennedy to suggest a premise that the female-only cast found agreeable (he wryly adds 'I should have just asked them straight away').

In between this creative work with the student company, he is running sessions for pupils on GCSE and A-level theatre courses, facilitating workshops for members of staff interested in creative writing, and employing his skills as a writer in other curriculum areas such as English. The research and development for the plays has achieved a presence beyond the confines of the rehearsal room, into the day-to-day workings of the school, its alumni community and geographical location. The second play, *Stolen Secrets* (2008) was a series of five dramatic poems for performance each developed from voluntary suggestions placed within specially-designed 'secret boxes' placed around the school. Kennedy, director Julia Voce and the cast would empty the boxes in rehearsal and identify potential starting points for stories that had come from within the school's community. Students were also sent out 'on location' to research characters and come back with suggestions. This extended relationship with the community's populace, geography and culture is vital in creating not only an environment of trust between the host community and the visiting artist, but also the opportunity for the writer to gain an intimate understanding of that community's internal dynamics.

All of Kennedy's plays for Mulberry are characterised by the predominance of a poetic, direct address storytelling style that often frames the action, allowing students to play multiple roles and transform themselves swiftly from narrator to character. It is a form of dialogue that is highly effective in performance, communicating an immediacy and desire to share stories; it is also rooted in the lives of the teenagers and their engagement with both culture and social activities. 'Their main point of reference in dramatic storytelling is soap-opera naturalism', explains Kennedy, 'and if we gave naturalism to them it didn't always tend to work to their strengths, as you got a sort of sub-EastEnders imitation of drama'. The result is a fluid, open text, which can be populated by any number of actors; also a pragmatic choice if the cast size fluctuates through rehearsal, as it did with *Stolen Secrets*:

East London
Our ends
Is built on secrets
Ancient secrets
Teenage secrets
Foreign secrets
Wartime secrets
They hide in tower block stairwells
Under stains on the carpet
In hoods
Gutters
Drops of rain
Between lines of faded newsprint
Or trickling out the drains
Sometimes the whispering gets so loud
It hangs there like a thundercloud.[35]

Kennedy describes the genesis of this style as part of the social world of the cast, 'playground stuff, telling tales and gossiping and with multiple narrators falling over each other, correcting each other, and with a momentum that's performative – audiences really respond to the immediacy of it'. Style of expression, content and community are bound together in the Mulberry plays – whilst they each chronicle the imaginations and experiences of East End Bengali teenagers, the stories are fictionalised in both form and content, presented as 'their extended world, not themselves literally'. This was particularly true of the final play of the trilogy *The Unravelling* (2009), which unfolded as 'a sort of meta-theatrical parable about the power of mastering storytelling as a means to take control of one's life.' In this sense it echoes Bond's desire to allow audiences to step away from themselves and their surroundings. As Fisher corroborates, 'storytelling and narrative enables individuals to consider and critique their own subjective relationships to the community of which they are part' and as such, the fictionalisation of raw material – the ideas provided by the cast that stem from their life experience in that community – can liberate individuals and change their value systems.[36]

Just as Bond has been given the opportunity to test his contemporary theory of drama through collaboration with Big Brum, Kennedy has found collaboration with young people an opportunity to experiment with his writing in a way a traditional commissioning structure would not allow, where 'you'd be sent off on your own and expected to deliver in six months'. The poetic and expressive style has found its way into his writing for adult audiences and, as such, develops his own artistic voice. The Mulberry residency is a reciprocal relationship, and one that can influence mainstream British theatre through both process and production.

In comparison to Kennedy's working environment of close collaboration, writers on the National Theatre Connections programme are commissioned to deliver a play without a structured programme of contact with young people. The majority of development or research comes from the writer's own experiences. Paul Miller, director of the three Connections plays selected from the portfolio for performance at the National Theatre in 2008, lauds this process for allowing experienced writers to create a 'singular vision', and suggests that the sheer variety of voices and styles across each year is one of the great joys of the programme.

The Connections programme was created in the early 1990s by Suzy Graham Adriani and was designed to make new plays available for performance by young people, offering something that had hitherto been less available. The long-term goal was to create a lasting body of work that could be accessed by young people in the future; over 200 companies of young people perform the plays each year, and each annual volume is published and a copy sent to every school library:

> Young people weren't well served. We had the adult canon of work: huge, rich, brilliant, then the world of literature for teenagers that was great, but theatre wasn't paying attention to them. There was theatre for young people, TIE, but nobody was writing theatre for young people to perform themselves.[37]

Being commissioned to write for young people still offers a space to stretch artistically. Writer Lin Coghlan points out that whilst enthusiasm for young people and young audiences is helpful for the writer 'it's also an opportunity to write a huge play which you normally would never get asked to do'.[38] The challenge of scale can also present itself from the other direction, as writers are asked to provide scripts with a maximum playing time of one hour. Roy Williams sees this time constraint as a tool and a challenge that 'really allowed me to be much more focused on this piece than probably I have on other plays [where] you can afford to indulge yourself a little'. Dennis Kelly's initial engagement with the project stems from a remembrance of his own time in youth theatres and the value he invested in that experience, so 'being able to write something for people in youth theatres to perform was a very direct way of being able to talk to people who, like me, might have needed it at that time.'

The three plays presented very different scenarios and are distinct not just in their content but also their form, each grounded in a particular style of theatrical language. Williams' *Baby Girl* is ostensibly about the cycle of teenage pregnancies from mother to daughter, but is also an exploration of the gulf between the different stages of teenage life from thirteen to eighteen. It is presented in his characteristic street-realism, and structured around the months of pregnancy leading up to the day of the birth. The action is located in immediately recognisable settings (a park, a dilapidated flat, the street, a hospital) and the dialogue has a distinctly urban swagger, communicating the fast-thinking cut and thrust of characters jostling for status. The play becomes a journey towards grudging acceptance for young mother Kelle, a final choice born of the simple need to survive in the world.

Deoxyribonucleic Acid (DNA) by Dennis Kelly also has a linear structure, moving between a wood, a field and a street, as a group of school friends conspire to cover up a death they have caused. However, in the execution of their complicated plan to create a story around the death and absolve them from any connection, they accidentally frame a man for murder, thanks to DNA found on an item of clothing that is part of their cover-up. A final complication is the reappearance of the friend they thought dead, who has been living in the woods in a semi-feral state. The play captures the interdependence of the 'pack' with stark clarity; the bonds that tie them together are stretched to breaking point when collective responsibility is compromised by individual need.

The language of the play departs from Williams' gritty back-and-forth naturalism and is littered with long monologues, fragmented sentences and overlapping dialogue, creating a heightened and poetic style that captures the high tension and nervous energy of the situation the characters are facing. Contemplative ringleader Phil, often silent for long periods, is consistently pursued by the chatterbox Lea, who speaks as she thinks. This dynamic between the two creates a fascinating stream of consciousness, drawing in expansive images and ideas and extending the imaginative reach of the play beyond the situation itself:

> I mean, please, don't gimme all that, carbon dioxide? Carbon dioxide, Phil? And look at the rest of the universe. Venus, Phil, there's a, look at Venus, what about Venus, hot enough to melt lead or Titan with oceans of liquid nitrogen, I mean stars, Phil, a billion nuclear reactions a second, I mean to be

honest it's all either red hot or ice cold, so, so, so . . . No. It's
life that upsets the natural order. It's us that's the anomaly.[39]

Finally, the structure of Coghlan's *The Miracle* is a combination of
flashbacks, live action and narration, with a character list nearing
fifty that comprises a community with a young girl, Ron (Veronica)
at its centre, who believes she has acquired special powers. The
play tells the story of the community's reaction to this revelation,
and illustrates our collective need to have belief in the transcen-
dental and spiritual even when we live in a secular age. The community has previously suffered a natural disaster when a huge flood
hits the town, and halfway through the play a young soldier – a son
from one of the families – returns; it is through him that Ron can
depart from the mysterious chain of events that she has apparently
set in motion.

The play thrives on ambiguity and mysticism, reflecting its
subject matter, and the structure has a feeling of alchemy about
it: characters, scenes and situations conjured up from nowhere
arrive to create a tapestry of interconnected narratives. The
story (and backstory) reveals itself to the audience through the
framing device of narration by Ron's best friend Zelda, and
gathers together a huge variety of characters in depicting the town.
There is a lively and spontaneous rhythm to the play that reflects
Coghlan's process in writing it from scratch and discovering it as it
unfolded before her, 'watching the world of the play as it began to
come into focus'.[40] The ambiguities and questions the play raises
are open ended, but linked closely to Coghlan's interest in characters at the age of Ron and Zelda, who are constantly asking 'who
am I going to be . . . am I going to be the way everybody tells me
I'm meant to be?'

Although the commissions could be accused of being adult com-
mentaries on the experiences of young people as they see them,
the plays escape from being patronising because they deal with
complex experiences from young characters' perspectives. They
remain at the centre of the plays' stories, and manage to 'tackle
moral issues without being moralising'.[41] The dangers of moralising are recognised by Kelly, who implicitly supports Bond's
maxim that 'drama teaches nothing' in stating 'to think I know

more than a fourteen-year-old about morals is preposterous' – an attitude that is evident in the open questions left by the characters' experiences in *DNA*.

What connects all three case studies is the point of view from which the stories are written. The world is presented as experienced from a young person's point of view; it is the same material world we inhabit as adults, but articulated differently. It honours experience above power of expression. Elwell cites Michael Dalton of Pop-Up Theatre on the subject of understanding, who warns that 'we forget young people's level of comprehension is at an adult level, although their level of expression is not'.[42] This is why, in theory, it is entirely possible to write a play about suicide bombers for 4-year-olds. How do those image and ideas arrive in the mind of a child? What do they look like and how are they understood? How do they make sense of them in relation to their own lives? Young people exist in the same globalised world as adults, so it is crucial that theatre can recognise these experiences within their frame of reference.

WHAT NEXT FOR YOUNG PEOPLE'S THEATRE?

Of all the genres explored in this book, theatre for young people has had one of the most intimate relationships with politics since its emergence in the 1950s. Funding, artistic direction, diversification, changes in the curriculum and government policy have all come to bear directly on the types of work that are on offer. For many practitioners, the fierce economic market that was encouraged in the 1980s still comes to bear not only on young people's theatre, but on the culture and lives of young people themselves. Consumerism is rife and young people are often the target of its promises of fulfilment and instant gratification. Tony Graham of the Unicorn Theatre expresses his fear that childhood 'has been undermined by the relentless activity of global capitalism', and that the work we make for children should not avoid the most difficult questions we face as adults, suggesting that 'great artists paint a world which might be informed by morality (or emotional truth), yet refuses to patronise, moralise or "educate"'.[43]

What theatre also provides is an alternative to global consumerism and the digital age. In Kennedy's words, it matters 'precisely *because* everything else is on a screen and pixellated and moved down millions of miles of cable: it's got liveness on its side'. Not just liveness, but the ability to capture the universal in the specific and transcend cultural and geographical boundaries, perhaps even using globalisation as a tool to unite experiences. In response to the analyses invited by Bond's plays, Coult suggests that 'the problems a kid in London faces may be felt less sharply than his counterpart in an Iraqi village, but increasingly they stem from the same social and economic forces, over which neither has much control'.[44] The ability of recognisable human experience to bridge cultural divides is also evidenced in Theatre Centre's production of *Souls* (2000) by Roy Williams, which tells the story of three Black British brothers living in West London. The play was taken to local schools in Tower Hamlets, East London, with the brothers transposed to be Bangladeshis – the play was just as effective, as 'human commonality filtered through cultural specificity came into focus'.[45]

The theoretical attention given to the work of TIE by Bond and Cooper at Big Brum, the deep involvement of writer, cast and community at Mulberry School and the determination to capture a specificity of teenage experience in the Connections plays suggests that the medium could not be anything other than political. Kennedy's fascination with young people is inherently political in motive:

> I'm interested in the bigger political ideas about multiculturalism, and they're [London's young people] making that manifest in a theatrical way, through youth culture and the sort of fusions you get there – be it Asian hip-hop or funky modern clothes companies who do trendy hijabs – I just love it, it's fascinating. Teenagers bring playfulness to the politics of the situation in which they find themselves.

This level of commitment and belief in an audience comes from a deep-seated belief in the power of theatre to change society at a grass-roots level. At its best, it does this by creating stories that problematise our common situation as human beings, but from a young person's perspective. As a result – either through an interactive development process or witnessing the play in production – it asks us to see ourselves in the world more clearly.

CHAPTER SUMMARY

The progress of theatre for young people has been linked to education policies and theatre funding streams since Theatre in Education (TIE) began in the 1960s. The 1980s saw control of budgets devolved from education authorities to individual schools, and although TIE dwindled as a result, different forms of theatre for young people developed to respond to the changes. In the last 10 years new theatre buildings specifically designed for children, a new canon of work for teenagers from the National Theatre Connections programme and the introduction of Artsmark and compulsory Citizenship classes in schools have advocated theatre for young people as relevant, sustainable and essential to their development.

Theatre for young people is often characterised through its involvement with the audience at either a development stage, collaborating with writers or companies to create new stories to perform or be performed by professional actors, or during performance, such as the workshops embedded in TIE programmes or simple techniques of audience participation. Conversely, this has also led to a long-held division in the perspective of theatre for young people, seen as either strictly educational, or as a professional form of theatre with artistic standards on a par with work for adult audiences. This division is often dissolved by the practices of TIE that see both workshops and play as part of an overall 'performance' programme, or the techniques of August Boal's Forum Theatre, where the audience is invited to create solutions for problems faced by characters in the drama.

All three case studies offer examples of young people being empowered by drama. They are empowered to create their own system of values and reason through the work of Edward Bond, overstepping taught ideologies to construct the world from their own point of view; they are collaborators and performers of stories from their own lives in the work of Fin Kennedy, sharing their fictionalised lives with a wider public, and they are the performers of work written exclusively for their generation by leading professional writers in the Connections programme. The pursuit of a young person's perspective is shared among all of these writers, and leads to drama that communicates a distinct vision of the world.

NOTES

1. Stuart Bennett, *Theatre for Children and Young People* (Twickenham: Aurora Metro, 2005), p. 12.
2. Dan Urian, 'Drama in Education: from Theory to "Study Cases"', *Contemporary Theatre Review* 10:2, 2000, pp. 1–9 (2).
3. David Davis, 'Edward Bond and Drama in Education' in David Davis (ed.), *Edward Bond and the Dramatic Child* (Staffordshire: Trentham Books, 2005), pp. 163–80 (p. 167).
4. Persephone Sextou, 'Theatre in Education in Britain: Current Practice and Future Potential', *New Theatre Quarterly* 19:2, 2003, pp. 177–88 (177).
5. Chris Elwell, 'Theatre and Education' in Stuart Mackey (ed.), *Practical Theatre: A Post-16 Approach* (Stanley Thornes: Cheltenham, 1997) pp. 239–77 (241).
6. Sextou, 'Theatre in Education in Britain', p. 181.
7. Ibid., p. 187.
8. Extract from 'Citizenship: Programme of Study for Key Stage 3 and Attainment Target', Crown Copyright 2007, available www.qca.org.uk/curriculum (accessed 24 September 2009).
9. Sextou, 'Theatre in Education in Britain', p. 178.
10. Artsmark information from www.artscouncil.org.uk/artsmark and on Creative Partnerships from http://ofsted.gov.uk (both accessed 24 September 2009).
11. Oliver Birch, 'En Masse Theatre – The Shelter: Fun in Strange Places' in J. Sumsion (ed.), *The Skeleton Key* (Cheshire: Action Transport Theatre Company, 2007), pp. 13–17 (15).

12. David Wood, *Theatre for Children: A Guide to Writing, Directing and Acting* (London: Faber and Faber, 1997), p. 21.
13. Anthony Clark, untitled paper delivered at 'The Quality of Children's Theatre' conference, Birmingham Rep, 9 July 2002. Published by Arts Council, November 2003.
14. Edward Bond, *Reality Has Lost Its Voice*, DVD, recorded by Andy Marshall at 'Imagination in Action': 25 years of Big Brum Theatre in Education, 2007.
15. David Allen, '"Going to the Centre": Edward Bond's *The Children*', Studies in Theatre and Performance, 27:2, 2007, pp. 115–36 (118).
16. Paul Miller; all further quotations from Paul Miller are from interview with author, National Theatre, 26 August 2009.
17. Elwell, 'Theatre and Education', p. 239.
18. Edward Bond, keynote speech, 'The Quality of Children's Theatre' conference, Birmingham Rep, 9 July 2002. Published by Arts Council, November 2003.
19. Anthony Jackson, *Theatre, Education and the Making of Meanings: Art or instrument?* (Manchester: Manchester University Press: 2007), p. 146.
20. Augusto Boal, *Theatre of the Oppressed* (London: Pluto Press, 1979), p. 155.
21. Bennett, *Theatre for Children and Young People*, p. 19.
22. Jackson, *Theatre, Education and the Making of Meanings*, p. 149.
23. Fin Kennedy: all further quotations from Fin Kennedy are from interview with author, Lewes, 24 August 2009.
24. Chris Cooper, Artistic Director of Big Brum TIE Company: all further quotations from interview with author, Birmingham, 7 September 2009.
25. Georges Bas, 'A Glossary of Terms Used in Bondian Theatre' in David Davis (ed.), *Edward Bond and the Dramatic Child* (Staffordshire: Trentham Books, 2005) pp. 201–20 (216).
26. Davis, *Edward Bond and the Dramatic Child*, p. 13.
27. Jackson, *Theatre, Education and the Making of Meanings*, p. 29.
28. Tony Coult, 'Notes and Commentary' in Edward Bond, *At The Inland Sea* (London: Methuen, 1997), pp. 35–81 (39).
29. Edward Bond, *At The Inland Sea* (London: Methuen, 1997), p. 15.

30. Coult, 'Notes and Commentary', p. 38.
31. Edward Bond, *Plays: 8* (London: Methuen, 2006), p. 201.
32. Amanda Stuart Fisher, 'The Playwright in Residence: A Community's Storyteller', *The Drama Review* 48:3, 2004, pp. 135–49 (137).
33. Ibid., p. 139.
34. Quotation from www.finkennedy.co.uk/blog.htm (accessed 15 August 2009).
35. Fin Kennedy, *Stolen Secrets*, unpublished play text.
36. Fisher, 'The Playwright in Residence', p. 136.
37. Suzy Graham Adriani: quotation from interview with author, London, 29 September 2009.
38. Unmarked comments from Lin Coghlan, Dennis Kelly and Roy Williams are from a panel discussion recorded and transcribed by Theatre Voice, Theatre Museum, 26 March 2008, www.theatrevoice.com (accessed 24 July 2009).
39. Dennis Kelly, 'Deoxyribonucleic Acid (DNA)', *NT Connections 2007* (London: Faber and Faber, 2007), pp. 231–83 (254).
40. Lin Coghlan, *The Miracle* (London: Oberon, 2008), p. 54.
41. Paul Taylor, Review of *Baby Girl / DNA / The Miracle* at the National Theatre, *The Independent*, 4 March 2008.
42. Michael Dalton in Elwell, 'Theatre and Education', p. 250.
43. Tony Graham, untitled paper delivered at 'The Quality of Children's Theatre' conference, Birmingham Rep, 9 July 2002. Published by Arts Council, November 2003.
44. Coult, 'Notes and Commentary', p. 69.
45. Thomas Kell, 'Theatre Centre and New Writing' in Stuart Bennett (ed.), *Theatre for Children and Young People* (Twickenham: Aurora Metro, 2005), pp. 131–9 (139).

CHAPTER 6

Adaptation and Transposition – Reinterpreting the Past

WHAT IS ADAPTATION?

Drama has always been a magpie of storytelling forms, stealing and borrowing from existing narrative sources to create new ones. The characters and plots that comprise many of the tragedies from the most prominent Greek dramatists – Aeschylus, Sophocles and Euripides – have their roots in the '*muthoi* (myths or stories) which were expressed in the older narrative epic poems':[1] *The Iliad* and *The Odyssey*, ascribed to Homer and charting the escalation of events leading to the Trojan War and the long return home of the soldier Odysseus. In addition, we usually encounter both versions – the poems and the plays – in our native tongue, the texts subject to further disruption and alteration through the act of translation. The stories told through Shakespeare's plays can also be traced back to other sources, with many of his plays 'shown to follow, broadly or closely . . . earlier texts that he had read or otherwise knew of'.[2] The most famous example is likely to be *Romeo and Juliet*, originally a fifteenth-century Italian novella and the plot of which Shakespeare probably encountered through an adaptation itself: a verse narrative titled *Romeus and Juliet* by English writer Arthur Brooke.[3]

Adaptation is best understood for the purposes of this chapter as the act of taking an existing book, play text or screenplay and transposing it to another context. It is useful to consider context here in three different ways. First, the context of the medium: a book might be transposed to the stage. A simple example to begin with is the recent transposition of Primo Levi's first-person prose account of surviving the Holocaust *If This Is A Man* (1947) into the one-person play *Primo*, adapted and performed by the actor Anthony Sher in 2004 at the National Theatre. The production was widely acknowledged for its respectful treatment of Primo Levi's original account, reflected in Adam Scott's review for *The Independent* on 5 October, who witnessed 'a night of startling theatricality, a salutary lesson in stage minimalism'. The play maintains a level of fidelity to the source text in its manner and tone, and the world of the drama is also set in the same time and space as the book. The artistic medium has completely shifted.

Second, one can consider the context of the story within the original source text: the world in which the characters of the drama are placed. Harold Brighouse's 1915 stage play *Hobson's Choice* is set at the end of the nineteenth century, and follows the story of Henry Hobson and his three daughters in a shoe shop in Salford. Hobson's 'choice' is to marry off his eldest daughter to the shop's best boot-maker, but he must face the consequences and show his humility when their new rival business drives him into a state of impoverishment. In 2003 writer Tanika Gupta adapted the play – retaining the medium of the stage – but relocated the story to the present day, in a modern Asian fashion shop. 'I was amazed when I first sat down to read the play how easily it transposed' she says, referring to the chauvinistic attitudes of Hobson and how quickly this put her in mind of the contemporary world.[4]

Gupta's version retains the dramatic structure of the original play, but transposes some of the characters' ethnicities from white to Asian – using one culture and time with frustratingly patriarchal values to reflect another. Despite the gulf between the career choices available to an Asian woman in the twenty-first century, and the insistence of Hobson's eldest daughter in the original play that she simply be married, Gupta still retained the story of the source text, explaining 'I didn't want to go too far from the original play because then it wouldn't have been an adaptation'. In Gupta's play the context of the story changes, but the dramatic structure and the medium of communication stay the same.

An alternative approach to transposing the context of the story world – where it is fractured and almost completely removed from its original structure – can be found in Mark Ravenhill's play *Handbag* (1998), where five of the characters from Oscar Wilde's play *The Importance of Being Earnest* (1895) end up colliding with characters from *Handbag*, which is a contemporary drama about the role of parenting in an age of sexual diversity. The source text of Wilde is employed by Ravenhill as a commentary of sorts, juxtaposed in the earlier part of the play through independent scenes, then illuminating both sets of characters and their parallels and dissonances by combining them within the same timeframe and narrative by the end.

Third, one needs to consider context as a factor that lies outside either the source text's story or its medium, looking instead at the time and place in which it was originally encountered by an audience. This is an unavoidable contextual shift in all adaptations. The historical or cultural conditions in which the source text was first seen can never be directly replicated, but is often the stimulus that governs transpositions of story, structure or medium. The challenge of ensuring that a text from a different time and space can speak with relevance to a contemporary audience takes its lead from the 'strictest sense' of the word adapt, describing 'the task of an organism finding itself in a potentially hostile setting and seeking to fit in'.[5]

On occasion, relevance is self-evident in the themes and content of the story, which seems to reach across temporal or historically-specific boundaries. Part-funded by the British government, Lawrence Olivier's film adaptation of Shakespeare's *Henry V*, which features a rousingly patriotic call to arms in the famous 'St Crispin's Day' speech, was released in 1944 and coincided with the Normandy landings towards the end of World War II. Effective transposition in this case was governed by a factor external to the creative act of adaptation: a time of war across much of Europe and the need for propaganda to boost morale.

The practice of adaptation is a vast creative playground, with multiple choices facing the adapter. As shown above, the subsequent 'reading' of an adaptation can be equally complex for the audience and almost always double-coded, as we interpret not only the meaning of a play in its own right, but also its relationship to an original source text. Linda Hutcheon offers a distillation of the options into three distinct areas which echo the categories of 'context' described above: first, 'an acknowledged transposition of a recognizable other work or works', such as Sher's adaptation of Primo Levi's account which maintains story and setting; second, 'a creative *and* an interpretative act of appropriation/ salvaging' such as Gupta's updating of Brighouse's 1915 play to the present day and culture; and third, 'an extended intertextual engagement with the adapted work', such as Ravenhill's radical deployment of characters and situations from Wilde's source text in an original play of his own making.[6] Writers have a long history of appropriating source texts and using them to satisfy their own needs, taking the raw dramatic material and sculpting from it something that will speak to the audience of their own time.

Adaptation in contemporary British drama is not confined to the act of writers changing or updating source texts into a modern style: texts can also stay unaltered, but be radically reframed by the work of a director. This is often achieved through changing the costumes or setting, couching a classic play within a contemporary cultural or political landscape and encouraging an audience to find new readings of even the most well-known texts. Frantic Assembly's radical restaging of *Othello* (2008) cut large portions of the play to create a lean and aggressive version of the original, but what remained of Shakespeare's verse was moved from Venice to the present day, in a dilapidated pub in a working-class area of a Northern town.

The effect of this transposition on the reading of the play was to haul its themes and ideas into the present day, the use of verse creating a vivid comparison between gang rivalry and the currency of loyalty among white working-class males, and the unrelenting drive for status and power orchestrated by a seventeenth-century soldier. Critical responses to this contemporary setting, alongside the company's usual boisterous performance style (see Chapter 3), were broadly positive: although the text had been given 'an expert gutting' there was a feeling that 'Shakespeare hasn't been buried, but honoured and imaginatively reinvented for 21st-century audiences'.[7] This may suggest an unfair assumption regarding the

ability of a contemporary audience to watch Shakespeare unadulterated, but it does honour the laudable qualities of theatrical
adaptation, and its enabling of dramatic literature to transcend 400
years of history.

Recontextualisation of this kind is a method of stage adaptation
that signifies a clear difference from literary adaptation: the restaging of a text can maintain fidelity to the spoken word – the text's
literary qualities – but draws on the plastic and three-dimensional
nature of performance to alter its meaning. As an audience we
are interpreting an associative structure, creating subtextual conversations between the contemporary world as know it, the contemporary world as depicted through the chosen setting of the
adaptation, and the original world from which the source text is
taken. Adaptation is a complex conversation between the past, the
present and the world of the story, enhancing our understanding
of all three: but the nature of that conversation is mediated by
performance choices made in the present and the reading intended
by the adapter. It is why this form of adaptation – transposing the
setting but maintaining the text – exploits the existing openness
and complexity of live performance further than a completely new
piece of work, as 'the remounting of any drama text in another time
and circumstance will change its semiotic content and reception
even more extensively'.[8]

Transposition of setting is not a prerequisite of reviving a classic
for a contemporary audience. The National Theatre's two revivals of Sophocles' *Oedipus* in 1996 and 2008, and the relationship
between the style of text and the staging offer a useful comparison.
The first was staged by director Peter Hall during a production of
all three Oedipus plays, each employing the use of Greek masks as
would have been adopted in the original performances in Ancient
Greece. Hall's reasoning for the use of masks was completely
embedded in the style of the text and the treatment of emotion by
Sophocles, a matter which he extends to consider the presence of
'mask' beyond the material object:

> There is a mask in all great tragic drama, including
> Shakespeare. For me Shakespeare's verse is his mask. His
> form is the mask. You can't do Shakespeare in a mask and

it's quite interesting why. Because it's like putting a mask on a mask. The text is too complex and too metaphorical to exist behind the mask. You ask me why [the production uses mask]? I believe it's to enable us to deal with horrible, horrible emotions at an intensity that would not be possible without the mask.[9]

In the case of Greek tragedy, the face of the mask enables intense emotions to be directly stated through its contours and design. The text, which expresses the emotions of the character poetically, can therefore be delivered without the performer 'being' the character. Emotional verisimilitude in the performer is less important than our understanding of the language articulating that emotion – an articulation that may be disrupted through a more naturalistic performance. In complete contrast, the version in 2008 stripped away the rhyming couplets preferred by Hall and commissioned a new text from Irish writer Frank McGuinness. This resulted in a production with 'a language of brutal simplicity', accompanied by modern dress with performers dressed in sharp suits.[10] McGuinness' contemporary rendering of the action communicates the story through a modern text, for unmasked actors to speak to a modern audience, and is thus complemented by an appropriate visual language. The act of adapting the text affects the performance style, creating a more complete sense of adaptation than a simple transposition of space; the structure of the story remains intact, but the text and the production choices are teased away from their origins.

The 'modern language' adaptation is a common tendency not only with Greek tragedy, but with other texts where the original language of performance is not English. With Shakespeare this sort of practice is far less common: the original language of the play is Elizabethan verse and the main translation that occurs is from page to stage, as an ancient and unfamiliar performance language is imbued with meaning through action and inflection. If any changes do occur they are more often than not contextual. Striking examples from recent history can be found not only on stage but in the cinema as well: Baz Luhrmann's *William Shakespeare's Romeo and Juliet* (1996) parachutes the text directly into present-day North America, and Kenneth Branagh's *Love's Labour's Lost* (1999) creates a musical out of Shakespeare's original text in 1930s Hollywood style. Branagh's film is also set just as World War II is about to break out, showing some fidelity to the source text's political backdrop and 'providing its audiences with a more recent historical context of conflict than the Shakespearean play's interaction with the late sixteenth-century French Wars of Religion'.[11]

With classics from a foreign language, the process of adaptation may involve a focus on updating both text and context simultaneously, with the writer transposing setting and language in their new version. New 'versions' of a source text will very often be commissions for known writers, some of whom have a track record for their own translations and will undertake the task of adaptation alongside. Martin Crimp, for example, has translated plays by Molière (*The Misanthrope*, 1996), Ionesco (*The Chairs*, 1997) and Chekhov (*The Seagull*, 2006) and adapted Greek tragedy as well (*Cruel and Tender*, 2004, from Sophocles' *Trachiniae*). Referring to his work on *The Misanthrope*, Crimp raises the question of fidelity to the source text by quoting an extract from Molière's play *La Critique de l'Ecole des Femmes*: 'if you don't make recognisable portraits of the contemporary world, then nothing's been achieved'.[12] This outlook is reflected in Crimp's straightforward approach to the act of adaptation – 'opt for a contemporary setting, and then explore the consequences, whatever deviations and departures from the original that may involve' – which, together with Molière's advice, suggests adaptation requires a necessarily adventurous and imaginative approach, and rather than alterations being destructive, they are in fact essential to constructing relevant and meaningful drama.[13]

The first three case studies in this chapter embody adventure in adaptation, and have been identified as projects where production choices have guided the form of the performance rather than the influence of a writer-adapter. As a result, their reworkings of known source texts are often innovative and radical, challenging the boundaries between audience and performer and between the mediums of theatre, dance, music and film, leaning heavily on Hutcheon's third category of the 'intertextual' adaptation.

IMAGINATION AND ADVENTURE: FILTER, PUNCHDRUNK AND KNEEHIGH

Established in 2001, Filter Theatre's first show *Faster* was itself an appropriation of a source text, inspired by the novel *Faster, or the Acceleration of Just About Everything* (1999) by science writer James Gleick, a non-fiction publication exploring the increasingly fast pace of the modern world. Transposing Gleick's investigation into a hurtling fictional narrative about a three-way love story, the play combined elements of physical theatre, spoken text and what appeared to be real-time performance choices, dictated by the rhythms and music created by company members on various instruments. This dynamic reflected the company's 'central tenet . . . that electronic and live sound-effects should form each scene's core, rather than lurking on the periphery'.[14] *Twelfth Night*, originally commissioned as part of the Royal Shakespeare Company's 'Complete Works' season has been touring intermittently since 2006 and 'takes Shakespeare's dark, poetic comedy as the jumping off point for a dramatic and musical jam session'.[15]

It is likely that *Twelfth Night* was originally written for the 'twelfth night' of entertainment following Christmas Day, and Filter honours this intention wholeheartedly. The play is performed on a stage dressed only by a jumble of wires and cables connecting various instruments, and presents Shakespeare's love story of mistaken identity and entanglement through a small group of performers and an extensively pared-back text (as with Frantic Assembly's *Othello*), accompanied throughout by the live music and sound effects created by on-stage sound designers Ross Hughes and Tom Haines. At the play's opening, the familiar lines 'if music be the food of love, play on, give me excess of it' become audible through a crackling transistor radio and are spliced with the recognisable phrasing and intonation of the late-night shipping forecast. The performers then turn to the audience to gather spare clothes and costume to provide a disguise for Viola, as she enters the service of Duke Orsino posing as a young boy, Cesario.

This element of audience contact is continued throughout the play, reaching its peak in the original 'party scene' of Shakespeare's text, Act II Scene 2, where a Clown entertains Sir Andrew Augecheek and Sir Toby Belch with song. In Filter's version it is orchestrated by Sir Toby Belch, who, drunk and staggering around the back of the stage searching for revellers, gradually encourages his friend Sir Andrew into joining in, at which point the performers don Velcro headgear and throw fluffy tennis balls into the audience to help whip up the riotous atmosphere. Audience members are invited on stage to drink (real) tequila shots and fresh pizza is suddenly delivered to the auditorium; all the while the music continues and the performers invade the auditorium with wild chases and, on the occasion the author attended, a brief food fight.[16] The interruption of Malvolio to cease the festivities creates a shared disappointment that ripples through the theatre, momentarily involving the audience directly with the plight of the protagonists.

The anarchic storytelling style is not without its complications; the characters of Viola and her twin brother Sebastian, in love with Duke Orsino and Olivia respectively, are played by the same actress, resulting in a tongue-in-cheek resolution to the play's original story as one performer stands hand-in-hand with both of his/her lovers. For a source text that delights in gender-swapping and role-reversal, however, the casting choice is also rather appropriate. Nevertheless, the stripped-back text and enjoyably chaotic staging does mean a prior knowledge of the source text is something of an advantage, and as one reviewer puts it, 'there are occasions, particularly towards the end, when the doubling of characters is awkward and, rather than illuminating the play, starts to make it seem unnecessarily complicated'.[17]

The dramaturgy of Filter's adaptation allows for a particular form of experiential theatre, where game-playing and risk-taking are shared between performer and audience, but at the potential cost of compromising the source text's fundamental shape by obscuring the actual story from view. In which case it is no small feat that Punchdrunk Theatre's adaptation of Goethe's *Faust* and Marlowe's *Dr Faustus* still communicates the story of Faust's bargain with the devil and Mephistopheles' ultimate revenge; there is barely any spoken text at all and the audience choose where to explore, what to touch, who to follow and which level of an expansive installation across five storeys to navigate first.

Punchdrunk Theatre formed in Southwest England and each of its productions has honoured a clear artistic policy: to create immersive experiences where audiences make choices, and are honoured in the theatre-making process as much as any other element, enticing us 'to rediscover the childlike excitement and anticipation of exploring the unknown and experience a real sense of adventure'.[18] Like Filter, its production archive until *Faust* in 2006 shows a record of previous productions based on existing texts; *The Cherry Orchard* (2000), *The Tempest* (2003) and the hybrid *The Firebird's Ball*, inspired by both Stravinsky's music for the ballet *The Firebird* and Shakespeare's *Romeo and Juliet*, and which along with *Faust* also transformed a large empty building into an expansive performance space. Artistic Director Felix Barrett explains the attraction of these established texts and their subsequent fragmentation through performance by referring to a key element of the adaptive text – the conversation it creates with its source:

> [It's] the complexity that's in these great works and the richness of the text. The detail, the minutiae of the text is then scattered over the piece, we make that the experience so it's a complex journey through. The reason why we use these great classics is, for a start the audience need a hook because the conventions take some getting used to. In order to empower the audience they need to feel that is a puzzle, a conundrum that they can grasp. They need to be able to piece together the history. That's why we never write a piece from scratch, there has to be that awakening, where it clicks for each individual.[19]

The production was staged in a warehouse on Wapping Lane in London, and upon entering the building's ticketing area, before the performance began, audience members were provided with a piece of paper containing a brief synopsis of *Faust*. Whilst only for reference, and feeling largely insignificant compared to the sheer extent of the performance space, it ensures that any audience member unfamiliar with the story can put what is a fragmented version of the play into some sort of context. The adapted text is made visible, and the enjoyment of the performance perhaps enhanced by being able to compare – before or after – how this particular adaptation transposes the plot of the source text. Julie Sanders believes that this is an essential element for the audience to obtain a complete reading of the adaptation, suggesting that 'the spectator or reader must be able to participate in the play of similarity and difference perceived between the original, source, or inspiration to appreciate fully the reshaping or rewriting undertaken by the adaptive text'.[20]

The reshaping and rewriting in the case of Punchdrunk's *Faust*, however, is partly the role of the spectator. Required to wear identical white masks for the duration of the performance, the audience in *Faust* become anonymous figures, blending into the space but therefore liberated from the restrictions placed upon them by more traditional audience–performer relationships. Barrett acknowledges the dual function of this technique, the convention creating community and autonomy simultaneously because 'the mask allows you to work for yourself if you want to, but equally, they encourage you to feel all the more a unity because you're all made the same'. From the minute they don their masks and are plunged into one of the vividly cinematic landscapes, with characters and scenes happened upon depending on where they turn, the audience is practically engaged in the act of adaptation. The chronology of the narrative is dictated largely by the audience's selected route as they roam freely throughout the space.

The scenes that occur do not contain spoken text, communicated instead through choreographed movement or dance. Longer sequences accompanied by music and other, shorter and more subtle sequences performed to 'their own sound, the impact of body against body and the body in space'. This transposition of spoken text to movement is a move from the cerebral to the visceral, relocating story from the literal sound and sense of language, to the lateral and visually arresting image of dance. This sort of interpretative performance work that begins with text is similar to the directing style of Katie Mitchell, whose production of *Iphigenia at Aulis* 'foregrounds the visceral experience of affect rather than affect's mimesis . . . the result is the distressing, disquieting body that rushes, retches, panics, feels *too much*, and makes *us* feel too much in the process'.[21]

For Barrett, this adaptive choice is linked closely to the

performance environment and the overall language of a space where spoken text may not be able to compete. It is a search for 'a performance [that was] big enough to match the space . . . the danger element that comes in that hard, fast, staccato physicality, that's assaulting in the same way that the spaces were'. Although the audience are given an element of choice, what is offered is still dictated by a particular performance strategy, with several of these sequences looped and repeated in cycles. This allows different groups to witness the same sequence at different times, and occasionally to collectively witness sequences as an entire audience, such as the final descent of Faust into hell, which brought together every member of the audience to the basement floor of the site.

With Filter's *Twelfth Night*, criticism was levelled at the points of narrative focus being obscured by other elements of the play's style and structure. However, Punchdrunk's desire to isolate moments of narrative transition (or closure) for the entire audience can also be interpreted as an interruption to the overarching dramaturgy of the piece, suddenly imposing a conventional 'theatrical frame' and 'provoking expectations that work against the spatial structures of the event'.[22] The suggestion is that these sudden shifts in performance style create unhelpful tensions, the free-flowing atmosphere of the event suddenly paused. Looking at the performance as adaptation, however, these focal points are essential to encouraging a reading that recognises the 'play of similarity and difference' between narrative source and adaptive text that Sanders describes.

This sense of playfulness is extended further into self-conscious referencing during Kneehigh Theatre's *Brief Encounter* (2008), which is an adaptation of three sources at once: the songs of Noel Coward; Coward's short one-act play *Still Life* (1935); and David Lean's iconic film adaptation of the same play, *Brief Encounter* (1946), starring Trevor Howard and Celia Johnson. The screenplay was written by Coward, Lean and Anthony Havelock-Allen – the trio later winning an Oscar nomination for Best Original Screenplay – and was underscored throughout by a single piece of music, Rachmaninoff's passionately romantic Piano Concerto No.3. The film is widely recognised as a well-loved classic, with the

British Film Institute ranking it second in the top 100 British films of the twentieth century.

The story is simple: following a chance meeting at a railway station, Dr Alec Harvey and a woman from an unremarkable suburban marriage, Laura Jesson, embark on a romantic affair that is ultimately cut short by the former's decision to move to Africa for work. The story is told after the event from Laura's point of view, in flashbacks whilst husband Fred sits completing the crossword in their front room. Laura's voice-over acts as a narrative guide, linking scenes and often interrupting the action, gifting the audience with a private subtext and commentary and providing an intimate understanding of her character's position.

The film was first seen as a stage adaptation in the West End in 2000, when London was already entertaining various versions of well-known screenplays including *The Lion King*, *The Graduate* and *The Witches of Eastwick*. The play was a drily naturalistic transposition of the film's script, written by Andrew Taylor and directed by Roger Redfarn without any new theatrical touches to ease the transition from screen to stage (unlike the inventive and still-running *The Lion King*), and as Mark Shenton recorded in his What's On Stage review of 12 September, the duo in adding 'precisely nothing . . . have detracted from the cinematic experience'. Laura's monologues, for example, accompanied with close-ups of her face wracked with worry and indecision in the film, became amorphous and distant as the actress was temporarily isolated on the stage to listen to her own voice.

The contrast with Kneehigh's attempt could not be bigger, as their show 'switches between live action and film footage, and between moods of clipped, clenched pain and wild music-hall exuberance in order to dramatise the passion heaving under all that middle-class restraint, and in order to contrast the anguished and thwarted love between the duty-bound central duo . . . with the slap-and-tickle high-jinks of two other couples among the rail staff'.[23] The playfulness of Kneehigh's production adheres closely to Hutcheon's positive description of adaptation, offering 'repetition but without replication, bringing together the comfort of ritual and recognition with the delight of surprise and novelty'.[24]

Kneehigh's adaptation not only adapts the story, but transposes the spirit of the film *Brief Encounter* and celebrates the multiple contexts surrounding its original incarnation. The high-camp of Coward's music is captured during singing vignettes in front of a portable red curtain; the orchestral qualities of the film find life in an arch but perfectly delivered acapella group harmony of Concerto No.3 behind an old upright piano, sung by the railway waiting-room staff; the cinematic heritage of the original is referenced when Alec and Laura come to sit in the front row of the audience, watching projected images of themselves on stage; and the scenic language is, where possible, evoked through associative images. Laura's final descent into the isolation of her secret sees the actress swirling into a video backdrop of pulsating ocean waves. Where it is deemed not possible, it is affectionately imagined; the announcement of the train departures is accompanied by a draw-string wooden toy train pulled across the stage by the station master. Emma Rice, Artistic Director of Kneehigh, explains the reasoning behind the layering of performance styles as a conscious decision to not try and replicate the film:

> Why would you do that? It's a brilliant film that people can watch, so that was never the aim. But because it is such an iconic British film, my first idea about the piece was that it had to be really referential to that film. But it also had to be very referential to theater. I wanted to boldly play with both those forms so that the audience would delight in the live event. This is why at times the curtain will come down and performers entertain in front of it – that's a very British theatrical tradition. But we've also got the big cinema screen with people bursting in and out of it. I thought this had to be totally about film and totally about theater all in one evening.[25]

The use of digital media and film has been a particularly prominent feature in theatre productions since 2000, though often serving a purely scenic function in drama by providing digitally-enhanced backdrops, like the huge cyclorama in Tom Stoppard's 2002 *The Coast of Utopia* trilogy at the National Theatre with its virtual depictions of raging oceans, snow-covered cities and affluent

Russian estates. Its inclusion in Kneehigh's *Brief Encounter* is notable beyond its purpose as an indicator of story location: interplay of live performance and film communicates the dramatic subtext of the story and the subtext of the act of adaptation. At one point whilst in search of his errant wife, Fred walks up to the black and white image of a room and then melts into it, giving the illusion of the actor seamlessly carrying on his search within the projection. Fred is suddenly isolated within the screen, and separated from Laura's secret recollections which continue to fill the stage. The moment emphasises Fred's emotional distance from Laura's experiences, through actual separation, but also visually; he is in monochrome whilst the story is in vivid colour.

This 'intermedial' form of presentation blurs the boundaries between setting and dramatic composition, offering new challenges to audiences and new ways of reading theatre performance as '*mise-en-scene* and dramaturgy are less easily disentangled . . . the use of recorded media and live relay multiplies the scope of possible incidents, source materials, interactions, intertexts and issues, and the ways of presenting and perceiving them'.[26] The properties that dictate setting and location have an interactive role in the composition of performance, not only the plot structure.

The three companies above engage with multiple adaptive strategies, reframing the source text with non-theatre spaces, varied performance languages, challenges to the role of the audience and a particular interpretation of the source text's application for a contemporary audience. None of them, however, has a writer at the helm, and choices regarding content and form are dictated by a much broader set of criteria, applying the text as inspiration for immersive experiences or multidisciplinary approaches, rather than treating it as a strict guideline. For writers who choose to adapt a play but retain a conventional mode of performance – audience separated from the action and text the dominant mode of communication – there are particular benefits to following an existing guide. Carl Grose, who has collaborated with Kneehigh on several adaptations but has a growing profile of solo-authored plays, suggests that adaptation not only provides a template but is also quicker than starting to write a play from the very beginning:

Ultimately it's easier . . . if you're working with a structure, a lot of your choices are made for you, and even if you choose not to do what Euripides suggests or Shakespeare has written, you have the choice to go the other way. With playwriting, because there is rarely a pre-existing structure, you may find that your initial choices are wrong, and you have to rip apart the foundations and start again.[27]

The next two examples consider the writer's choices when adapting an existing play, offering more detailed textual comparisons and analysing in particular the relationship between the adapter's choices for a contemporary audience, and the source text's effect on its original spectators.

TEXT AS TEMPLATE: NORTHERN BROADSIDES AND HEADLONG THEATRE

Northern Broadsides is based in Halifax, West Yorkshire, and was created in 1992 by Barrie Rutter who still works as their Artistic Director. Always performing with their regional accents, the company brings classic plays to new audiences in unusual spaces – previous sites include a cattle market, a church, a disused mill and an indoor riding stable. Over the years the company has developed a unique style of performance for classic work that escapes a forced or mannered delivery and revels in the idiosyncrasies of Northern dialect on a pared-down stage, encouraging 'both established and new audiences to enjoy Shakespeare regardless of language or theatrical convention'.[28]

In 2007 they produced *Lisa's Sex Strike*, Blake Morrison's new adaptation of Greek playwright Aristophanes' anti-war comedy *Lysistrata* (411 BC) in which the women of Athens, led by the industrious Lysistrata, refuse sex from their husbands in a protest against the tragic failures of the war between Athens and Sparta, which at the time of its first performance had been running for 20 years. With the older women of Athens, Lysistrata's plan is to launch an assault on the Acropolis and prevent any more money being spent on the war. As Morrison points out, the play would have been received with extreme scepticism by an Athenian audience, the majority of whom were male and 'would have regarded what the women were doing as ridiculous fantasy, whereas now it seems much less so – there have been a number of sex strikes across the globe in recent years'.[29] Aristophanes' plays are often characterised by their fierce political satire, lampooning individual politicians and their handling of the city's governance, and despite the likely sentiments of the Greek audience expressed above some translators find that *Lysistrata* would have offered them 'a brilliantly unexpected slant: funny enough to get around the warmongers and serious enough to make them think'.[30]

Morrison's version transposes the story to a small town in Yorkshire in the present day, with a multi-ethnic cast of women planning the occupation of a factory where their husbands are employed – a factory which turns out to be supplying weapons parts to the arms trade. Aristophanes' plays are written in verse, but verse 'that shifts from one intricate meter to another throughout', and some English versions opt to present a contemporary conversational style of dialogue as a result, avoiding the pitfalls of literal translation.[31] Morrison opts for the opposite, employing a poetic structure and writing almost the entire play in rhyming couplets whilst retaining the Northern inflections desired by the company. The excerpts below, one from a translation that creates a naturalistic style of dialogue, and one from Morrison's version, are both from an early scene in the story where Lysistrata / Lisa announces her plan to round up the women for support:

CALONICE: Tell me Lysistrata dear, what is it you've summoned this meeting for? Is it something big?

LYSISTRATA: Very.

CALONICE: [*thinking she detects a significant intonation in that word*]: Not thick as well?

LYSISTRATA: As a matter of fact, yes.

CALONICE: Then why on earth aren't they here?

LYSISTRATA: [*realizing she has been misleading*]: No, not that kind of thing – well not exactly. If it had been, I can assure you, they'd have been here

as quick as you can bat an eyelid. No, I've had
an idea, which for many sleepless nights I've
been tossing to and fro –

CALONICE: Must be a pretty flimsy one, in that case.
LYSISTRATA: Flimsy? Calonice, we women have the
salvation of Greece in our hands.[32]

LISA: I know all that. But when summat big's at stake.
CAROL: Big? *How* big?
LISA: Massive.
CAROL: Why didn't you say?
         When it's massive, us lasses come right away.
LISA: It's all I think about, night and day.
CAROL: Same here, love. No need to be ashamed.
LISA: It's up to us. The future's in our hands.
CAROL: You take the future, I'd rather hold some man's.
LISA: The town's as bad as Sodom and Gomorrah.
CAROL: (*flicking through magazine*) I'm off to have a
         manicure tomorrow.[33]

Here Morrison captures the Northern dialect but the rhyme also
emphasises the theatrical nature of the play, whereas Sommerstein's
version employs a naturalistic tone without the heightened, performative aspect of the language. A vital element of Aristophanes'
original is its theatrical absurdity, with giant phalluses appearing
on stage and the employment of song and music to accompany the
comedic aspects of the story. Morrison's process of transposing
(not translating) the play was a serious undertaking, involving consultation of numerous versions and translations in other languages
including German and Italian, and careful study of the notes
sections that accompanied each text:

I'd have a half a dozen translations around me, and compare
passages, and usually I'd end up feeling dissatisfied with
what they'd come up with! The problem is that translations
so quickly become dated. There has to be some conviction to
the language – words which actors can speak without sounding stilted. What I hope to do is provide a modern version in

which the speech has a life and energy about it. Some of the more 'correct' academic versions you could never hear actors get up and deliver.

Whilst Morrison finds a justifiable equivalent for Aristophanes' stylistic choices, there were problems with the structure of the original play that required changes rather than equivalent versions. 'The characters in the first half didn't reappear' he explains, 'and once you've got the sex strike established, the second half doesn't really go anywhere'. The solution was to carry the character of the Magistrate, a member of the committee for the safety of the state in the source text, transposed in the adaptation as Mr Prutt, the factory owner, into the second half of the play. This created a moment of redemption at the end of the play that required him to change his outlook on the world. For Morrison, Prutt's role was also about maintaining tension and keeping a visible conflict between the women and the men on stage. The problem with the source text is 'the lack of a single dominant male figure to oppose Lysistrata. There was a sense of satisfaction in bringing this one person back so the sense of conflict could be continued'.

As well as key structural changes that adapt the source text's dramaturgy and apply a more contemporary shape to the story, the smallest details can inspire a context for the new, adaptive story world. Before Morrison's adaptation had found its dominant contemporary equivalent of a multicultural Northern factory town, in one of the many translations and versions surrounding him was a passing reference to a 'snood', used by the figure of the Magistrate when he finally loses patience with Lysistrata and her friends during their occupation of the Acropolis and yells: 'Silence for you, you wench, when you're wearing a snood? I'd rather die'.[34] Upon researching the etymology of the word and consulting other translations, the equivalent of a 'veil' emerged. At the time of writing, the image of 'a male authority figure refusing to converse with a woman because of her choice of headwear' was irresistible. The media was rich with debates responding to former foreign secretary Jack Straw's refusal to talk to a veiled Muslim woman from his own constituency in Blackburn, referring to it as 'a visible statement of separation and difference'.[35]

This led to Morrison amassing a wealth of news items on Islamophobia, gang wars, veils, hoodies and sex strikes as well as finding a connection with the racial tensions implicit in Straw's comment, and the emergence of separatism in some Northern towns with large ethnic communities. A contemporary equivalent with *Lysistrata* also emerged: her allies all come from different communities but overcome personal differences to fight for peace – ergo, the 'sisters' in Morrison's version become united across ethnic and religious divides. The seriousness of the equivalent subject matter in the present day, however, distracted Morrison in his initial drafts from the absurdity and extravagance of Aristophanes' comedy, 'so much so that I was in danger of turning a comedy into a tragedy'.[36] The prose-driven first drafts were slowly transformed into half- and then full-rhyming couplets, helping to recapture the theatricality and humour of the source text and honouring the intention of Aristophanes: to get away with sensitive anti-war subject matter by framing it with deliberately extravagant theatrical touches.

Morrison is adamant about the adapter's need to 'respect the spirit of the original' but also acknowledges that this sometimes means 'respecting its lack of respect – the departure from the norms of the time that made it a classic in the first place'.[37] It is important to note the relationship implicit in Morrison's comment, between the spirit of the source text's intrinsic qualities, and the spirit in which they were received in performance – what might be referred to as the 'spirit of reception'. Recognition of the latter was a prevailing force in Headlong Theatre's adaptation of *Six Characters in Search of an Author* (2008, Chichester Festival Theatre), Luigi Pirandello's Italian tragicomedy from 1921. Associate Director Ben Power and Artistic Director Rupert Goold were joint adapters of the play, with Goold directing the production. 'The original in the early twenties had provoked riots, it was an incendiary play', says Power 'but people saw it now as a boulevard comedy. We wanted to discover how we could reconnect with that sense of danger that really arrived in two parts: the Oedipal content of child abuse, and the excitement of a form that was ahead of its time'.[38]

In the original text, a theatre company rehearsing another of Pirandello's plays is interrupted by the arrival of a mysterious family, led by the character of the Father. They state that they are in search of an author and are waiting for their story to be told. When they persuade the director of the company to allow a re-enactment, they reveal a darkly tragic tale: the Father has unwittingly visited his step-daughter in a brothel and the two youngest children of the family subsequently commit suicide. The actors from the company try in vain to recreate the scene themselves, but fail miserably; artifice is no replacement for lived experience or real life. This tension between art and reality is a predominant feature of Pirandello's plays, but the theory of creativity inspiring *Six Characters in Search of an Author* can be found in the short essay from 1899 *Spoken Action*, which predates any of his writing for the stage:

> A play doesn't create people, people create a play. So first of all one must have people − free, living, active people. With them and through them the idea of a play will be born, its shape and destiny enclosed in this first seed; in every seed there already quivers a living being, the oak and all its branches already exist in an acorn . . . the less each character is enslaved by the author's intention and style, by the demands of an imaginary plot, the less he is the passive instrument of an action, the more individual he can be, freely displaying in every action his full, specific personality.[39]

Pirandello's play has been referred to as 'one of the great works of twentieth-century modernism, as significant in its way as the discovery of cubism in art and the development of jazz and serialism in music'.[40] It is no surprise, therefore, that Headlong Theatre gravitated towards the play with their artistic policy of 'exploring revolutionary writers and practitioners of the past . . . to push the imaginative boundaries of the stage'.[41] Headlong's version transposes the rehearsal room of the theatre setting to the production office of a documentary film company, struggling against the clock to complete a docu-drama about a 14-year-old boy undergoing euthanasia at a Danish clinic. This new choice of setting is rooted in multiple factors, each addressing what Mark Musa refers to as the 'three levels of drama' in the source text; the human drama the six characters own, the drama of their search for an author, and Pirandello's dramatic frame for communicating the overall story, the form of which was so hotly debated by audiences.[42]

The human drama of the six characters 'hinges on incest, suicide and sibling murder', and whilst Pirandello's plays are often considered the dusty work of a theatrical philosopher and intellectual, the undertones of death and family tragedy signpost the emotional depths of his storytelling, and are impossible to ignore.[43] The adaptation therefore keeps the structure of the family's story intact; it is only the context for these characters' arrival, shifting from rehearsal room to film studio, which is changed. The subject matter of death and the way it is framed by the Father, however, fascinated Power in its suggestion that characters of fiction, as fixed beings, could somehow 'transcend the ugliness of death', playing once again on Pirandello's blurred line between art and reality. In the Father's words:

> . . . he who has the luck to be born a live character can even laugh at death. He will never die. The one who will die is the man, the writer, the instrument of the creation. The creation never dies . . . they live eternally, because, being live germs, they had the good fortune to find a fertile matrix, a fantasy that knew how to raise and nourish them, to make them live for eternity! [44]

This refers directly to the second of Musa's 'levels' of drama: the family's re-enactment of the story in the hope of finding an author. This re-enactment is, in the source text, compared directly to the failure of the theatre company's actors to perform it accurately. They cannot recapture the emotional detail of the six characters' lived experience, the paradox of their performance only ever showing what the Father describes as 'something that would like to be the same, but at the same time is not!'[45] The paradox suggested for Power and Goold not only the contemporary equivalent of documentary drama, the edited 'reality' of fly-on-the-wall footage, but also the unreliability of editing when it creates a misleading version of events. It was here that another link between the source text and the growing concept for the adaptation was identified:

the subject of death. 'Accounts of death have a high dramatic currency in docu-drama' says Power 'and the themes of death, doubt and reality suddenly collided with present-day media coverage of particular events'. His comments lead us beyond Musa's third 'level' of the overarching drama of Pirandello's story into a fourth, additional frame of drama – the real-life media dramas that could be freely referenced by a contemporary audience in comparison to the action of the play.

Of striking relevance was the discovery in July 2007 that ITV's proposed docu-drama *Malcolm and Barbara: Love's Farewell* had not, as seemed to have been indicated by the footage, captured the 'live' death of Alzheimer's sufferer Malcolm Pointon on screen. Pointon actually died two and a half days later in hospital, but the documentary appeared to indicate the former. Film-maker Paul Watson expressed he had 'never intended to imply the footage portrayed the exact moment of death' but the incident was one of many being hauled into the media spotlight.[46] On 5 October 2007, the controller of the BBC Peter Fincham resigned over publicly broadcast footage of the Queen that appeared to show her storming out of a photo session 'in a huff'. News reports revealed that this misleading account was a result of documentary footage altering the real order of events, although the BBC denied any desire to deliberately misrepresent the Queen's actions.[47]

Despite the adaptation resisting any tampering with the story of the six characters, the contemporary frames of reference settled upon by Power and Goold quickly extended to have a direct impact on the form and content of the play. Echoing Morrison's concerns with Aristophanes' dramaturgy and the inconclusive journey of the Magistrate, the adapters felt that one of Pirandello's central figures, the theatre company's director, required a conclusive journey that could more vividly express the effect of the six characters' visit to his rehearsal room. They wanted their docu-drama director (who is female in the adaptation) to 'move on to being more of a protagonist, where the actions of the six characters unmoor her from reality', rather than the source text's story structure, which sees the director simply abandoning rehearsal after confusion over the suicide of the youngest member of the family, The Young Boy. Their decision finds life in 'a vortex of legitimate self-reflexiveness' where the director is plunged into what Power refers to as a 'rabbit hole' of different levels of reality.[48]

Carrying the body of the boy and with a hand-held video camera filming her every move, where Pirandello's play finishes, Headlong's adaptation takes the director into a completely new epilogue act, beginning with an exploration of the neighbouring theatre which we see projected on a screen on stage.[49] She returns to the auditorium where the end credits of the play are rolling up the stage, and then the entire stage is superimposed with a DVD extras menu screen for the play 'Six Characters in Search of an Author'. She finds herself in the first scene of the play again, yet this time totally invisible to the rest of the cast and with a director's commentary playing over the top. The lines we heard her speak at the play's opening are to her surprise involuntarily vomited up when required; the other characters are then strobe-lit and appear to 'rewind' in the manner of a frame-by-frame video search. Before long we are treated to the appearance of Pirandello himself, struggling to finish a play, and a conversation between the 'real' producer of the play and the writers of the adaptation. The final moments show the character of the director, through a tiny window of the film studio's back room, being injected by the six characters, apparently subjected to the fate of her documentary's subject.[50]

Whilst its touring production in autumn 2009 was referred to in John Peter's 11 October review for the *Sunday Times* as 'flashy, pretentious, self-admiring . . . and a pointless "version" of a great play', this cynical reception overlooks two areas: first, the determination of Headlong to recreate a production that, like Pirandello's, pushed the boundaries of contemporary theatrical expectations; and second, the necessity of creative adaptation, in response to dramaturgical choices made for an audience nearly a century earlier. Their celebration of the 'spirit' of the source text in all its contexts, particularly in the adaptation's ambitious new act, is close enough to Pirandello's intentions to allow Musa's perspective on the source text to speak as clearly for Headlong as it does for Pirandello:

Having intuited a new dimension, Pirandello must construct his play in a new way. That which may appear as illogical

construction or disordered dramatic development is instead
the resolution of the true drama of the creating author . . . he
wanted something more from his art, and that something was
absent.[51]

THE PAST IS THE FUTURE: A FOOTNOTE TO ADAPTATION

In their 2002 title *Theatre in Crisis?* editors Maria Delgado and
Caridad Svich describe adaptation as a cycle of renewal, part of a
'long-held tradition in theatre of reworking stories, reconfabulat-
ing them, and re-configuring them for a new generation'.[52] In a
theatre culture that is admittedly nurturing the large-cast play back
onto the stage – Jez Butterworth's state-of-the-nation triumph
Jerusalem, Lucy Prebble's *Enron* and David Hare's *The Power of
Yes* are all recent examples from 2009 – adaptations of classics
can continue to permeate the imagination of writers and encourage them to take on bigger themes with broader brushstrokes.
'The large casts and often large landscapes of classic drama allow
for a breadth of inquiry' write Lichtenfels and Hunter in the
same title above, and 'offer an allegorical ground for sorting out
contemporary problems'.[53]

Theatre makers are responding to the time and place in which
they live, communicating with a living audience. This means
taking into account social and political environments, the dynamics
of the theatre culture at the time, the economics of theatre production and the impact created by a performance within these spheres
of influence. We have seen in preceding chapters that the work that
defines our more recent theatre history exists in an intimate relationship with the culture of the time, and to come full circle with
the current chapter, Shakespeare's was no different. He wrote for
a company of actors he knew intimately and many of his parts were
written to serve particular performers. His royal patrons were often
subjects of flattery within his work: the representation of King
James I's Puritanical outlook on human justice via the morally
forthright but dramatically flawed Duke of Venice in *Measure for
Measure* is a prime example of a dramatic narrative influenced by

those who could fund its production. His cycle of history plays, revived recently in their entirety by the RSC, have resonance in the modern world with their overarching theme of Britain's unstable sovereignty and Empire-building dreams coming under threat, but are born of an Elizabethan history when any sense of unified 'Britishness' was also a distant fantasy and the country looked to divert civil unrest through the creation of an 'external enemy'.[54] To an audience of the time these plays engaged with their collective and present history, but through metaphor, allegory and an artistic filter.

Rebellato suggests that theatrical representation is inherently metaphorical, its artifice always exercising the strategy of being 'invited to see (or think about) one thing in terms of another thing'.[55] Adaptation, in this sense, will always carry a meta-theatrical echo as one text is seen and heard through another. Directors and writers will doubtless continue to look towards the classics for inspiration, keeping the literary pretensions of British theatre alive, but that canon of work that belongs to a literary heritage is being consistently challenged by the non–literary language of contemporary theatre. Multi-media, dance, improvisation, music, installation and site-specific languages can only serve to reinvigorate our perception of not only drama in the present, but also the dramas of the past.

CHAPTER SUMMARY

Adaptation of existing narrative sources is a habit of dramatic literature dating from the Ancient Greek tragedians, involving the transposition of a story from one medium to another. Transposition of a source text to another context can occur through different processes: changing the context of the medium, such as a book into a stage play; changing the context of the story world in which the characters are placed by updating the timeframe; or altering the source text completely in an attempt to recapture the response to its original production. The act of adaptation does not necessarily rely on a writer; classic works are often restaged in contemporary dress to clarify the connection between the source text and the modern world. Adaptations encourage a 'double-reading' for an audience, as we interpret the new, adaptive text in its own right, and its relationship to the source text as well.

Strategies of adaptation are multiple, with particular companies choosing overtly theatrical styles to re-imagine classic texts for a contemporary audience. Filter Theatre, Punchdrunk and Kneehigh are all companies who have transformed source texts through bold and imaginative performative choices, including improvisation and audience participation, integration of film and live performance, use of multiple sources to create intertextual adaptations and immersing the spectator in the story world through a huge performance installation. The danger with ambitious choices is that the source text can become obscured or unclear in the desire to create a theatrical experience rather than a conventional drama.

In situations where writers are deciding on the transposition of the source text, sensitivity towards the theatrical function of the language is often important. In transposing the verse comedy of Aristophanes to the present day, writer Blake Morrison retained the use of rhyme but with contemporary dialects: without the rhyme the text became too serious and lost its playfulness. Similarly, the dramatic structure may be flawed or the impact of the original text dated, and new material is created to ensure that the source text can still have the same impact; Headlong Theatre added an entirely new act to the end of their version of Pirandello's 1921 play *Six Characters in Search of an Author* to help achieve this. Adaptation relies on creativity as well as the search for exact equivalents, and choices will always be dependent on the adapter's individual understanding of the source text's intentions.

NOTES

1. Graham Ley, *A Short Introduction to the Greek Theater* (London: University of Chicago Press, 1999), p. 5.
2. Richard Proudfoot, A. Thompson and D. Scott Kastan (eds), 'Shakespeare's Reading and Reading Shakespeare', *The Arden*

Shakespeare Complete Works (Surrey: Thomas Nelson and Sons, 1998), p. 10.

3. Ibid., p. 1005.

4. Tanika Gupta, this and subsequent quotation from *Woman's Hour*, 7 July 2003, www.bbc.co.uk/radio4/womanshour/2003_27_mon_03.shtml (accessed 4 December 2009).

5. Paul Edwards, 'Adaptation: Two Theories', *Text and Performance Quarterly* 27:4, 2007, pp. 369–77 (369).

6. Linda Hutcheon, *A Theory of Adaptation* (Abingdon: Routledge, 2006), p. 8.

7. Lyn Gardner, Review of *Othello* by William Shakespeare / Frantic Assembly, *The Guardian*, 29 September 2008.

8. Mark Fortier, *Theory / Theatre: An Introduction* (London: Routledge, 1997), p. 91.

9. Peter Hall, Platform Paper 'The Oedipus Plays', Peter Hall and Peter Stothard, National Theatre, 21 September 1996, transcription from http://www.nationaltheatre.org.uk/2626/platform-papers/peter-hall.html (accessed 4 December 2009).

10. Michael Billington, Review of Sophocles' *Oedipus*, directed by Jonathan Kent, 16 October 2008.

11. Julie Sanders, *Adaptation and Appropriation* (Abingdon: Routledge, 2006), p. 21.

12. Molière in Martin Crimp, *Plays Two* (London: Faber and Faber, 2005), p. 98.

13. Ibid., pp. 97–8.

14. Fiona Mountford, Review of *Faster* by Filter Theatre, *Evening Standard*, 8 April 2003.

15. Charles Spencer, Review of *Twelfth Night* by Filter Theatre, *The Independent*, 4 September 2008.

16. The author attended a performance at the Tricycle Theatre, London in September 2008.

17. Lyn Gardner, Review of *Twelfth Night* by Filter, *The Guardian*, 21 August 2008.

18. Punchdrunk Website, www.punchdrunk.org.uk/about.htm (accessed 3 December 2009).

19. Felix Barrett, interview with Josephine Machon, 2 February 2007, people.brunel.ac.uk/bst/vol0701/felixbarrett/felixbarrett.

doc (accessed 25 November 2009). All further quotations from Barrett attributable to this source.

20. Sanders, *Adaptation and Appropriation*, p. 45.
21. Kim Solga, 'Body Doubles, Babel's Voices: Katie Mitchell's Iphigenia at Aulis and the Theatre of Sacrifice', *Contemporary Theatre Review* 18:2, 2008, pp. 146–60 (150).
22. Cathy Turner and Synne K. Behrndt, *Dramaturgy and Performance* (Basingstoke: Palgrave Macmillan, 2007), p. 196.
23. Paul Taylor, Review of *Brief Encounter* by Kneehigh Theatre, *The Independent*, 19 February 2008.
24. Hutcheon, *A Theory of Adaptation*, p. 173.
25. Emma Rice, Interview with Dan Rubin, American Conservatory Theater, www.act-sf.org/site/DocServer/brief_wop_8.pdf (accessed 30 November 2009).
26. Greg Giesekam, *Staging the Screen: The Use of Film and Video in Theatre* (Basingstoke: Palgrave Macmillan, 2007), p. 10.
27. Carl Grose, interview with author, Royal Festival Hall, 15 September 2009.
28. Northern Broadsides Website, www.northern-broadsides.co.uk (accessed 24 November 2009).
29. Blake Morrison, this and further quotations from Morrison, unless referenced otherwise, from interview with author, Goldsmiths College, 20 October 2009.
30. Paul Roche, *Aristophanes: The Complete Plays* (New York: New American Library, 2005), p. 417.
31. Ibid., p. xiii.
32. Alan H. Sommerstein, *Lysistrata and Other Plays* (Harmondsworth: Penguin Classics, 1973), p. 181.
33. Blake Morrison, *Lisa's Sex Strike*, unpublished play text.
34. Blake Morrison, 'A 2,500-year-old sex ban', *The Guardian*, 10 September 2007.
35. Jack Straw's statement was quoted in various newspapers in October 2006. For an example in context refer to www.dailymail.co.uk/news/article-408770/Muslims-outraged-Jack-Straws-veil-veto.html (accessed 4 December 2009).
36. Blake Morrison, *Turning Classical Plays into Contemporary Theatre*, paper delivered at Archive of Performances of Greek & Roman Drama, Oxford University on 26 November 2007.

37. Ibid.
38. Ben Power, all further quotations from telephone interview with author, 19 October 2009.
39. Luigi Pirandello in Eric Bentley (ed.), *The Theory of the Modern Stage* (London: Penguin, 1968), pp. 155–6.
40. Charles Spencer, Review of *Six Characters in Search of an Author* by Ben Power and Rupert Goold, *The Independent*, 10 July 2008.
41. Headlong Website, www.headlongtheatre.co.uk (accessed 7 December 2009).
42. Mark Musa in Luigi Pirandello, *Six Characters in Search of an Author and Other Plays* (London: Penguin, [1921] 1995), p. xi.
43. Michael Billington, Review of *Six Characters in Search of an Author* by Ben Power and Rupert Goold, *The Guardian*, 16 September 2008.
44. Pirandello, *Six Characters*, p. 14.
45. Ibid., p. 47.
46. Owen Gibson, 'ITV under pressure after revealing truth about Alzheimer's death documentary', *The Guardian*, 1 August 2007.
47. BBC News online, 5 October 2007, news.bbc.co.uk/1/hi/7029940.stm (accessed 25 November 2009).
48. Charles Spencer, Review of *Six Characters in Search of an Author* by Ben Power and Rupert Goold, *The Independent*, 10 July 2008.
49. In the version attended by the author at the Gielgud Theatre in September 2008, this journey consisted of a foray into the Palace Theatre next door where the director is seen descending the Gielgud's backstage staircase, and then traversing the stage of *Les Miserables* mid-performance; yet she moves through unnoticed by its cast.
50. Luigi Pirandello, Rupert Goold and Ben Power, *Six Characters in Search of an Author* (London: Nick Hern Books, 2009), pp. 73–87.
51. Musa in Pirandello, *Six Characters*, p. xii.
52. Maria Delgado and Caridad Svich (eds), *Theatre in Crisis?* (Manchester: Manchester University Press, 2002), p. 12.
53. Lichtenfels and Hunter in Delgado and Svich, *Theatre in Crisis?*, p. 53.

54. William Maley, '"This Sceptred Isle": Shakespeare and the British Problem', in John J. Joughin (ed.), *Shakespeare and National Culture* (Manchester: Manchester University Press, 1997), pp. 83–108 (99–101).

55. Dan Rebellato, 'When We Talk of Horses: Or, what do we see when we see a play?', *Performance Research* 14:1, 2009, pp. 17–28 (25).

Conclusion

READING CONTEMPORARY DRAMA

The aim of this book was to share a vision of contemporary British drama that illustrated the approaches different writers were taking when creating new work, and the variety of ways in which spoken and written text was used in performance. The examples contained within the six chapters point overwhelmingly towards a theatre ecology that is brimming with possibilities, supporting writers of new drama through a diverse range of processes and forms. British theatre is able to sustain work from the Aristotelian school of dramaturgy such as Burke's *Gagarin Way*, with its unities of space and time and political subject matter. It has created a vehicle for reporting and reconstructing domestic and global current affairs through tribunal and verbatim plays such as *Bloody Sunday* and *Guantanamo*. The fusion of dance and text in *Stockholm* and the lateral theatrical imagery of Neilson's *Relocated* indicate an audience that is becoming theatre literate, able to link image and text beyond the confines of linear story.

The works of Gupta, Bhatti, Kwei-Armah and tucker green tackle the politics of a multicultural Britain and construct new aesthetics and languages within the theatrical mainstream, whilst Bond and Kennedy push the imaginations of young people in both the performance and preparation of their plays, leading to drama with immediacy and relevance for its audience. Finally, the companies and writers who engage in adaptation find ways to re-imagine classics which draw on all of the strategies above: transposing work to different cultural settings, collaborating with audiences and communities to both make and perform the work, exploiting theatrical (and filmic) languages to their fullest extent and where necessary relying on the power of 2,500-year-old words to speak to the contemporary world.

In finishing the chapter subjects with adaptation and transposition, there are some deliberate questions being posed. How many more writers do we need? How many more stories are required? Can drama be simply the retelling of old stories in new ways, or new stories told in a never-ending arrangement of different forms and structures? Is it even about stories being told to us at all – can we equate some drama with the habits of the art gallery or museum, where stories exist in the mind of the audience alone as they encounter an environment of objects and artefacts? The progressive languages of theatre, particularly the use of digital media and the incorporation of live loops or pre-recorded film in performance as practised by director Katie Mitchell, Kneehigh's *Brief Encounter* and the work of Filter Theatre have transformed our definitions of drama, but are not unanimously praised. Barrie Rutter of Northern Broadsides is particularly passionate about maintaining the purity of language in classic work:

> I don't want two-dimensional screens, when you have rhyming couplets. I don't want screens telling you what to do – like [having] a seashore in *King Lear*. There isn't a bloody seashore, it's in the mind. All that literalness, two dimensional literalness that often goes in productions today – get rid of them . . . words are the thing about theatre . . . the discourse of human conflict, that's what's exciting.[1]

Although Northern Broadsides produced Blake Morrison's adaptation of Aristophanes' *Lysistrata*, as evidenced in Chapter 6 the emphasis in Morrison's script was very much on maintenance of language and its properties as a means of honouring the source text's original qualities. Rutter's vitriol is actually directed towards a vital component of theatrical performance: a demand upon the audience to imagine and interpret, rather than being spoon-fed with literalism. He is referring in particular to the static qualities of scenery in this case – creating the seashore in *King Lear* – but his reference point of the imagination manoeuvres us back towards one of the book's opening concerns: what we need to consider when reading contemporary dramatic text on the page.

The dramatic tensions in conventional dramas like Burke's *Gagarin Way* rely on the audience's ability to interpret the subtext of everyday speech. Consider this short exchange where security guard Tom is trying to stand but Eddie wants him to sit down:

Tom   I'm fine.
Eddie   Sit down.
Tom   I'm fine.
Eddie   I'd rather you sat down.
Tom   I can keep an eye on the door.
Eddie   It'll be a wee while yet.
Tom   I don't mind.
Eddie   I want you to sit down. (*Beat.*) So fucking sit down.[2]

The shape of the exchange – avoidance, request, avoidance, request, avoidance, request, avoidance, imposition and implied threat – tells us much more than the simple fact that Tom does not want to sit down. Not sitting down is a way of avoiding Eddie, of keeping his distance, of trying to find a way out of the situation. Eddie's repetitions reveal a character who is insistent and will not take 'no' for an answer. Tom does not say 'I'm scared of you' and Eddie does not say 'I'm potentially very dangerous' because the rhythm and shape of the text creates a space for the actors and audience to intuit these facts instead. This dynamic occurs through what is left out, the gaps in which the audience can interpret the 'real' meaning of what the characters are saying. Without this gap, text becomes lifeless and dull, telling the action rather than showing the action – it is literal, and leaves every question answered. Effective subtext will 'invite the audience in, to try to clarify what exactly is going on, what exactly is meant, what exactly is felt'.[3] It is a silent conversation between the audience and the text.

With many of the examples in this book, the principle of subtext must find a much broader application: these silent conversations are multiple and simultaneous, occurring between the performer and the character they are representing (*My Name is Rachel Corrie*, Chapter 2), the performance space and the action (*Sea/Worthy*, Chapter 3), the styles of performance from different cultures (Tara Arts, Chapter 4), the performer and the story they are telling (*Stolen Secrets*, Chapter 5) and the source text and the adapted texts (*Brief Encounter*, Chapter 6). In reading any of the written texts of these productions, these dynamics would not be immediately apparent, unlike the examples of subtext given in Burke's play which are constantly visible because the drama is driven by dialogue and is clear to see on the page.

Our tools for interpreting contemporary drama have to go beyond the relatively simplistic task of following a plot, deducing objectives and recognising characterisation from patterns of speech, and include an ability to understand how space, the body in performance, music, sound and political context might contribute to the performance communicating with an audience. The aim for the reader of contemporary drama, then, is to be literate in these silent conversations and allow them to inform an analysis of the work, assessing the potential of their impact in performance. When the dramaturg or professional reader brings these qualities to bear in their reading of a script, they are thinking simultaneously as audience, performer and director, able to imagine the text from multiple perspectives and appreciate fully its complexities. This is not to suggest that the dramaturg is in any way omnipotent or all-seeing when faced with a script, or that instinct is not valued as much as knowledge; Julian Meyrick, himself a dramaturg, reminds us that 'there is no position from which to deliver an absolute critical assessment of a show's potential meaning'.[4] Creative instinct must have legitimacy if British drama continues to diversify with the characteristics shown here, and it is essential that any student of theatre begins to develop an instinct for these languages, and experiences and discusses the composition of drama not only on the page, but also in performance.

THE CONTEMPORARY IN CONTEXT

Towards the end of the decade, the National Theatre of Scotland's Artistic Director Vicky Featherstone offered an encouraging appraisal of contemporary theatre, drawing on many of the areas already identified:

> The positive legacy of the Labour government is the cultural emphasis. There's been this shift from a sense of theatre as an elite, inaccessible art form, to a cross-art form which is about access and multiculturalism. We're really reaping the benefits of that commitment in terms of the plays audiences want to go to and the work artists want to put on stage. There's been a breakdown of the definition of theatre – now it's about an event, the live performance, it's no longer about the museum of the canon.[5]

The desire to continually redefine, develop and cross-fertilise theatre with other art forms, celebrating the live event, is a way of increasing its relevance and accessibility through diversification rather than simplification. Featherstone's recognition of a broad range of artistic influences supports the selection of work in the chapters above, indicating that both audiences and practitioners are now happy to look forwards in terms of theatre's 'increasing interdisciplinarity and the forms of representation it offers'.[6] Access is no longer the benchmark for quality, and a greater trust is being placed in the intrinsic artistic quality of the work creating accessible experiences for audiences. David Edgar is more sceptical, referring in particular to the McMaster Report on 'excellence' (see Chapter 3) and its future application promoting 'a patrician view of high art rather than diplomacy and access', suggesting a tension between the pursuit of artistic excellence and the ability of audiences to engage with it.[7] This seems a rather cynical view compared to the evident popularity of writers and companies in the last 5 years crossing artistic boundaries to offer audiences the unexpected, such as Caryl Churchill, Edward Bond, Hidden City, Anthony Neilson and Punchdrunk.

Continuing the atmosphere of positivity, in the last month of

2009 the Radio 4, *Newsnight* and *The Guardian* arts critic Mark Lawson proffered the suggestion that British theatre might be entering a new 'golden age'. His conclusion was drawn from contextual factors – a selection of sources including healthy financial figures in the commercial theatre sector, rising audience numbers defying the impact of the recession, and the arrival of original drama breaking through the 'wasteland' of new writing, battling an increasing tendency for revivals of classic plays with Hollywood-style star casting.[8] His optimistic outlook is carefully balanced with perspectives from professional theatre-makers, who warn of short-lived successes, the erratic nature of the theatre industry, and the increasing 'filmisation' of commissioning that sees the power of veto resting less with writers, and increasingly with the literary managers of theatres who are deciding whether or not to produce the work. The overall message is to proceed with caution; Lawson identifies changes that promise a healthy sector with a diverse range of work, but a need for writers and producers to remain vigilant regarding the factors that might influence their artistic choices.

The present culture of 'development' is symptomatic of the exponential growth of interest in new writing in and directly after the 1990s – there are more writers being nurtured, trained and developed and an industry of dramaturgy and workshop opportunities has emerged to support it – but the implications are far-reaching. Opportunities to be produced have not grown at the same rate, principally because an infrastructure for developing plays is much cheaper to sustain than an infrastructure for producing plays; the result is a critical mass of unproduced scripts, increased choice for artistic directors but not necessarily a more beneficial environment for writers. As David Eldridge points out, 'there's now a belief in the intrinsic value of development. It can work, everyone's had good advice, or a reading that's helped, but it's utterly small compared to the experience of having a play actually done'.[9] The surge of interest in finding new plays is only useful if the work can be produced in full for an audience.

Sierz identified the fad of 'yoof' as the predominant content of plays during the early years of the millennium, and it was a fashion reflected in the industry's desire to find young writers. In 2002, 17-year-old Neela Dolezalova saw her first full-length play *Playing Fields* produced at Soho Theatre, having been part of the writers' development programme since the age of 15. The trend continues to date: in 2008 at 21 years of age, Polly Stenham became the youngest writer to have a play produced in the West End since Christopher Hampton's *When Did You Last See My Mother* in 1966. Her account of dysfunctional upper-middle-class family life, *That Face*, was quickly followed by another commission and a second play *Tusk Tusk* in 2009, which continued her interest in recording the loyalties and betrayals of family life in a world far beyond the working-class sink-estates of In-Yer-Face drama. Stenham has been supported since her debut with further commissions, but the continued focus on youth carries with it an implication that it counts more than experience for the gatekeepers of producing theatres. Eldridge's concern about the realistic state of play for writers – in spite of the new generations of emerging talent – is supported by Lyn Gardner who finds it troubling that 'an industry claiming to support theatre writers may actually have created a situation where it has never been easier to become a playwright, and never harder to sustain an actual career'.[10]

It is vital for the future of British drama that opportunities for production can diversify to match the ever-increasing pool of writers, and support the variety of work arriving from less conventional routes than unsolicited manuscripts sent to producing theatres. The amount of work taking place in non-theatre spaces has been a popular solution, finding outlets for new writers to engage with audiences whilst expanding their theatrical vocabulary and working practices; there has also been a predominance of seasons of short plays, such as Soho Theatre's *Everything Must Go!* (2009) in response to the recession, or the Bristol Old Vic's curtain-raising *Short Cuts* in the same year to accompany new studio productions, but this could equally be viewed as reductive thinking. If the contemporary theatre is expanding artistically then a practical infrastructure to reflect this growth – which may also require a change in what is valued as theatre and drama – will be an important next step.

THEORY AND PRACTICE: A FINAL WORD

> There is nothing natural about academic theorizing. It is entirely composed, and behind its composition lie rules of discursive engagement which are binding and authoritative. To situate oneself outside the rules is to court not revolution but incoherence.[11]

In 2006 I started to attend academic conferences about contemporary theatre and drama. I sometimes found myself lost in a haze of words and theories that had yet to bear any relationship to the realities of making theatre professionally. Often there was little recourse to practical examples of professional work, or suggestions as to how papers might be relevant to it, but everybody seemed to be very interested and I duly kept quiet, convinced I was missing something. Those conferences did not seem to bridge the void between theory and the reality of professional practice. This was a paradoxical problem: I had been brought in to teach on academic courses principally because I was a professional practitioner. The situation did not appear to add up. I got on with my work, with the dramaturgy and the playwriting and teaching, but this thing called research I assumed was part of another world.

At the end of 2007, it was a complete surprise when the individual who had recommended me to the publishers sat me down in his office, asked what I thought I could write about, and I spent the next half an hour telling him and getting very worked up. Until asked, I hadn't realised that I had in fact been researching all the time – everything now seemed to have been research of a sort. What was missing from the conferences clicked into place: it was my ability and desire to assimilate abstract knowledge into practical actions – transforming theory into practice. This habit of assimilation is sometimes unconscious. The tracing of ideas and concepts through to practical activities and back again is often instantaneous, treated as 'inspiration' whilst we create new work. But we can form our own methodologies and theorise our own approaches to making theatre by increasing our awareness of both perspectives – theory and practice – and considering where they might meet, and where there might be helpful collisions or disjuncture, where our long-held values about what theatre and drama should or should not do can be disrupted. Our values must also be permitted a level of subjectivity. Research, theory, assimilation, practice and personal investment – a *care* for the work – are all required to create a model of good practice.

A book cannot tell you how to care about writing or studying drama or working professionally with writers, but it can suggest examples that indicate a level of care, passion and imagination in the work of others. This powerful triumvirate leads us to areas where, as Meyrick suggests above, we are flying in the face of received wisdom, where our creative experiments are alien to those who bear the rulebook in hand ring-fencing the imagination, rather than stimulating it to work harder. Theatre critic Claire Armitstead relates this attitude to a feeling of isolation or fear when faced by the unfamiliar, illustrating the grip that history holds on our values. Using Sarah Kane's *Blasted* as an example, she suggests that when we are faced by a play which 'fundamentally challenges the very precepts by which you write: linguistic, logical, linear narrative structures the instinct is to feel intimidated and react by saying "this is not theatre"'.[12]

The ability to describe our work in relation to our values – what we believe drama is actually for – leads to a final practical suggestion. I recommend and reiterate the importance of having both care and imagination in our practical and theoretical endeavours, and embracing every opportunity to challenge and defend our values about the work we see and make. If we care, we bring the detail and rigour that the work deserves, and then we are on the way to creating drama of lasting value.

NOTES

1. Barrie Rutter, 'A National Narrative' panel at *All Together Now? British Theatre After Multiculturalism*, 13–14 June 2009, Warwick University www2.warwick.ac.uk/newsandevents/ audio/more/atn/ (accessed 25 July 2009).
2. Gregory Burke, *Gagarin Way* (London: Faber and Faber, 2001), p. 11.

3. Rib Davis, *Writing Dialogue For Scripts*, 2nd edn (London: A&C Black, 2003), p. 70.
4. Julian Meyrick, 'The Limits of Theory: Academic versus Professional Understanding of Theatre Problems', *New Theatre Quarterly* 19:3, 2003, pp. 230–42 (235).
5. Vicky Featherstone in Hermione Hoby, 'Is British theatre booming?', *The Observer*, 14 June 2009.
6. Nadine Holdsworth and Mary Luckhurst (eds), *A Concise Companion to Contemporary British and Irish Drama* (Oxford: Blackwell Publishing, 2008), p. 1.
7. David Edgar, 'Access Schmaccess', *All Together Now? British Theatre After Multiculturalism*, 13–14 June 2009, Warwick University, www2.warwick.ac.uk/newsandevents/audio/more/atn/ (accessed 25 July 2009).
8. Mark Lawson, 'Bravo!', *The Guardian*, 2 December 2008.
9. David Eldridge, interview with author, see Chapter 3 Notes.
10. Lyn Gardner, 'Youth should not be valued over experience in theatre', *The Guardian* Theatre Blog, 3 August 2009.
11. Meyrick, 'The Limits of Theory', p. 231.
12. Claire Armitstead in Graham Saunders, *'Love Me or Kill Me': Sarah Kane and the theatre of extremes* (Manchester: Manchester University Press, 2002), p. 10.

Student Resources

ELECTRONIC RESOURCES

Although it is difficult to obtain full copies of play texts electronically, there are a number of useful sites for general reference regarding contemporary British drama, which are regularly updated and often offer archived material. Transcribed or recorded interviews, reviews of plays, and longer articles and papers are available across the following sites, and many of them include detailed online discussion pages that are kept visible long after contributions have closed. The popularity of blogging over the past decade has meant that reviewers and the arts media offer an immediate view of the theatre landscape in a way that printed references cannot sustain, offering alternative and wide-ranging resources for students and professionals. This brief selection gives some indication of what is available.

Arts Council Publications

www.artscouncil.org.uk/publications
The publications section of the Arts Council's website offers free downloads of numerous publications across all art forms, including consultations, conferences and funding recommendations. The most recent are also the most pertinent to this book, including *Writ Large: new writing on the English stage*

2003–2009 and *New Writing in Theatre 2003–8, an assessment of new writing within smaller scale theatre in England,* both published in December 2009.

British Theatre Guide

www.britishtheatreguide.info
An eclectic selection of interviews, articles, reviews, news and training opportunities, this website offers a broad view of the British theatre scene and offers an archived index of articles from 1997.

Dramaturgy Forum

www.dramforum.com
A small selection of articles and discussions can be found on this website, dating from around 2004 and exploring the role of the dramaturg in a range of contexts.

Dramaturgs' Network

ee.dramaturgy.co.uk
Running since 2002, the Dramaturgs' Network site is primarily a resource for advocating and discussing the role of the dramaturg, and recording working processes, panel discussions and conferences. It is updated with notices on a regular basis, and with a newsletter three to four times a year which usually offers more detailed articles on the growth of this role in British theatre.

In Yer Face Theatre

www.inyerface-theatre.com
Aleks Sierz's website accompanying his publication *In Yer Face Theatre: British Drama Today* offers an extensive overview of theatre during the 1990s and up to the present day, including numerous links to supporting sites for guidance on writers, directors, theatres and other publications. The archive section contains interviews and opinions from leading writers and commentators

on new writing up to 2003, whilst the bibliography is regularly updated with new publications.

Modern Theatre and Playwrights Online

doollee.com
At the end of 2009 doollee.com offered a listing of over 32,000 writers and 108,000 plays on its online database, each with categories to show where and when plays were first performed and if they are available in print. This is a very useful resource for finding out a playwright's full body of work, as it contains a record of many performances that may not be in print.

National Theatre Platform Paper Transcripts

www.nationaltheatre.org.uk/8237/platforms/platform-transcripts.html
The National Theatre website holds information on productions past and present down to the cast lists and technical crew, but for study the most useful (though slightly limited) area of the site is the Platform Papers: a selection of transcribed interviews from 1990–2004.

Shenton's View

blogs.thestage.co.uk/shenton
Part of the weekly industry newspaper The Stage, Mark Shenton's blog is updated almost daily and offers reviews, comment and opinion on theatre matters from the quirky to the serious.

The Guardian Theatre Page and Blog

www.guardian.co.uk/stage/theatre
The Guardian remains Britain's leading broadsheet advocate of the performing arts, offering an extensive archive of the articles, reviews and interviews that have appeared in print copy, and a daily blog frequented by many professionals, who regularly comment on issues as well as writing the blog copy. Offering links

to other sites and features, this is a very quick way to read around a particular topic.

Theatre Record

www.theatrerecord.org
Whilst immeasurably more useful where found in print, Theatre Record's website offers critic Ian Shuttleworth's fortnightly critical overview of new work and emerging topics, and an archive facility that lists which plays have been reviewed.

Theatre Voice

www.theatrevoice.com
Theatre Voice is updated very frequently, offering recorded interviews and panel discussions with writers, directors, producers, actors and companies about new theatre in Britain, offering an archiving service dating back to 2003 with over 690 conversations available. There is also a blogging section with guest contributions. Some but not all of the interviews are available as transcripts.

What's On Stage

www.whatsonstage.com
What's On Stage offers regular review round-ups for a quick glance at current theatre and the media's opinion, and also has an idiosyncratic theatre blog updated weekly or more, written by theatre critic Michael Coveney.

QUESTIONS FOR DISCUSSION

Chapter 1

New Writing, Then and Now

- Why were cultural commentators so quick to criticise the categorisation of In-Yer-Face writers only a few years after it had appeared?

- Do contemporary writers have a responsibility to offer solutions to political problems, or only to articulate existing problems more clearly?
- What are the benefits of social realism as a form of drama that more expressly theatrical forms may not be able to offer?

Simon Stephens, Gregory Burke and Caryl Churchill

- What commonalities can you find between Stephens' plays from Chapter 1 and the more recent plays of *Sea Wall* and *Punk Rock*?
- As a multidisciplinary form of theatre, how far do you think Gregory Burke is actually attributable as the author of *Black Watch*?
- How might different stagings of Caryl Churchill's *Seven Jewish Children* alter the politics of the play?

New Writing Tomorrow

- How does an audience's relationship to a performed text change if they are contained within the walls of the stage design and story?
- Why is more drama being produced in site-specific locations and how does this relate to the criticisms of new writing through the past decade?

Chapter 2

A Climate for Verbatim

- Why does theatre assume greater authority than journalism as a medium for upholding the 'real' version of events?
- How far does our familiarity with reality TV formats and Internet social networking sites assist an analysis of verbatim theatre?

Research, Editing and Truth

- Why does a writer use verbatim theatre to explore a particular event, rather than using their imagination to create a fictional drama based on the same verbatim research?

- Is it possible to collate verbatim material that is objective at source?

Problems in Performance

- Is there any situation where verbatim material becomes too sensitive or personal to be recreated as public performance?
- In what performance contexts might verbatim sources be used if they were not spoken by actors?

Dealing With Limitations

- Should verbatim theatre be concerned with exposing truth or promoting debate?
- Is verbatim theatre dramatic storytelling or theatricalised journalism?

Chapter 3

Drama and Collaboration

- What are the limitations of collaboratively written drama compared to a solo-authored play or a designated writer within an ensemble company?
- What strategies might you employ to maintain a collaborative approach to creating performance text despite having no single writer in control?

Writing as Devising

- How does the presence of multiple narratives in drama relate to what Philip Auslander calls our 'mediatized culture'? Are they useful beyond articulating a criticism of narrative's inadequacies?
- Why do collaborations between writers and other practitioners tend to lead to non-naturalistic work, and is there any reason why this should not be the case?

Case Studies

- How does David Eldridge's description of *Market Boy*'s development compare to the written play text, and is the play text an adequate representation of production?
- Taking Bryony Lavery's *Stockholm* as an example, how does non-verbal performance construct argument and debate alongside text?
- Take any play text discussed in Chapter 1: how might an audience's understanding of it be enhanced by a site-specific performance or a production that draws on the skills of a non-theatre practitioner?
- How might the long-form improvisation rules established by Cartoon de Salvo in *Hard Hearted Hannah and Other Stories* be applied to a devising process that involves an individual writer?

Future Narratives

- What are the different ways in which 'narrative' might be applied to the rituals, routines or cycles of everyday life to suggest dramatic structures for devising?
- What is it that experimental theatre is experimenting with?

Chapter 4

Separation, Difference and Terminology

- What attributes would you expect a text to have if you heard it described as a Black or Asian play?
- Would the establishment of a permanent home for exclusively Black theatre in Britain, supporting and training Black practitioners and producing their work, be a positive development?

Multiculturalism, Globalisation and Censorship

- Should theatres be given free reign to produce the work they believe has artistic merit, regardless of how it may be interpreted by particular communities?

- How does the shift in terminology from 'spectators' to 'consumers' change the way we apply value to drama?

Identity, Aesthetics and Language

- Is Andrew Lloyd Webber and A. R. Rahmann's *Bombay Dreams* exploitative of Asian culture or a useful way of bringing cultural diversity to a mass audience?
- How far does aesthetic difference in Black and Asian work serve the overall aim of British theatre being fully integrated and representative of the population?

Looking Forward

- Are development schemes that single out writers on the basis of their ethnicity a requirement to diversify British theatre, or the perpetuation of an unhelpful division?
- Would future seasons of solely Black and Asian work at flagship venues in Britain, like those at the Tricycle Theatre, assist integration to the mainstream or further ghettoise the work?

Chapter 5

A Recent History

- Should plays for young people performed in schools actively counter the curriculum or help satisfy its targets?
- Why historically has the work of TIE and theatre for young people been so politicised?

Commonalities and Challenges

- How does theatre for young people overcome the stigma of instrumentalism and achieve status as a professional genre in its own right?
- Does the pursuit of justice in theatre for young people exclude playfulness and entertainment as elements of the work?

Case Studies

- In performance, how might the objectives of Edward Bond's work for TIE fail to succeed in opening the gap for the audience?
- How does Fin Kennedy's work with Mulberry school connect with Bond's in terms of its engagement with young people's conception of justice?
- Are the National Theatre Connections plays interpretations of a teenage world from an adult point of view, or plays about the adult world from a teenage point of view?

What Next for Young People's Theatre?

- Does theatre for young people have to maintain a politicised agenda in order to communicate effectively with its audience?
- What might the differences be between theatre for young people and theatre for children or toddlers? How do the performance languages and topics change?

Chapter 6

What is Adaptation?

- How does a writer achieve fidelity to the source text but maintain their creative licence as the adapter? What controls are in place to govern decisions?
- Why do audiences and practitioners return to classic texts rather than seeking out new work?

Imagination and Adventure

- Does an adaptation that creates an effective theatrical experience but fails to express the drama clearly fail overall as an adaptation?
- Is it more important for contemporary practitioners to reinvent classic work for modern audiences, or for audiences to work harder at understanding classic work in its original form?

Text as Template

- What qualities do you think a source text might have to prevent it requiring alteration for a contemporary audience?
- Compare Goold and Power's adaptation to Pirandello's original play: is the insertion of a new act in Headlong's version of Pirandello's play justified or an intrusion on the source text?

The Past is the Future

- Why might adaptation be referred to as a lesser practice than creating original work, and how do we decide on the artistic value ascribed to each version?
- Director Katie Mitchell created a new version of Martin Crimp's *Attempts on Her Life* ten years after its first production: at what point is a source text ready for adaptation?

GUIDE TO FURTHER READING

This guide offers further reading beyond those references already cited in chapter end notes. Due to the contemporary focus of the book, these may include articles from recent theatre journals and print or online arts journalism, as well as other published volumes. Suggested reading appears beneath specific chapter sections where appropriate (see Introduction and Chapters 3, 4 and 5), otherwise sections have been collapsed to provide one comprehensive further reading list for a single chapter: see Chapters 1, 2 and 6.

Introduction

Writers, Theatre and Drama

BOOKS
Bennett, Benjamin, *Theater as Problem: Modern Drama and its Place in Literature*. London: Cornell University Press, 1999.

Page, Adrian, *The Death of the Playwright?: Modern British Drama and Literary Theory*. London: Macmillan, 1992.

Wu, Duncan, *Making Plays: Interviews with Contemporary British Dramatists and Directors*. New York: St Martin's Press, 2000.

JOURNAL ARTICLES

Barnett, David, 'When is a Play not a Drama? Two Examples of Postdramatic Theatre Texts', *New Theatre Quarterly* 24: 1 (2008), pp. 14–23.

Theatre and Theory

BOOKS

Bennett, Susan, *Theatre Audiences: a Theory of Production and Reception*, 2nd edn. London: Routledge, 1997.

Castagno, Paul, *New Playwriting Strategies: A Language-Based Approach to Playwriting*. London: Routledge, 2001.

Cobley, Paul, *Narrative*. London: Routledge, 2001.

Edgar, David, *How Plays Work: A Practical Guide to Playwriting*. London: Nick Hern Books, 2009.

Meisel, Martin, *How Plays Work: Reading and Performance*. Oxford: Oxford University Press, 2007.

Contemporary Theatre in Context – A Brief History

BOOKS

Eyre, Richard and Nicholas Wright, *Changing Stages: A View of British Theatre in the Twentieth Century*. London: Bloomsbury Publishing, 2000.

Lacey, Stephen, *British Realist Theatre: The New Wave in its Context 1956–1965*. London: Routledge, 1995.

Peacock, David Keith, *Thatcher's Theatre: British theatre and drama in the eighties*. London: Greenwood Press, 1999.

Rebellato, Dan, *1956 And All That: The Making of Modern British Drama*. London: Routledge, 1999.

Chapter 1: In-Yer-Face Theatre and Legacies of the New Writing Boom

BOOKS

Ansorge, Peter, *From Liverpool to Los Angeles: on writing for theatre, film and television*. London: Faber and Faber, 1997.

Aragey, Mireia, Hildegard Klein, Enric Monforte and Pilar Zozaya (eds), *British Theatre of the 1990s: Interviews with Directors, Playwrights, Critics and Academics*. Basingstoke: Palgrave Macmillan, 2007.

Devine, Harriet, *Looking Back: Playwrights at the Royal Court*. London: Faber and Faber, 2006.

Fitzsimmons, Linda, *File on Churchill*. London: Methuen Drama, 1989.

Kritzer, Amelia H., *Political Theatre in Post-Thatcher Britain 1995–2005*. Basingstoke: Palgrave Macmillan, 2007.

Kustov, Michael, *theatre@risk*. London: Methuen, 2001.

Turnbull, Olivia, *Bringing Down The House: The Crisis in Britain's Regional Theatres*. Chicago: Chicago University Press, 2009.

JOURNAL ARTICLES

Leach, Robert, 'The Short, Astonishing History of the National Theatre of Scotland', *New Theatre Quarterly* 23: 2 (2007), pp. 171–83.

Ravenhill, Mark, 'A Tear in the Fabric: the James Bulger Murder and New Theatre Writing in the 'Nineties', *New Theatre Quarterly* 20: 4 (2004), pp. 305–14.

Sierz, Aleks, 'Can old forms be reinvigorated? Radical populism and new writing in British theatre today', *Contemporary Theatre Review* 16: 3 (2006), pp. 301–11.

Chapter 2: Verbatim Theatre – The Rise of a Political Voice

BOOKS

Forsyth, Alison (ed.), *Get Real: Documentary Theatre Past and Present*. Basingstoke: Palgrave Macmillan, 2009.

Ridout, Nicholas, *Theatre and Ethics*. Basingstoke: Palgrave Macmillan, 2009.

Schweitzer, Pam, *Reminiscence Theatre: Making Theatre From Memories*. London: Jessica Kingsley Publishers, 2007.

JOURNAL ARTICLES

Botham, Paola, 'From Deconstruction to Reconstruction: A Habermasian Framework for Contemporary Political Theatre', *Contemporary Theatre Review* 18: 3 (2008), pp. 307–17.

Canton, Ursula, 'We May Not Know Reality, But It Still Matters – A Functional Analysis of 'Factual Elements' in the Theatre', *Contemporary Theatre Review* 18: 3 (2008), pp. 318–27.

Jeffers, Alison, 'Refugee Perspectives: the practice and ethics of verbatim theatre and refugee stories', *Platform* 1: 1 (2006), pp. 1–17.

McDougall, Gordon, 'Theatrical truth: the dialogue between audience and performance', *Studies in Theatre and Performance* 22: 2 (2002), pp. 107–17.

Soto-Morettini, Donna, 'Trouble in the House: David Hare's *Stuff Happens*', *Contemporary Theatre Review* 15: 3 (2005), pp. 309–19.

ARTS JOURNALISM

Ascherson, Neal, 'Whose Line is it Anyway?', *The Observer*, 9 November 2003.

Edgar, David, 'Secret Lives', *The Guardian*, 19 April 2003.

Hare, David, 'Why fabulate?', *The Guardian*, 2 February 2002.

Chapter 3: Writing and Devising – The Call for Collaboration

Drama and Collaboration

BOOKS

Ackerman, Alan and Martin Puchner (eds), *Against theatre: creative destructions on the modernist stage*. New York: Palgrave Macmillan, 2006.

Bicât, Tina and Chris Baldwin, *Devised and Collaborative Theatre: a practical guide*. Marlborough: Crowood, 2002.

Govan, Emma, Kate Normington and Helen Nicholson, *Making a Performance*. London: Routledge, 2007.

Itzin, Catherine, *Stages in the Revolution: Political Theatre in Britain Since 1968*. London: Eyre Methuen, 1980.

Oddey, Alison, *Devising Theatre: A Practical and Theoretical Handbook*. London: Routledge 1996.

Whitmore, Jon, *Directing Postmodern Theater: shaping signification in performance*. Ann Arbor, Michigan: University of Michigan Press, 1994.

Writing as Devising / Case Studies

BOOKS

Etchells, Tim, *Certain Fragments: Contemporary Performance and Forced Entertainment*. London: Routledge 1999.

Graham, Scott and Steven Hoggett, *The Frantic Assembly Book of Devising Theatre*. London: Routledge, 2009.

Helmer, Judith and Florian Malzacher (eds), *Not Even a Game Anymore: The Theatre of Forced Entertainment*. Berlin: Alexander Verlag, 2004.

JOURNAL ARTICLES

Babbage, Frances, 'Performing Love: a week's discourse with Forced Entertainment', *Contemporary Theatre Review* 12: 4 (2002), pp. 63–76.

Mendus, Clive, '"Competitive Co-operation": Playing with Theatre de Complicite', *New Theatre Quarterly* 23: 3 (2006), pp. 257–67.

ARTS JOURNALISM

Anthony Neilson, Interviewed by Caroline Smith, *Brand*, 02, 2008, www.brandliterarymagazine.co.uk/editions/02/contri butors/01/extract.pdf

Chapter 4: Black and Asian Writers – A Question of Representation

Separation, Difference and Terminology

BOOKS

Gilbert, Helen and Joanna Tompkins, *Post-colonial drama: theory, practice, politics*. London: Routledge, 1996.

Ugwu, Catherine (ed.), *Let's Get It On: The Politics of Black Performance*. London: ICA Publications, 1995.

Una, Roberta (ed.), *The color of theatre: race, culture and contemporary performance*. London: Continuum, 2002.

JOURNAL ARTICLES

Feature Issue: 'A Forum on Black Theatre: The Questions: What Is a Black Play? and / or What Is Playing Black?', *Theatre Journal* 57 (2005), pp. 571–616.

Holdbrook-Smith, Kobna, 'What is Black Theatre? The African-American Season at the Tricycle Theatre', *New Theatre Quarterly* 23: 3 (2007), 241–50.

Multiculturalism, Globalisation and Censorship

BOOKS

Kelly, Paul (ed.), *Multiculturalism reconsidered: 'Culture and equality' and its critics*. Cambridge: Polity Press in association with Blackwell Publishers, 2002.

Rebellato, Dan, *Theatre and Globalization*. Basingstoke: Palgrave Macmillan, 2009.

Goldberg, David Theo (ed.), *Multiculturalism: a critical reader*. Oxford: Blackwell Publishers, 1994.

Identity, Aesthetics and Language

BOOKS

Arana, R. Victoria, *'Black' British Aesthetics Today*. Newcastle-upon-Tyne: Cambridge Scholars Press, 2007.

JOURNAL ARTICLES

Adebayo, Mojisola and Valerie Mason-John, '"No Straight Answers": Writing in the Margins, Finding Lost Heroes', *New Theatre Quarterly* 25: 1 (2009), pp. 6–21.

Aston, Elaine, 'A Fair Trade?: Staging Female Sex Tourism in *Sugar Mummies* and *Trade*', *Contemporary Theatre Review* 18: 2 (2008), pp. 180–92.

Goddard, Lynette, 'West Indies *vs* England in Winsome Pinnock's Migration Narratives', *Contemporary Theatre Review* 14: 4 (2003), pp. 23–33.

Godiwala, Dimple, '*Kali*: providing a forum for British-Asian women playwrights', *Studies in Theatre and Performance* 26: 1 (2006), pp. 69–83.

Starck, Kathleen, '"Black and female is some of who I am and I want to explore it": black women's plays of the 1980s and 1990s', *Studies in Theatre and Performance* 26: 1 (2006), pp. 49–67.

Chapter 5: Theatre for Young People – Audiences of Today

A Recent History

BOOKS

Bennett, Stuart (ed.), *Theatre for Children and Young People in the UK: 50 Years of Professional Theatre in the UK*. Twickenham: Aurora Metro Publications, 2005.

Heathcote, Dorothy and Gavin Bolton, *Drama for Learning: Dorothy Heathcote's Mantle of the Expert Approach to Education*. Portsmouth NH: Heinemann, 1995.

JOURNAL ARTICLES

Scullion, Adrienne, 'The Citizenship Debate and Theatre for Young People in Contemporary Scotland', *New Theatre Quarterly* 24: 4 (2008), pp. 379–93.

Commonalities and Challenges / Case Studies

BOOKS

Bond, Edward, *Theatre & Education*. Basingstoke: Palgrave Macmillan, 2009.

Bond, Edward, *The Hidden Plot: notes on theatre and the state*. London: Methuen, 2000.

Jackson, Tony, *Learning through theatre: essays and casebooks on Theatre in Education*. London: Routledge, 1993.

JOURNAL ARTICLES

Billingham, Peter, 'Drama and the Human: Reflections at the Start of a Millennium, Edward Bond in conversation with Peter

Billingham', *PAJ: A Journal of Performance and Art* 87 (2007), pp. 1–14.

Bond, Edward, *Young Civilization*, Short Essay Contribution for Big Brum's 25th Anniversary, available at www.bigbrum.org. uk/archives/cat_events.html.

Wallis, Richard, 'Louder than words: making and performing theatre cross-culturally with young people. The Cædmon Project 2003', *Studies in Theatre and Performance* 25: 2 (2005), pp. 145–51.

ARTS JOURNALISM
Children's Theatre: TheatreVoice Forum. A discussion with John Retallack, David Wood and Annie Wood, Theatre Museum, 11 February 2005, transcript available at www.theatrevoice.com/tran_script/detail/?roundUpID=20.

Chapter 6: Adaptation and Transposition – Reinterpreting the Past

BOOKS
Allen, Graham, *Intertextuality*. London: Routledge, 2000.

Auslander, Philip, *Liveness: Performance in a mediatized culture*. London: Routledge, 1999.

Desmet, Christy and Robert Sawyer (eds), *Shakespeare and Appropriation*. London: Routledge 1999.

Kidnie, Jane Margaret, *Shakespeare and the problem of adaptation*. Abingdon, Abingdon: Routledge, 2009.

Scolnicov, Hanna and Peter Holland (eds), *The play out of context: Transferring plays from culture to culture*. Cambridge: Cambridge University Press, 1989.

Zatlin, Phyllis, *Theatrical Translation and Film Adaptation: a practitioner's view*. Clevedon: Multilingual Matters, 2005.

JOURNAL ARTICLES
Ley, Graham, ' "Discursive embodiment": the theatre as adaptation', *Journal of Adaptation in Film and Performance* 2: 3 (2009), pp. 201–9.

Milton, John, 'Between the cat and the devil: Adaptation Studies and Translation Studies', *Journal of Adaptation in Film and Performance* 2, 1 (2009), pp. 47–64.

USEFUL FORTHCOMING PUBLICATIONS 2010

Aston, Elaine and Elin Diamond (eds), *The Cambridge Companion to Caryl Churchill*. Cambridge: Cambridge University Press.

Freeman, John, *Blood Sweat and Theory: Research Through Practice in Performance*. Faringdon: Libri Publishing.

Ley, Graham and Sarah Dadswell (eds), *British South Asian Theatres: A Documented History*. Exeter: University of Exeter Press.

Wooster, Roger, *Contemporary Theatre in Education*. Chicago: Chicago University Press.

Index